The Butte learnt t

Trish Mitchell

Copyright © 2023 Trish Mitchell

ISBN: 9781916820111

All rights reserved, including the right to reproduce this book, or portions thereof in any form. No part of this text may be reproduced, transmitted, downloaded, decompiled, reverse engineered, or stored, in any form or introduced into any information storage and retrieval system, in any form or by any means, whether electronic or mechanical without the express written permission of the author.

This is a work of fiction. Names and characters are the product of the author's imagination and any resemblance to actual persons, living or dead, is entirely coincidental.

The views expressed in this work are solely those of the author and do not necessarily reflect the views of the publisher, and the publisher hereby disclaims any responsibility for them.

Thank you ..Sue, for all your support. Having never written a book before Sue gave me a wonderful opportunity to write this book. I will be forever grateful to you. X

Thank you .. To my life long friend Max, for all your help and guidance, it is so much appreciated. And for all your support when I was going through those dark days, I never ever thought I would see lighter days again. X

'Let yourself get introduced to your soul
 It wants to help you heal from the abuse
 And suffering you have endured'

'Then watch the beautiful Butterfly
 Wings unfold to empowerment'
 Freedom to own who you are.

Trish Mitchell.

About the Author

Trish Mitchell was born in Bexley, Kent in 1955, and now lives in her happy place in Westgate on sea, on the South East coast.

She has been an Aromatherapist and Reiki Master for many years, and continues to work as a Spiritual Life Coach, Spiritual and Ascension Guide, Intuitive energy and tarot card reader and a Psychic and Clairvoyant.

TO MY GORGEOUS FAMILY:

Kerry, Steve, Son in law Michael, Daughter in law Carly

My precious Grandchildren:
Charlotte, Holly, Sophie and Stanley

With love always

Mum & Nanna

CHAPTER 1

Matilda Fellowes sat on her bench by the sea, quietly reflecting on her journey. She had completed a full circle, back to Bamburgh in Northumberland, on the beach where she had many happy memories of a time gone by from when she was a child. Looking out at the beautiful calm sea on a warm July evening, the sun gradually going down behind the clouds, the spectacular colours of orange, purple and red all blended together to make a magnificent sunset, that last sparkle of light glistening on the sea, the sun slowly disappearing below the horizon. Tilly sighed.........Oh how peaceful she felt and contented, for Tilly had not known this feeling for a while. She had always been chasing the dream of the perfect life to be loved more than anything, but now understands, if you stand still and look within yourself long enough, you start to begin to find who you are, you begin to love yourself, it's the best thing ever. If we don't love ourselves first, then how can somebody else love us?

"Tilly"...... "Tilly"......... "HELLO" called a voice way down the beach, Tilly looked round in surprise. 'Isla,' she called back, seeing her best friend from her school days walking down to greet her. Tilly stood up, and walked towards her, giving each other the biggest hugs ever. 'Oh Isla, how lovely to see you,' Tilly said, feeling rather emotional at seeing her childhood friend stand before her.... 'How are you?' 'Yes I'm doing ok,' Isla said feeling emotional too. 'It must be a few years since we last saw one another. You have not changed a bit Tilly, you look really good, you still have your beautiful long blonde hair, you look really well.' 'I knew it was you by your voice. You look good too Isla. You have not changed much either, love your pixie haircut, it really suits you.' 'I just fancied a change, never had my hair this short before.'Replied Isla. 'So Tilly, how are you doing?' continued Isla.

'Yes... I am fine Isla, a few bumps in the road, and some white knuckle rides along the way but to be honest, it has made me who I am today. I feel a lot more content now than I have ever been in my life. Isla we must have lunch, we have so much to catch up on.' Isla loved the idea, 'So how long are you up here for?' enquired Isla.... Tilly looked at her .... 'I'm staying up here for a while,' Isla's face lit up and a big smile appeared. "REALLY" 'does that mean we can be the bestest friends, like when we were young girls, like when we started primary school together, when we used to play tricks on your sister.' Isla was so excited, she just kept reciting all the things they had done together. 'So Isla, where are you living now?' said Tilly, putting her sunglasses on, as the sun was so strong it was hurting her eyes. 'Oh not far,' 'I live in Alnwick. I have lived there for 2 years now. I did live abroad for a while in Italy. I wanted to come back to the UK as I found the sun was sometimes too hot for me especially in the summer months. Our children and grandchildren live here. I suppose I am about twenty minutes from Lucy and thirty minutes away from Jane, so lovely to be able to see more of them, seeing my grandchildren grow up is such a pleasure.' Isla continued, 'I cannot believe how our paths have crossed again, after all these years. Shall we make a date now?' Tilly was as excited as Isla.' Yes let's do that now' said Tilly, as they rummaged through their handbags, trying to find their diaries, they could not stop chatting to each other. 'Have you got time now for a catch up now Isla?' 'Yes, I have an hour or so, I need to get back, I am looking after my granddaughters later this evening.' 'That's fine,' said Tilly. They had both calmed down now knowing that their friendship would last forever.

They both sat down on the bench, where Tilly was sitting. They were both playing with the smooth soft sand still warm from the Summer sunshine with their bare feet. The gentle breeze every so often would blow, each of them brushing the hair from their faces, freeing their mouths so they could each continue the never ending conversation. Isla looked wistfully at Tilly as her mind wandered..... 'I have to say Tilly, as I looked at you earlier you seemed a million miles away, not even on the planet, are you ok?' 'Isla, you have not changed, you have always been very intuitive.' 'Tilly do you remember when I had my first kiss, then I got all silly about it, even got upset? You gave me a big hug saying that it was normal at thirteen to feel silly when you have had your first kiss, you had already had your first kiss,'... Isla replied,' still smiling at Tilly. 'Of course I do, I remember all our memories, it was so much fun. I reckon every time we meet up, something from our memory box will appear.' replied Tilly. Isla laughing as Tilly stated exactly what Isla had thought. 'So Tilly come on, I could tell from that distance that you had things on your mind.'…. 'Well actually Isla, I was really thinking how is has taken me so many years to find who I am as a woman, I know it's crazy'… 'certainly not' piped up Isla, we are all on our own unique journey sometimes it's rough terrain, sometimes it's a smooth pathway, some people have lots of white knuckle rides while others just have bumps in the road.' 'You are so right Isla', Tilly replied. 'Now I hope that it will only be a few bumps, and should a white knuckle ride appear, I will now know how to stop and get off the ride.' Tilly continued, 'for the first time in my life, I feel happy and contented, its as if I don't need to search anymore, I have come home to myself. 'Oh Isla, I so wished I was like that in my thirties, all the things I would and could have done, but my confidence and worrying about what I looked like I put limitations in my life. Oh on second thoughts,' Tilly paused... 'Maybe it's best now and not when I was in my thirties, I dread to think where I would have ended up.' They were both laughing. 'Tilly I think you could be right' looking at her wise friend. 'You had a very adventurous mind, and probably still do.' 'Yes but if I did not have those hangups, I could have had a more peaceful life,' replied Tilly. Isla continued 'As I said earlier, you have had to have had those experiences, it's part of your soul journey.' 'Yes I totally agree with you Isla, but it's been so painful' replied Tilly, Isla continued 'but you know it's all part of life's tapestry, I'm sure you must have had many fun times too.' Tilly laughed of course, 'I could write a book on my experiences when touring with the band.' "WOW " said Isla looking at Tilly in amazement. 'You've been in a band, you actually got to do what you loved and wanted to do.' Tilly explained that she became a lead singer, played piano and guitar. Isla was in awe of Tilly. 'You see Tilly, 'I don't feel I have ever achieved anything in my life, I have used my creative skills as an artist, but could never do it full time, I had to work in stuffy offices to make ends meet.' Tilly reminded her of what she had said earlier that life is a journey, a unique journey, no two souls have the same journey. 'But Isla you have lived in Italy, a beautiful country, painted, enjoyed a peaceful life, I would have given anything to have had that, but now I fully understand my life's path.' said Tilly.

Isla has a lot of wisdom about her, she is very spiritual, she has dabbled in most areas of spirituality, tarot cards, astrology, crystals, healing, she is very intuitive, and empathic. Tilly in her own way is very similar, they had just gone down different paths in life. They are kindred spirits, who have found each other again. Isla looked at her watch, she gasped ... 'where has all the time gone it's 6.30pm, I have to go Tilly.' They exchanged phone numbers, making that precious lunch date that was going to be important for both of them, as they began to help each other to grow and evolve together. The date is 12th August 2008, the place is the cafe they used to go to when they were teenagers which is called Daisy's Pantry, nestled between the beach and the castle, down a cobbled street where there were a few shops with houses and cottages in between. Daisy had passed away, so Daisy's granddaughter Angela now owns and runs the cafe, and it still has the same name. She still uses the recipes that her nanna had passed down to her. The pretty curtains and nets at the window, tied back very neatly with curtain ties. The floral tablecloths, vases of fresh flowers that adorned every table, were in keeping, when her nanna ran the cafe. It was Angela's pride and joy, she did not want to change the cafe, everybody loved it just as it was, she wanted to keep it like that. The only thing that Angela updated was the coffee machine. The aroma of the coffee smelt wonderful as you entered the cafe. The cakes all displayed in order of size, and the famous bread pudding. It always felt warm and cosy once you stepped inside.

The day had arrived, both Tilly and Isla were beside themselves with excitement, although they had spoken on the phone a few times. They hugged and walked into Daisy's Pantry, 'Ahhh how lovely' said Isla it has not changed at all,' 'I know' said Tilly, the smell of the coffee tingling her nostrils. 'Oh Isla, look at those cakes we must have some after lunch. It feels so good to be somewhere where it has not changed.' Tilly and Isla found a quiet corner and cosied up, ready to catch up on the years they had not seen each other, with many more lunch dates at their favourite cafe. As their lives unfold together of the emotional pain and hurt, the fun times, how they survived and healed their souls. Sitting in their cosy corner of the cafe, just gazing at one another, Isla sighed....'Tilly I cannot believe we are sitting here together, never thought this would ever happen.' 'Ok ladies' said the waitress, 'who is having the chicken hotpot and fresh vegetables' 'me' Tilly replied, 'thank you'… 'ahh that looks lovely and smells delicious.' In no time at all, the waitress was by the table serving Isla her steak pie and vegetables. 'Ohh that smells gorgeous, I used to have this when I came here with my mum and dad many years ago.' replied Isla, cutting into the Steak pie topped with a lovely golden puff pastry topping. The smell of the food was totally opening up the aromatic senses of both Tilly and Isla. 'So,' Isla inquired in between mouthfuls of food, 'where do we start?' Tillly replied. 'How about us reminiscing when we were younger, the fun times, the things we got up to, I feel I just want us to share, it's so cathartic.' Isla and Tilly both came up with the same word at the same time. They were both taking in the surroundings of the warmth and cosiness of the cafe, hearing people laugh, chattering, gossiping, and most of all enjoying the beautiful food.

'Isla do you remember the Christmas parties at Bamburgh Castle? I think we were about five when we started going, all dressed up in our pretty dresses, my brother and sister were with us as well. I always felt on edge at the parties, I think because my dad worked at the castle, I always felt he had his eye on me, it made me feel tense, that I could not let myself go and enjoy myself.' said Tilly looking down at her food. 'Funny you should say that Tilly, I actually did notice how sometimes you were a bit quiet.' Isla looked across at Tilly, who seemed to be somewhere else, in between eating her meal, she was staring into the abyss. 'You ok Tilly?' asked Isla, 'you seemed so far away then,' 'Yes sorry Isla, I did not realise that just by talking about the Christmas parties, what feelings and emotions had come to the surface.' Isla looked so surprised, she had never heard Tilly speak like that before. 'Oh Tilly,' Isla broke in. 'Whatever you are saying that for, you had a lovely childhood, seemed the perfect family'....'Well Isla,' Tilly replied, 'yes to the outside world, but nobody really knows what goes on behind closed doors do they!' 'I guess not,' Isla replied in a quiet sort of shocked voice.

She sensed that Tilly had something on her mind, but did not want to press her further, as they had only just met up again. 'I am thoroughly enjoying chatting about the fun times we had.' Isla, trying to move the conversation back to the fun times. 'You know Till's one thing I remember about you at school' said Isla, Tilly let out a long' yesss!!!!!!!'. 'I remember your singing voice and your love of playing music, you were always asked to play in the school choir singing solo with some of the Christmas carols, in front of all the parents, while I stood on the sidelines watching everybody else, when I look back I have probably done that most of my life, lived on the planet but never really feeling I belonged anywhere.' 'Oh don't say that Isla' replied Tilly, putting her hand on Isla's arm. 'You were great at school, always seemed to help the other kids in trouble, always gave a hug. I remember in class one day a little boy who was crying because he had lost his biscuits for break time. You went straight to him and put your arms around him, you helped him to find his biscuits, they were in his coat pocket and he had forgotten to take them out. The big smile on his face said it all, we are all different Isla,' Tilly paused....'We all have our strengths and weaknesses, the best thing to do is to build on your strengths, look at your weak areas, see how you can work on them, to utilise them to make you stronger. We cannot clear everything in life, Isla you of all people know that with your spiritual background.' 'I know you are right Tilly,' replied Isla, looking out of the window thinking about what Tilly had just said, 'but then, Isla continued 'you have done the things in life that have made you happy, as I have said before, I don't feel like I have achieved much in life.'

'Isla please don't feel like that, you have achieved many things, had a happy marriage, lived abroad, you are very creative, have managed to have a fairly balanced life, with the bumps of life that appear every so often, I feel I have been on a white knuckle ride, with painful lessons and challenges all of them on a emotional level, mainly relationships. I clearly made one hell of a mess in a past life, obviously was not interested in my soul growing and evolving, so they have thrown the book at me in this lifetime. ' Tilly laughed as she was speaking. 'Isla your life is how it was supposed to be' ….'mmm.' smiled Isla. 'Yes I suppose so.'

'Hey!! Tilly,' who was that lady that used to come down and visit your mum, I think she had a son, cannot remember his name though.' 'Oh you mean Morag,' replied Tilly, 'she is still my mum's best friend. They lived in the same street, in fact they were neighbours. They lived in Scotland when they were children, it seemed when her husband passed away, she would come and stay for a few days, Jack was her son,' Tilly continued. "Oh yes… , ' I remember now, you seemed to get on really well with him,' Isla said smiling as she remembered Jack coming down and taking her out in his car. 'Yes, we did from a very young age, as you know he was the first boy I kissed, he was a few years older than me. I remember when he learnt to drive, and the first time he came down in his car, we went to the ice cream parlour in the next village. I felt so grown up listening to pop music on the jukebox Gene Pitney, Beatles, Rolling Stones, Kinks, The Who, to name but a few. I loved them all, music was and still is my passion.' 'Yes I remember that day Tilly, you were so excited. Have to ask …. Did your mum and dad know where you were going?' Tilly looking sheepish lowered her head and spoke a quiet 'no'…. 'I just told them we were going for a drive. My dad would have gone mad if he knew, he was quite controlling when I was young, in fact all my life, even when I was older I always felt he was sitting on my shoulder, felt like that for years. Jack and I used to write to each other' Tilly continued, 'I used to have such a crush on him, I guess he was the first boy I loved, we just seemed to get each other, it was always easy and comfortable being with him, I remember when he wrote and told me about having a girlfriend, I cried for days.' 'Yes I remember' Isla replied 'you were heartbroken.' 'Yes I was' continued Tilly. 'When I look back it made me want to see what else the world had to offer,

Then you and I planned to go to London, to get work. We ended up working in cafes, a few offices. Yes, we had a great time, London was certainly the place to be, the fashion, the monochrome look, flared trousers, shift dresses, psychedelic coloured tops and trousers. The white knee high boots, the short hairstyles. Twiggy ruled the fashion world, we all wanted to be a Twiggy' they both laughed. 'What about the clubs? ' Tilly continued with excitement, 'They were the best,' Isla replied. "Goodness we went to so many, my favourite has to be the Marquee club, all the groups playing live, packed every night.' 'Yes' said Tilly, 'it was my favourite club too. When I think back, life was so free and easy going. We certainly enjoyed the six months we spent in London. It was quite a shock when we came back to Bamburgh, not sure if I ever really settled back home, probably why I left again a year later' as Tilly was sipping her coffee, and in her head back in London, thoughts and memories came flooding back about Bob. She moved back to London to be near him. 'I did miss you Tilly' said Isla 'when you went again, I guess that's when our paths started to divide, you went to London to be with Bob.' 'I know Isla, I missed you too, but living in Bamburgh was not enough for me and besides I wanted to be with Bob,' said Tilly. 'I do get that Tilly, you were always the one who wanted adventure. One thing that stuck in my mind was when you went to start singing lessons, as you felt your voice was not as good since leaving school, you were physically shaking with nerves. The tutor asked you to sing your favourite song, your voice came out all shaky and squeaky, so high pitched, you could not even remember the words, I was laughing standing at the back, I know not funny for you, you sounded like a cats choir, I had to put my fingers in my ears,' Isla still giggling as she was telling the story. 'Your determination to show that teacher you could sing, led your voice to being pitch perfect. You said one thing that you wanted to do, was to maybe sing with a band, or just solo.' 'Yes I was so disappointed that did not happen up here,' said Tilly 'but then my path would have been completely different, a bit like that film Sliding Doors' Tilly replied. 'Maybe that's why I felt the need to go back to London, I then ended up singing in Bob's band.' 'I remember being at school,' Isla continued with her account of singing in the school choir, 'I scraped through having to sing do-ray-me to the music teacher, but then I did not always sing in the choir, I just stood there and mimed, occasionally I would sing,' by this time Isla was laughing so much, as she took herself back to their school days. They were both laughing out loud, 'Oh Isla I am so enjoying meeting up and going over the years gone by.'

The waitress came over and interrupted them, both still giggling. 'Have you both finished your meal?' said the waitress, 'empty plates, looks like you both enjoyed your meals?' 'Yes' they both replied, 'it was delicious' The waitress added 'You both looked like you were so engrossed in your conversation, I did not want to disturb you.' 'Oh, you should have' Tilly replied smiling. ' We are just going back over our school days.' 'So ladies,' the waitress chirped up, 'would like more coffee, and maybe some pudding?' 'mmmm… yes please' both nodded their heads in agreement. They both decided on sticky toffee pudding with a generous amount of homemade custard, both touching their tummies as they were rather full, but knowing they each had just about enough room to squeeze in the pudding. Any ideas of following diets, went completely out of the window that day. The waitress was back in a flash with another two coffees. 'It won't be long and your puddings will be with you.' 'No problem' said Tilly. 'We are just enjoying being here.' Still in their cosy corner, they felt right at home, looking around the cafe, it seemed to have emptied out, looking out of the window the sun kept making an appearance, as the clouds gently drifted over the sun with beautiful blue skies randomly appearing. 'Shall we go down to the beach to walk off our calorific lunch?' asked Isla, holding her full tummy. 'Yes, that would be lovely,' replied Tilly. You know we have not stopped talking, have we?' 'It's a wonder we managed to eat at all.' Isla laughed as she spoke.

'Yes, I know, but then we have not seen each other for god knows how many years and we are still at the beginning.' 'Yes I know,' Tilly replied. 'It's been great, I am so pleased we can pick up our friendship after all these years.' 'I have to say Isla, I have always thought about you, but had no means of contacting you,' Isla added, 'me too,' 'here's to many more years of our friendship, now we have found each other. Maybe we can get our families together, and meet up. Obviously everybody leads such busy lives, but we can plan well in advance, somewhere a gap will appear, and it will fall into place,' 'Yes', 'that sounds like a good idea. Tilly' replied as she was gathering all the plates together for the waitress to collect. They had both finished their coffees and that delicious sticky toffee pudding. Isla and Tilly sat quietly for a few minutes both feeling quite emotional about the meet up, both realising that the friendship was as strong as ever. It felt like it was only yesterday they saw each other. They always say that true friendship never ends in between the gaps called life. The waitress came over, and jolted them out of their daydreams, 'so how was the pudding' asked the waitress, they both replied with big smiles on their faces, 'it was so delicious, we will be back for more.'

Isla started to tell the waitress that they were both born and lived in Bamburgh and that this is the first time they had met up for over three decades. 'Oh really?' enquired the waitress. 'So who are your parents' excited to know if she knew of them, Tilly spoke first, 'my dads name was Wilfred Harrison and my mum's name is Edith Harrison, I have a brother Edward and a sister Adele.' 'Oh you know those names ring a bell in my head' putting her hand to her head trying to find the memory link... 'Ah ha, I know,' the waitress said, 'your dad worked at Bamburgh Castle.' 'Well.. yes he did.' Tilly was surprised that she knew of her dad. 'How did you know that?' replied Tilly, 'Would you believe it, my grandad worked at Bamburgh Castle. As a child he used to tell me stories about the castle, how the gardens were kept so beautiful, and the haunted goings on that went on in the castle. Your dad's name did come up a few times, from what I can gather they were good friends at work.' Tilly looked sad, as she said that her father had passed away five years previous. 'Oh sorry to hear that,' the waitress gently put her hand on Tillys shoulder to comfort her. 'Yes my grandfather also has passed away, sad really,' replied the waitress. 'I have always lived here, never really ventured out of the village, it is in my blood, I am well and truly rooted here' she laughed.

'I have just moved back from London, replied Tilly. 'Having just recently got divorced, my mum still lives here. I have come back to live with her, so I can help her, she's quite frail now. I feel I need my roots back here too.' Tilly smiled feeling lucky that she still had her mum around. 'How about you lass,' looking at Isla 'Yes' continued Isla, 'I was born and bred here too. My dad was a Blacksmith, he worked in the nearby village of Shoreston Hall. Tilly and I met at school, this is our first meet up. We chose this cafe, as we used to come in here with our parents, and then when we were teenagers. We love the fact that it has not changed much.' The waitress nodded her head in agreement. 'Glad you enjoyed your lunch, can I get you anything else?' asked the waitress. 'Actually' Isla asked, 'could we please have the bill, we want to wander down to the beach and work off the lunch, the diet has gone completely out of the window today.' giggling as she spoke. 'Yes of course' the waitress said, 'I will go and get that done for you.' She turned around, smiling that she could talk about her grandfather whom she had loved very much. Tilly looked at Isla, 'such a small world.' 'Yes it is' replied Isla. 'Well let's get the bill paid, my treat' said Tilly, 'are you sure?' Isla enquired. 'Yes of course, we can take it in turns to treat each other next time we meet up.' 'Good idea Tilly, so lovely coming here today, let's hope next time we can get the same cosy corner.' Isla replied. They paid the bill and said goodbye to the waitress. 'Nice to have met you both, hope we see you both again?' the waitress added. 'Yes you will definitely be seeing us again. ' 'Bye take care' they both said.

On the way down to the beach both taking in the warm sunshine, walking on the side of the street where it was sunny, stopping to look at the quaint shops that they remembered as girls. Now owned by different people, with various types of retail. As they walked down, they came across a complementary health clinic, where they did aromatherapy massage, reiki, counselling, reflexology, and crystal healing. 'Oh look' Isla squealed in delight. 'Never thought I would see one of these shops here in Bamburgh, how lovely I will be booking an Aromatherapy massage soon, I could do with a good massage Tilly. I used to have regular treatments, the massage worked wonders for my back.' Isla checked on the opening times and made a note so she could book asap. 'Tilly, have you ever had an aromatherapy massage?' 'Er, no Isla, never really thought of ever having a massage.' 'The aroma of the oils are to die for' added Isla, in a dreamy voice. 'I do have trouble with my neck and shoulders,' said Tilly, touching her neck and feeling her tense muscles. 'So let's book one together' replied Isla. 'You will love it Tilly. 'Sounds good,' she replied.. 'I will ring tomorrow and get it booked'. Isla said eagerly, 'I have got the number now. As they continued to walk to the beach, Tilly just stopped.... 'Isla, how lucky are we to have been born here and have the beach a five minute walk away.' Taking in the sea air, the gentle breeze was blowing the tiny granules of sand into their faces, the sea was glistening, the sun beating down on them, the sun still high in the sky with a few white fluffy cotton clouds drifting over the bright blue sky, they found a bench to sit on. Isla started to feel all the tension in her body disappear, 'This is lovely Tilly my body does not feel so tense how amazing and healing the sea is.' Isla sighing as she was talking. Tilly on the other hand was trying her hardest to relax. She had found the breakup of her marriage very distressing. It had not been the happiest of marriages, but Tilly had loved and adored him. They had two children, a boy and a girl, both of whom have grown up and have their own families. Tilly felt very discombobulated when she first split from Bob, he was really all she had ever known, she had a best friend Peter who was in the band, but they had lost contact with each other. Peter had always held a candle for Tilly, but she only ever had eyes for Bob. Bob was the lead singer. Tilly played guitar alongside Peter who was lead guitarist, and Dave who was the drummer. The band was called Blue Fairground. Tilly loved the band days, always hoping that Bob would change, but he never did. Gradually Tilly found her body relaxing and taking deep breaths in, and breathing out the stress she felt in her body, like Isla was doing. It seemed that both women needed today, both women in their early sixties, and dealing with the change of lifestyle, but in different ways. Tilly had lived in London for 40 years and not long been divorced. Isla was still adjusting to not living in Italy, and the problems it had brought with it.

They both opened their eyes and let out a big sigh, it seemed quite a time since they had felt the energy of the sea. All around them, children playing, laughing splashing in the water. 'Do you remember those times Tilly when we were young,' seeing herself as a little girl building sandcastles with her dad. 'Yes of course,' replied Tilly. 'Those were the best days of my life.' 'Tilly, how on earth did you survive living down in London for all those years.' 'Isla you know, when I look back I really don't know how I survived.' 'I did long to be back to my roots, but my situation and all that went with it, meant I did not have much of a choice in the matter. I did come back to visit Mum and Dad, Eddy and Adele, but just for holidays. 'Everyone thought I had this fabulous life, but actually it was far from that, anyway,' Tilly, putting on a positive voice, that is behind me now, I need to move forward to a more positive future.' Isla smiled, 'Here's to your new chapter Tilly' Isla knew there was more to the divorce then Tilly was letting on. She knew her friend well enough to sense those things. Tilly was not someone who openly shared her private life, she had to process the emotions. Isla respects Tilly and the way she deals with her feelings, for they run very deep. 'Isla, I had better get back to mum,' 'Yes' replied Isla 'Brian will be wondering where I have got to. 'It's just been brilliant with us meeting up, let's hope we can meet up as much as time allows us,'replied Tilly. 'I don't see why not, I think booking the massage is first on the agenda' Isla continued, thinking about the massage. 'I can't wait for one of those soothing massages too,' said Tilly. 'Ok I will book a massage for us both tomorrow, once it's booked I will ring you and give you the date and the time' Isla replied. They gave each other a hug.'Thanks for today Isla, it was so good to catch up,' 'Same here' Isla replied. 'Bye Isla,' 'Bye Tilly' They both went their separate ways, back into the here and now.

'Tilly Tilly' called her mum. 'Yes Mum,' said Tilly, 'what can I get you?' ' Could you bring my blanket down, pet, it is on my bed. I am feeling a bit cold, while you are upstairs, it would take me ages to get up those stairs.' 'No problem I will be down in a minute,' 'ok,' no problem pet, when you are ready'. Tilly came down the stairs. 'Oh it does feel a bit chilly, here you go Mum, let's put this around you,' 'I am going to get dinner ready soon.' No sooner had she put the blanket around her the phone rang. She quickly answered the phone. 'Hi Til's, it's me Isla,' 'good news, I have booked the aromatherapy massage treatments. We are in luck, there are two therapists on that day, which means we can have a treatment at the same time.' 'Oh Isla,' replied Tilly.' That sounds delightful, I cannot wait, I'm so looking forward to a massage,' 'It's for this Friday at 2.30pm. Would that suit you?' said Isla, 'Yes that's perfect Isla, I have never experienced the oils and a massage before.' Tilly replied. 'Oh you will love it. It will release all that tension you are feeling in your body,' Isla said with a dreamy voice Tilly sighed, 'that sounds brilliant, to have my body not feel so tense would be great. I am going to have to go, I am helping my Mum.' 'No problem, shall we meet outside the therapy centre,' replied Isla. 'Yes that's perfect,' replied Tilly, looking forward to a new experience.' 'Bye Tilly see you Friday' 'Bye Isla.

Tilly walked back into the room "Ooh" said Tilly, her mum sensing that something that Tilly was looking forward to. 'So where are you off to pet?' ' Isla has booked an aromatherapy massage' " Mum" 'I cannot wait. I need this,' Tilly replied. 'I know you do, I can see how stressed you are, I have not said anything as I feel you have needed some time to settle down, where are you going for your massage?' 'There is a new therapy centre that has opened up in one of the little rows of shops tucked away by the cafe, it's so convenient to get to,' replied Tilly. 'It's so lovely that you and Isla have found each other again. After all these years,' replied Edith. 'She was your very best friend at school. I remember when you announced that you were both going to London together, I was frantic with worry, but I know how headstrong you are, if you want to do something, nothing will stop you, your dad and I did try to stop you as we felt you were to young to go to London, but we relented and off you went the two of you, Tilly you would have gone anyway' her mum replied, knowing how stubborn her daughter is. 'Yes but Mum,'

Tilly said urgently. 'It was not that I was going for good, but I needed to see London and experience a new way of life. I was only there for 6 months, and we both came back, but I always had a yearning to go back and live there. That era has finished for me now, I need my roots especially as I've got divorced from Bob, I have found it particularly hard dealing with the grief of ending a marriage of many years, family breaking up, my two kids, and grandchildren, I did want to marry for life Mum.'said Tilly feeling emotional. 'I know you did' said Edith 'but to be honest Tilly I did have my reservations about him, when you first brought him up here to meet us, when your mind's made up Tilly it is hard for you to see another way I know I am your mum, but you seemed so in awe of him, somehow you got lost in love and when that happens, you are so immersed and cannot see the red flags that are waving in front of you.'Tilly sat listening to her mum sitting in the chair opposite her, with the blanket wrapped around her mum's legs looking frail, not the strong robust women she used to be, but did not know that her mum felt like this.

Her mum was right, but Tilly also remembered her mother going through the same type of marriage she had been in. Bob was controlling, but to Tilly it was a feeling of being loved and cared for. Tilly did not have a good relationship with her father, she loved him, but never felt properly loved by her father, he could be very abusive and Tilly being very sensitive, it made her feel fearful and anxious. She saw how her mother was controlled but it was not recognised as control back then, it was a totally different era. Tilly went back into her past of how she met Bob, and the chemistry they had, wondering how it all went wrong, and how her brother and sister lives have turned out so different from hers.

Her sister Adele was a grounded person, she was a free spirit like Tilly but Adele was not as sensitive as her sister. She never accepted her father's bullish ways, she gave as good as she got, she was determined he was not going to control her or her future. She certainly was the epitome of the 60's, she took drugs, loved boys and the attention, had sex with most of them, although her father was controlling, she was the most rebellious out of the three of them, the more he told her not to, she did it even more, she loved dancing and had a charisma about her. She was not bothered about being in love, she just loved the freedom of life, as she grew up, she became fiercely independent, and concentrating on what made her happy in work, which was unusual in that era, as you were expected to leave school find yourself a job, either hairdresser or banking etc, then you met a boyfriend, got engaged, married and had children, so Adele did not fit the normal image of a 60's girl, unlike Tilly who wanted to get married and have a family.

Her brother Edward was a very forward thinking boy. As he grew up he was a very motivated man, always striving to be better, he was never in touch with his emotions, even as a young boy, he also like Adele, did not let his father get the better of him, especially as he reached his late teens. By the time he was in his mid Twenties he had done some travelling, eventually ending up living in Canada for almost a decade before returning back to Bamburgh, then emigrating to Australia. Tilly always felt the odd one out in her family, she was very different from her siblings. She had a wonderful bond with her mother, for they were very similar. She was very sensitive, and never really ever got to do what she wanted, she loved sewing and helping out in the community, baking for the family. Wilfred never really liked her doing anything unless he was there, he liked her at home, where she should be, as he always stated when a row ensued. But as Edith got older and the children grew up, she found her strength to become who she wanted to be, she loved doing all her hobbies and helping out when she could.

Both Edith and Tilly loved to sew. Her mum would spend hours with her showing how to make clothes, curtains, cushions, in fact everything that her mum knew how to make. She trained in her younger days as a seamstress, this was one of the many gifts her mum gave to her, as Tilly loved the 60's look, the floral dresses, little jackets, the monochrome look, of Black and White, the beatle caps, White high boots with a platform. Tilly so enjoyed making her own clothes and making new designs. They were very close and shared a deep bond with each other, and still have to this day. In Tilly's eyes Bob opened up a new world for her, she loved singing, playing piano and guitar. When Tilly met him, it was her first time in London. He was a solo singer in venues that had live music, he also played in a band. Their paths crossed when Tilly and Isla first went to London and found lots of music venues, but found a pub where Bob used to sing and play his guitar, they used to smile at each other, Tilly blushing everytime he sang a song, his eyes looking straight at her eyes, making Tilly feel awkward. One night when they were both in the pub, Bob came over when taking a break during his session, and started talking to them Both. Isla knew he fancied Tilly, and she knew Tilly fancied him, as it always seemed to be this pub she wanted to go to….."So girls can I get you a drink,' Bob asked looking at Tilly. 'Yes, that would be lovely thank you' they both said together. 'So what are your names and where do you come from?' He enquired 'Oh before you tell me what you would like to drink,' 'err… I will have a Cinzano and Lemonade please,' replied Isla.. 'Can I have a Martini and Lemonade please with ice?' muttered Tilly, still blushing from him coming over. 'So now we have drinks sorted, what are your names?'. 'Mine is Bob, and yours,' he asked 'Oh I am Tilly,' 'and I'm Isla,' we both come from Bamburgh in Northumberland,' Isla continued. 'Wow, you are a long way from home, what brings you down here,' Bob enquired. "We both wanted to experience living in London for six months or so. We are loving it, it's lively, loads to see and do, and we love the music scene.' 'Where do you come from?' Isla enquired, 'I come from Welling in Kent, I was born and bred there, it's a train journey away that's all.' 'Hey girls, enjoy the rest of the evening. I have to go back on stage in a few minutes to set up, hopefully see you again soon,' looking totally at Tilly as he was saying it, a broad smile came on his face as he was looking at her. 'Yes that would be lovely,' replied Tilly as she put her face downwards with her big Brown eyes looking directly at him under her fringe. 'Isla, I think I'm smitten with him, he is just gorgeous,' Tilly smiled as she was talking, 'Yes he does seem like a really nice guy Tilly. '

'Well we can come next week and see him if you like, ' Isla replied, knowing Tilly would love to speak with him again. Tilly and Bob had really gotten to know each other, just by meeting in the pub every week, she had never spent any time with him. It was a few months later, when Tilly and Isla were going back home, this was to be the last time she would see Bob. She felt very upset, but he never mentioned going out together so just thought he just liked her. When Bob came over that night, he noticed that she seemed very quiet, he asked her if she was ok. Tilly told him that they were both going home at the weekend, and would miss London and the bright lights, he seemed quite upset that she was going back home. 'Hey Tilly don't worry, we can exchange telephone numbers if you like.' 'Would your mum and dad mind if I rang you at home?' he enquired, hoping that he would get her phone number. 'My Mum would not mind, but my Dad might, not unless you can ring me during the day, I need to find a job when I get back' Tilly replied.' 'No problem, that is better for me as I tend to work in the evenings,' Bob replied back. They exchanged numbers and kept in contact with each other, Tilly was smitten with him, she wanted to sing and play piano and do what Bob was doing, he was her dream man. Although Bob was only a few years older than her, he was definitely more streetwise than Tilly.

Tilly and Isla were on the train home, both looking out of the window and seemed to be in their own worlds, they both loved the last six months of their lives. It really opened their eyes after living in the tiny village of Bamburgh. Tilly knew she had fallen for him, she was in deep thought of trying to understand how she could have these feelings. We have never been out on a date, never kissed, never been on our own together, but the chemistry was something else, I can feel it, he's in my head all the time. The train gently came to a halt at Bamburgh Station, Tilly all of sudden realising the journey had come to an end, both girls, getting their luggage, making their way back home. Tilly, already working out in her head as to how soon she can get back down to London. Bob rang Tilly as often as he could, and Tilly would keep in contact, she went down to London every few months to meet him, and he would come up to Bamburgh, but it was quite a while before he could stay at her home, after a year of this back and forth, Tilly decided to go back to London, she had been itching to get back down there, although she would miss her Mum, the bright lights of London kept calling her back, she got herself a job, a place to live, Tilly and Bob had got closer together. Bob proposed to her one night after a gig had finished on the stage in front of the audience. Tilly thought all her dreams had come true, she loved and adored Bob. Eventually they got married in the pretty village church in Bamburgh, their reception was held in Bamburgh castle as her Father still worked there. They stayed for a few weeks, then moved in together at Tillys Flat, in London. She started singing in the band alongside Bob, playing guitar beside Pete, and played the piano when needed.

'Tilly, are you ok,' enquired Edith 'You seem like you are in another world, have I said something to upset you, if I have I never meant to,' she asked quietly. 'No, no it's ok Mum, I was miles away, just remembering when I first met him, and the feelings I had, and how Adele and Edward's lives have been so different to mine. To be honest I never knew you felt like that when you met Bob, it sort of upset me I suppose.' she said gently with a hundred thoughts going round in her head at the same time. 'Tilly I never meant to hurt you, but what I saw was the same type of man like your pa I did love him, but I could never be myself, your pa had controlling ways as you know only to well Tilly, I just never wanted you to have the same life as me, that's all. We are very similar Tilly, your brother and sister had a harder shell so they did not let their pa get to them, you on the other hand are like me, you are very sensitive, feelings of hurt go straight to your heart pet, and you cant let them go. The one thing I have learnt, Tilly, we all need to follow our own path in this life, sometimes it cannot be changed until the change is done, your marriage came to an end, and that is what has happened to you, you have got older, wiser and stronger. therefore you were ready to make the decision to divorce, and start a new life. Tilly do you not realise how much strength and courage it takes to leave a controlling relationship, especially the amount of years you were with him, you became codependent and lost yourself, I could see that years ago pet, but how could I give advice when I was in the same position, but when me and your pa married, divorce was not an option it was for better or worse. You can now start a new life. Tilly, don't punish yourself, it takes time to recover and heal from any marriage breakup, let alone one like you experienced,' as Edith put her blanket back in place on her legs 'so there you go Tilly.' 'Where did all that come from.' Edith added.

   'Actually Mum I was thinking the same, I did not know you had such wisdom,' as they both laughed together. 'Call it old age,' said Edith. 'When you children got older, I wanted to get divorced, but it was not an easy thing to do, I was fearful of how I was going to support myself, I never worked, whereas you have and have your own finances.' 'I know mum,' replied Tilly.' You are right, it's just weird how I saw you controlled when I was a child, and vowed I would never let it happen to me and it did' said Tilly. 'I know I am an old lady now, but I am here for you always, I love you and want you to be happy.' 'Thanks Mum, 'Tilly continued, 'I was not sure how you would take it, if I started talking about my past, I now realise how much I have bottled it all up for years. Since I have met up with Isla, just talking to her has made me realise how much I have suppressed in my life, I don't think that I have ever really looked at myself that closely, have just continued and accepted what was happening to me, now I feel this is the right time to heal myself, so I can move forward with my life, make new memories, enjoy my family and grandchildren, not feeling in a constant state of low anxiety, feeling on edge all the time.' Tilly replied, smiling at her mum. 'Now pet, in time you will be happy again, I can feel it in my bones.' 'So how about I put the kettle on and make us a nice cuppa Mum? I know I could do with one,' Tilly said, as she went over to her mum and gave her the biggest hug and a kiss on the cheek, tears in her eyes, 'I love you Mum, thank you.' 'Now then pet, that is a good idea let's have a cuppa. 'Tilly, 'her mum continued, 'that was a lovely hug and a kiss, I have missed your hugs Tilly you were always good at giving them.' Whilst Tilly was waiting for the kettle to boil, she was thinking that she had never heard her mum talk like before, she realised how wise and intuitive she was, it felt like a weight had been lifted from her being able to speak to her mum and share her feelings. The kettle had started to boil,

Tilly was preparing the dinner, it was all in the oven, Now for a cuppa and a biscuit while it is cooking. Tilly and her mum sat together while enjoying their cup of tea, they were both quietly reflecting over what had just been spoken about earlier. It had brought up memories for Edith, about her marriage to Wilfred. In her generation divorce or separation happened very rarely, you really just got on with it, and lived life the best you could, so Edith was happy that Tilly had found the strength to walk away.

After Wilfred had passed away, Edith did manage to have a type of life, she joined in community events making clothes and knitted toys. She was famous for her beautiful, homemade jams so she kept herself busy selling her homemade crafts to raise money for community projects. She made new friends, using her creative talents, it gave her back her freedom. Wilfred was a husband who wanted his wife at home and only went out as a couple, which Edith adhered to and brought the family up; she could see for herself that Bob was very similar to Wilfred. Meanwhile, Tilly, was enjoying her cuppa, her mind on the aromatherapy massage in a few days time, she could feel the tension leaving her body just thinking about the massage, In fact she lost track of time, she glanced across to see her mum having one of her naps, forgetting the dinner was in the oven, she quickly got up and saved the dinner from forming burnt edges in the nick of time. Edith was in her middle 80's, but Tilly could see she was getting more frail, and she did love her cheeky naps during the day, but her mind was still very sharp. 'Mum wake up,' gently tapping her on the shoulder, 'dinner is ready.' 'lovely thank you pet,' "er" Tilly interrupted her, 'Mum' I hope it tastes ok, I sort of forgot the dinner was in the oven,' Edith looked down and laughed and replied 'well you don't often get smoked haddock with slightly burnt edges, but the poached eggs look perfect. See Tilly you can always find a positive out of everything in life.' They both settled down to watch the TV chatting in between programmes when the adverts appeared. Tilly and her mum had really bonded back to how they used to be, Tilly feeling more comfortable talking to her, as she gradually opened up and her feelings came to the surface ready to be released and healed.

CHAPTER 2

Tilly's alarm clock went off at 8am on the dot. Tilly, still in her slumbers, put her hand out to turn off the alarm. No it can't be Tilly thought to herself, I don't even feel I have even gone to sleep, she turned over on her side pulling the duvet over her head. Tilly had not been feeling so good, feeling a bit low and depressed trying to come to terms with her divorce, her past coming rapidly to the surface, to be looked at, made her feel lost within herself. She gradually opened her eyes to the sun shining through her window, with a slight breeze from the window that was slightly ajar. Her bedroom overlooked the lush green fields where cows and sheep graze in the pastures yonder on the hill. She pulled herself up and looked out of the window looking at the sheep and cows minding their own business, cows chewing the cud, the sheep merrily pulling at the grass. She took a long hard look at this glorious place she called home now quietly feeling grateful for being back in her homeland, but wondered why she had lost that feeling of peace and contentment, she knew it was there, for she had felt that feeling. She knew intuitively it was suppressing all the emotions trying to keep everything buried so she did not have to deal with the past. A big smile appeared on her face, it was the day she was to meet Isla and have the Aromatherapy massage. Ever since Isla had booked the treatments she was so looking forward to experiencing the massage using the essential oils, but also aware that her emotions could surface, emotions that she had held inside for most of her life and just imagined the aroma of the oils as she entered the relaxing and calming therapy room.

Tilly had breakfast out in the garden. It was so peaceful, the warmth of the sun on her body, the birds singing, just drinking up the energy. "Ahh, this is just what I need, to start the day she thought." Whilst in the garden she rang her daughter Sarah and her son Stanley for a catch up, to make some arrangements for meeting up, it seemed ages since she had seen them and her grandchildren, so much had gone on. Her children were very supportive of her, they knew what she had been through, living with it in their own childhoods. They have now both grown up into the most caring and responsible adults, with their own families. Stanley is motivated and driven very much like her brother Edward. He is now a married man with his own family, a very responsible husband and father, who looks after his family. Her daughter Sarah, equally motivated and driven, is slightly different. Sarah, has always been an independent girl, studied at school, very creative, a bit of a rebel with a cause, but now she is all grown up, married with her own family too.

Although she loved her father, she did struggle to have a close connection with him, and sometimes feared him. Unfortunately her relationship with her father changed when he met someone else. A new wife who had a son and a daughter. Tilly could see that her daughter was feeling left out, and it was hurting her badly, unfortunately, Tilly did not know how to deal with this situation. Tilly herself had nervous breakdowns, agoraphobia, panic attacks, depression and anxiety, from the abuse she had received over the years. And felt so useless, and worthless that she could not help her daughter. Tillys world got smaller and smaller and she never really went out much, and when she did, the panic and fear that just rose up in her, it would make her feel so unwell she would head back to the safety of her home yet in reality it was not safe at her home either. She has lived like this for years, never really knowing how to get out of the marriage and even when her and Bob split up, which happened a few times, she always went back, he always promised to change, but never did. Sarah especially, when her father remarried, tried to please him all the time, she was so scared of losing him, no matter what he was still her father, but everytime she got close, another drama would occur, Tilly hated what she was seeing, but was trying to heal from the abusive relationship herself.

'OK, that's great,' said Tilly. 'That date is in the diary. I can't wait to see you, Martin, Hallie and Lyla, I will ring your brother, and give him the date. Will ring you tomorrow to let you know. Your nan will be so excited to see you all.' 'Ok' replied her daughter Sarah, 'enjoy your massage, love you Mum,' 'love you too Sarah very much, give the girls a kiss from their Nanna.' ' Will do,' Sarah replied. Tilly was happy that her daughter had found love, the love that she would have liked to have experienced, but never did, well, yes in the beginning, but once Stanley was born. Bob just turned on her. Sarah, her daughter when she got older, once said to her mother, the one thing she had learnt is that she did not want a marriage or a life like her mother. Sarah could never understand why her mother put up with it. Tilly can see that Sarah has made the right choices and decisions in life. Her and Martin are an ideal couple, they support each other, and have a wonderful family life with their daughters. The one thing that Tilly can see in Sarah, is the same type of mother that Tilly was when she had her young family.

Tilly looked at the time, it was 1pm, where had the time gone she thought, I had better get some lunch and sort out some clothes to wear. Tilly got dressed and was ready to go. She started her walk to the shop, she seemed to pass everyone she knew, typical she thought just when you need to be somewhere on time. As she turned the corner she saw Isla waiting outside the therapy centre. Tilly finally got to Isla, 'I am so sorry I am a bit late, I just seemed to have met everybody on my way here,' Tilly said out of breath, 'No problem, just get your breath back Tilly it's not 2.30 yet, we have a few minutes,' replied Isla. Tilly, now composed, took hold of Isla's arm as they went through the door of Aromasense, the health centre. As soon as they walked in, the aroma of the oils wafted under their noses, tickling their senses. 'Oh Isla, the oils are just beautiful,' 'I know,' replied Isla, ' they are very powerful and uplifting.'

'Hello I am Sophie the receptionist, are you Tilly and Isla for your 2.30 appointments for the two aromatherapy massages?' 'Yes that's us they replied together,' with excited voices, 'Ok' said the receptionist, 'Isla you are booked in with Holly and Tilly you are booked in with Charlotte, please take a seat, they won't belong.' Tilly made herself busy by looking at the leaflet, giving all the available therapies that were on offer. 'Hey Isla look, they do reiki healing, I may book for this, it's very good for healing emotional problems, and feeling out of balance, they use crystals as well.' Tilly added. 'Yes I have had reiki before,' said Isla. 'I found it so calming and peaceful, it really helped.' 'Oh you have had reiki Isla?' Tilly asked, inquisitively, 'Yes, explained Isla, I have had quite a few treatments, and I have found them very helpful especially, when I was going through my spiritual awakening, where I was very confused about life, but knew there was more to life than this.' 'You have been through your spiritual awakening. I have felt something similar to that but have never really found myself on that level' Tilly replied. 'To be honest Tilly, it's a lifelong journey of self discovery, as you are always changing, but I love that side of me, and do my best to work on that level. So maybe we can have a chat, they do counselling and reflexology here as well as Til's, they certainly cater for all areas of well being.' Replied Isla. Little did Tilly realise that she would be a regular client in the near future, as the aromatherapy massage opened her up spiritually, emotionally, physically and mentally, and Isla would play a pivotal role in her life, in helping Tilly to understand her spiritual journey, and find a gift that was hidden beneath all the layers that had been protecting Tilly for many years, she often felt like she was looking at the world on the outside never really participating, the only exception to that was when she was singing and playing her music. Tilly loved and enjoyed having her family, she is so very much a family person. Unfortunately, what she had experienced in her childhood and her marriage to Bob, made her feel insecure, not worthy, lack of confidence, feeling like she was going mad, had robbed her of having the idyllic family life she dreamed of as a child. She has not sung or played her guitar for years. She knew deep down she had to heal herself first before anything else could move forward in her life.

Tilly's healing journey has begun. 'So, who is Tilly?' enquired the therapist. 'Me, I'm Tilly.' 'Nice to meet you Tilly, I am Charlotte, your therapist for today, would you like to follow me?' Tilly very gingerly followed her, she felt excited but also a bit nervous, as she had to take her clothes off, in fact she had not taken her clothes off for a long time in front of someone she did not know, let alone her ex husband, she was conscious of her body, all the bits that were not in the right place, as she would say, everything has gone south. The very thought of it made her feel very vulnerable.

As Charlotte opened the door, the wonderful aroma of bergamot, chamomile, neroli and lavender filled the room, Tilly just stood there taking it all in. The room was light and bright, the couch positioned in the middle of the room. pink fluffy towels folded with perfection lay on the couch, couch roll, and a comfy pillow, Tilly looked at the couch and could not wait until she was up there enjoying the massage. She spotted a little oil burner, where the aroma of the oils were gently swirling around the room, creating a peaceful and harmonious ambiance to the room. pink ditsy curtains, hung at the windows, with crystals hanging from the window, everytime the sun shone through it created a beautiful prism of rainbow colours which adorned the walls. She also noticed a tray with a lot of bottles, base oil, small mixing jars for blending the oils, ready to be concocted for a new client, it all looked so magical. 'Tilly,' Charlotte called to her. 'Are you ready?' Would you like to sit in the chair over here?' 'You looked like you were soaking up the energies of the room.' 'This is so lovely and relaxing,' Tilly declared. 'Thank you Tilly, that's exactly how I like my clients to feel when they walk into the room, so come and take a seat, we need to do a consultation, so I can know exactly what oils to blend for you.' 'Don't look so worried Tilly, this is really a lovely therapy to be enjoyed, it will release all the tension in your body, and help you relax, some clients fall asleep.' A big smile came on Tillys face as she said that. 'I don't know why, but I feel very emotional. I am not normally like this, but having this massage feels right for me.' Tilly replied in a quavering voice. 'Hey Tilly, it's ok, don't feel embarrassed, most therapies can bring deep emotions to the surface, in fact Tilly, it's good to feel like this, "Erm" I mean it in the nicest possible way. I feel you are ready to release these emotions. Are you ok Tilly for us to start the consultation?' Charlotte said, looking at Tilly to register her emotional level. 'Yes I'm ok,' Tilly replied, still feeling a bit tearful. 'Sorry Charlotte,' Charlotte came in straight away, 'Tilly you have nothing to say sorry for, emotions are the most natural responses, when we are ready to release those tears, it is all part of the healing journey.' 'Thank you Charlotte.' Replied Tilly.

It felt like an eternity with the consultation, Tilly did not realise how in depth it would be, but as an holistic therapy, that is how it works, everything needs to be considered on every level. Tilly was shocked with herself at just how much came out, she just felt so relieved just sharing with a stranger she had never met before, and the information that she shared with Charlotte, who was very patient with her. Understanding her childhood of control and emotional abuse, then in a marriage with the same emotional and abusive control, had indeed left her bereft of herself knowing that she needed to start the process of healing and recovering from all of her past, which seemed like the biggest mountain to climb.

'Ok, Tilly, so let's get you on the couch, you will have a towel covering the areas that I am not working on.' Charlotte left Tilly to get settled as she went to blend the oils that thought were appropriate for Tilly on that day. 'Tilly the blends will be mainly for relaxation, and to help release some of the emotions that are ready to come to the surface. Is that ok for you Tilly?' enquired Charlotte. 'Yes' a muffled voice came from the pillow, as she was getting herself comfortable for the start of the massage. 'Those oils smell divine, what have you used today,' said Tilly. 'I have blended, geranium, lavender, bergamot, grapefruit and for your head massage, I will use frankincense and neroli, that is equally a beautiful aroma.' Tilly was laying on the couch, waiting for the touch of Charlotte's hands starting to unravel all the knots in her back, especially by her shoulder blades, and shoulders, the tension she felt in her neck. Having worked on her back, Tilly could feel already that a release had taken place. Just as she was getting used to this feeling of being undressed, the towel was lowered to show Tilly's bum, she felt very uncomfortable, at somebody seeing and massaging her bottom, but thankfully that feeling soon disappeared, as Charlotte's hands went up her back again, she could feel even more tension melting away, but is was so exhilarating, it made Tilly feel alive, as Charlotte moved to release the tension either side of her spine.

Tillys emotions had started to rise to the surface, she was lying on the couch, not sure what to do, she tried to control them, but in the end the tears fell silently down her cheeks making the pillow damp. She felt slightly frightened of how these emotions had overpowered her. Deep down she knew what was happening, it was to help her move forward in her life, but it still felt scary. She managed to get herself back in the moment of the massage, the aroma of the oils and the relaxation music. It was not long after that, that Charlotte had asked Tilly to turn over gently onto her back. As she turned over Charlotte could see that tears were falling down her cheeks. Tilly could not suppress them anymore, Tilly felt so silly and stupid as she was surprised at the reaction to the massage. Charlotte already knew that Tilly was upset, she could feel it in her body.' 'I'm sorry Charlotte.' 'Hey it's ok Tilly, it's quite normal. You have deep suppressed emotions that have been buried deep inside for a very long time. Sadness from the past will react to the areas I have worked on. When I started massaging your back, I could feel the knots on either side of your spine, this area in particular carries all the emotions of suppression, especially between the shoulder blades, that is where the tension is held, so I'm not surprised at all that this created the outpouring of emotions.' "Really" Tilly replied, not quite understanding what had happened to her. Charlotte put her hand on her shoulder. 'Tilly you did say in the consultation that you have not long been divorced after a long marriage, you have suffered emotional abuse, and had issues with your father, the emotions you have been through have been very traumatic. Most people who go through these experiences start to neglect their emotions by suppressing them, thinking that they will just go away, and just carry on with life, just blocking out everything. But actually the body keeps score on such emotions, they then become trapped in the body causing emotional mental and physical and spiritual imbalances that in turn creates fatigue, anxiety, fear, panic attacks, illness and disease, the list goes on, then the body feels the pain. Have you experienced any of these feelings?' Tilly thought for a moment, then slowly replied to Charlotte, 'well, yes I suppose I have, during the divorce and after, then I came up here and felt so much more content within myself, but just lately, starting to feel a bit anxious, low mood etc. I have never really thought that my past could create such emotions.' 'That's ok Tilly,' said Charlotte, 'at least you have some idea now, I am no doctor, but it seems you may be suffering some of the effects from your past. It may be worth discussing with a counsellor, or maybe seeking the doctor's advice.' Tilly again knew deep down that she was ready to see a counsellor but something inside was stopping her, could she face the pain that would come up. Today was the very first time she had ever openly discussed, it was a massive step for her today. But she felt lighter than when she went in for her massage. 'When you feel ready we do have a counsellor here, her name is Lucy, she is lovely and very spiritual, I feel maybe that is something you need to factor in as you are very spiritual yourself, of course if that is the path you would like to go down.' 'Yes I will look at that' said Tilly. ' Charlotte, how often would you recommend a massage?' 'Well to start with maybe once a month, then see how you go,' replied Charlotte.

Tilly got up and got dressed, her shoulders were so much looser, in fact her body felt like a new body. 'Thank you Charlotte for spending the time with me. I will book one when I go down to reception.' 'You're welcome Tilly, take care.' When Tilly got down to reception, Isla had been waiting for about 10 mins. 'Hey Tilly how was it?' 'It was just magical Isla, I loved it, you were right the aroma of the oils were just beautiful. I am just going to book another appointment for next month,' said Tilly. 'I think I will as well, I do feel so much better too' replied Isla. 'So shall we make these appointments every month together, then we get to see each other?' 'Why not Tilly, I think it's a great idea. They both paid their fees, made new appointments for the following month. They both said goodbye to Sophie and Tilly picked up a brochure with all the therapies that were at the centre, mainly looking for the information on the counselling. They both walked out into the little cobbled street and walked towards the beach. 'So Tilly, how was the massage?' Isla took Tillys arm, noticing the tears in her eyes, she was also talking in a very slow gentle voice. 'Whatever is wrong Tilly ?' Isla asked, 'I started getting upset when laying on the couch. I felt stupid, but

Charlotte was very good at helping me understand my emotions. I did not realise how much I have suppressed my emotions for so many years. When Charlotte started working on my back, she was massaging up up the spine It was like the floodgates had opened, that's when Charlotte explained that the trapped emotions that I have been carrying around with me, create tension in the body, I have always thought the head was the place for thoughts, making decisions, crying, and the pains in your body, were separate to the head, but now I understand that the mind and body are connected they weave and work together. Once we work with the head and body together as one, then they can work together to heal you.'

Isla, having more of an understanding of the spiritual side of life, knew there was more to this then Tilly was letting on, these emotions can be trauma from the past, abuse, childhood issues, not feeling part of the world, not feeling loved properly in relationships as well as family, these all play a pivotal role, as to whether we are confident and able to have the life we want and deserve, or we are shrouded from a joyful life, by all the negative layers that we have taken on from people who are close to us, that are meant to love us, but instead we take on their perception of us, and we become who they think we are, that is when we begin to feel disempowered, lack confidence, low self esteem, self doubting. 'Tilly, please stop punishing yourself,' said Isla, 'better that these emotions have come to the surface to be healed then to still be trapped in your body. You are very sensitive Tilly, so any type of emotional upset will affect you. But at least, you can start working on the areas that need to be released from you, so welcome to the start of your healing journey.' 'Yes I know, Isla, you are right, I should have realised this years ago, but I just got lost.' 'Tilly, we are near the beach, let's sit down, you can compose yourself, and take in the afternoon sun. Look Tilly, there is a bench there, go and grab it, and I will get us a cuppa and some cake. Cake always cheers us up, I will give you the bigger piece, as you need cheering up more than me,' Isla said smiling. 'How was your massage Isla?' said Tilly. 'Oh it was lovely and relaxing, it feeds the soul. I needed that, so glad that I have booked another one with you.' said Isla. They sat there together, basking in the sun, enjoying their cuppa and coffee and walnut cake, listening to the waves gently lapping up onto the seashore, both so happy that they had their friendship back and were there to support one another. Tilly had composed herself. She did not want to go home with her mum seeing her so upset, when she was supposed to be stress free from the massage. 'So Tilly, how was your Aromatherapy Massage?' Edith enquired, as Tilly sat down and nestled into the plumped up cushions on the chair. 'Oh mum it was so lovely and relaxing, all the knots have been ironed out of my shoulders and neck, the aroma of the oils are so beautiful, you feel you are in heaven,' Tilly replied, in a slow relaxed tone. 'That is good, pet are you going again?' 'Yes' replied Tilly, 'I am going every month, it is a lovely therapy centre, they do a lot of other therapies, I am thinking of trying some of them.'

Later that evening, when Edith had gone to bed, Tilly was sitting by herself, thinking about the massage, and how her emotions came out of nowhere. She knew she had to deal with her past wounds, from her father and Bob. She started to question herself, and how she had ended up being divorced. When she met Bob, she never knew he had so many problems. They were right in the beginning of the relationship. She did think that things did not feel right, but chose to ignore them. She loved and adored Bob, and just thought it would pass once the children came along, but in fact it got worse. She started going back to certain times, her thoughts were taking to times that clearly had made Tilly so anxious, and out of control, Tilly felt very uncomfortable at going back into the situations that had messed her up mentally, but not understanding how she had become a shadow of her former self, her self confidence had gone, the light had been turned off deep inside, in fact the light had been turned off for years, she had just got used to living like that, she felt numb, devoid of any emotions herself. She went back to the beginning, with Bob being a musician, when he played on his own at gigs, she saw with her own eyes, when she was in London with Isla how he had a following of women, they all seemed to flock to him, this was before he came over to introduce himself to her and Isla. He was tall, dark, and very handsome, blue eyes you just got lost in, everytime he looked at you, long dark hair to his shoulders with a slight curl, the trousers he wore, certainly showed of the the slim hips, and everything else around that area, the trousers flared down to the black boots with a slight platform sole, tight shirts with a snazzy waistcoat, with a bit of bare chest showing, he knew he had charm and charisma, he also knew that he exuded sex appeal, and my god did he play on that he could have any girl, they were his for the taking. Tilly did see him one night leaving the gig with a tall leggy blonde girl, in fact she saw this a few times, with different women, but Tilly being young and innocent, it did not register, the fact that he came over to her and Isla, he made it very clear, that he fancied her, Tilly just felt like the cat that got the cream, it boosted her confidence no end, he was a musician, so was Tilly, it was an instant attraction. As Tilly continued to think, she realised that actually she seemed to fit the sort of woman Bob liked. She was tall, long blonde hair, very slim, loved fashion, she certainly was a fashionesta of her time, she designed and made some of the clothes she wore. Tilly stood out in the crowd, she too had played a few gigs in her own home town of Bamburgh, and other villages around, she was used to being centre stage, and always looked gorgeous. The only difference was that she was a sensitive and empathic soul, how could she have known that this is what Bob honed in on.

Tilly had a controlling and abusive dad, unfortunately this paved the way for Tilly to attract someone like Bob into her life, her own father was the life and soul of the party, when out socially and gave help to other members of the village, he was well known, he was the head gardener at the Bamburgh Castle, Wilfred, Tillys Dad, as far as she knew, had not cheated on her mum, but was very unkind to her, he seemed to want everything his own way, he did raise his voice a lot, Tilly saw the other side of him, when he was in a bad mood, he would come home and hit her mum, he used to use the cane a lot to her and her brother and sister, he knocked all the confidence out of her mother, that she became someone, who did not go out much, she occasionally got away with joining in on some community events, but it was Wilfred who had to be top dog, he was fiercely competitive, so for her mum and Tilly, it had a mental effect on them both, but

Adele and Edward the reverse effect. So for Tilly she had no comparison of how a man should treat her, so it was familiar for Tilly how Bob was treating her with no love or affection. When they first met, he was so kind to her, bought her little gifts, but very subtly started to control, because Tilly played in the band with him by then, he made sure he would pick her clothes, Tilly saw this as love and care, and totally went with his decision, occasionally, she would change the top or dress just before going out on the stage, but it was to late for Bob to intervene, but when they got home he would make her feel bad about herself, saying she looked like a "whore," "who do you think you are dressing like that" "your to fat for that dress". Tilly did feel uncomfortable about the comments, but her dad had said similar things to her, so just accepted that this was normal. She also saw Bob flirt with other young women, she thought so naively that being the lead singer in a band, he was making sure that the band kept their following of fans, who came to see them on a regular basis. Tilly still deep in thought remembered some the Christmas's with their children, that he caused such great pain and sadness, with his drunken outbursts, which she had most nights, but at Christmas, he was worse, he created so many problems, smashing things in his temper in his drunken state, one Christmas, he decided to throw the food outside in the garden, because Tilly was not at home when he came in, she had taken the children out early on Christmas eve, to a carol concert when she got home, Stanley saw something shining out of the window laying on the grass, they went out and found all the food. Sarah and Stanley started crying another time he decided to punch the kitchen door which had the glass panels, severing the tendons in his hands, blood everywhere, glass smashed, Stanley had woken up, with all the shouting and noise, and sat on the stairs, confused, it was a ritual every night. He would arrive home drunk, he gambled, had so many affairs, was a sex addict, he would set upon Tilly, she was living in fear. He would kick and punch her, he never wanted Tilly to be better than him, so he would pull her apart, everytime Tilly got her strength back, he would bring her down again with his mental abuse, he knew her trigger points, so he knew exactly what his words and actions would do to her. Then he would be so lovely and loving, for a week or even a few months, but then he would revert back. She felt so guilty for putting her children through this, she never ever wanted her children to see what she had witnessed as a child.

Bob never abused the children, only Tilly, but he never really had any emotional connection to them. She was powerless to him, for over the years, he had totally disempowered her, she was lost, felt so unwell all the time, she had nervous breakdowns, panic attacks, and anxiety. She also had social anxiety, agoraphobia for years, after all the years of marriage, she was a shell of her former self. She did occasionally find the strength to leave a few times, or he left, but he always charmed her back, he always had affairs, throughout the marriage, her mind was closed down, and so was she, but she loves her children, more than anything in life, and tried to protect them, so she eventually led two lives, one of making sure the children never really knew what went on, and acted normally, but inside she was terrified of Bob, and trod on eggshells all the time, it became normal to her. Everytime the key went in the door when he came home from work, her anxiety would rise up within, her head in a whirl, to see what mood he was in, was it going to be peaceful or abusive, she knew she could never leave properly, and survive, for he dealt with all the finances giving her just enough money to buy food and clothes for the children. She had a beautiful house, to the outside world, it looked like she had everything she could wish for. Bob's business was doing well, they were comfortable, she had nice clothes, when he gave her money, especially if they were going out socially to a posh do, in social situations, he would be so attentive, nobody would ever know what went on behind closed doors.

All these memories came flooding back, just snippets of her life. She was crying so much the tears were cascading down her cheeks, she tried to be quiet, she did not want her mum to wake up, she never really knew the depth of what really went on in her marriage. Tilly lived in London, her Mum in Bamburgh, so they visited a few times a year, and when they did Bob was on his best behaviour, although Edith saw straight through him, she knew there were problems, it was like reliving her life all over again, but she did not want to cause trouble, she did not see her Daughter and Grandchildren that often, so wanted to make the most of making memories of the good times she would spend with them.

The next morning, Tilly went out to get some groceries, and decided to ring Isla. She told Isla how she had sobbed so much the night before, she had sobbed so much her body ached all over. She had a bad headache, she never knew there were so many tears inside of her. After explaining to Isla what had happened, she suggested maybe having some counselling sessions at the therapy centre. Isla did not know about all the abuse that went on, but she had a pretty good idea of reading between the lines when she and Tilly had spoken in the past few months since they had met up. 'Funnily enough' Tilly said, 'Charlotte had made the same suggestion to me when I had my massage. I have been thinking about it.' 'Tilly do you think that would help heal you from your past hurts?' 'Yes, I am happy to give it a try.' 'It would certainly help you move forward in your life now. Talking to a professional may start you on that journey. Your soul needs emotional healing. I am here as your friend, to support you, should you need that.' 'You know Isla, Tilly added, 'that is just what I need, I feel so guilty about my children's childhood, there is a part of me missing, in fact not a part, but a bloody great big hole,' Tilly laughed gently down the phone, I think it's my heart, it feels so broken' Tilly continued. 'Tilly, I think you are right. It's for you, to clear all the past hurts healing the wounds of your soul, You can thank Charlotte, she has a done good job on awakening you, working on your suppressed emotions, everything has a time, and this is your time now Tilly,' Isla added with an excited tone to her voice. 'You are right Isla when I get home I am going to book an appointment,' Tilly said with a voice that seemed positive and upbeat.

"AND" Tilly, Isla piped up, you know what we need don't you ? We need a break away, do you fancy going to London for a long weekend, go to the cafes, visit some old haunts, look round the shops, some retail therapy, you know we love bringing a few bags of goodies home,' Isla spoke in an excited voice at the thought of a weekend away. 'Yes, Isla I would love that,' Tilly said in an excited voice. 'Just what we need is a girly weekend.' I will ring you later, are you around ? enquired Tilly. 'Yes of course Tilly,' I am always around for my beautiful friend,' Isla spoke gently. ' Isla don't, you are making me cry again, you know I feel the same, I am always here for you too, I just feel so blessed we are together again,' Tilly replied with a few sobs in between her reply. 'Tilly, I didn't mean to make you cry, just wanted to let you know how much I value your friendship.' 'I know Isla.' said Tilly. 'I will wait to hear from you later today.' 'Take care Bye Tilly,' Isla said. ' I will Bye Isla.'

Tilly came home on a much happier note, the thought of a weekend in London, this is just what the doctor ordered. Tilly hunted for her diary, looking through it she found a date for a long weekend with Isla. Looking through her diary, she smiled to herself, only 2 weeks to go, and I get to see my children and grandchildren. She put down her diary, and was drawn to a box that she had not opened from moving to her mum's house. It looked quite old, the corners had been bashed about a bit during the move, Tilly was wondering what was inside this box, when she opened it, she found pictures of her and Isla at different stages of them growing up, pictures when they were in London, pictures of herself, her children when they were born, some pictures of her and Bob. Right at the bottom was some really old pictures taken with Jack, who she had known from such a young age, she sat and stared at them, they brought back such happy memories, he was the first boy she had kissed, he was part of the family really, his mum was Tillys mum's best friend. As she looked closer she saw some old letters still in the envelopes with a pink ribbon around them, she knew instantly what these were, they were letters from Jack from when they were young. She had lovely memories of Jack, she carefully put them back in the box. She started to move bits of paper around, seeing a book peering out of the papers. It was a book which had lots of phone numbers. She was scanning through the pages, when she came across Peter Appletons number, "wow," she was thinking, she could not remember when she last spoke to him. He was the guitarist in the band, Tilly and Peter really got on well together, she knew

37

Peter always held a candle to her, but Tilly never saw him like that years ago, he was a good friend to her. She always found Peter supportive, when they were in the band, Peter saw the way Bob spoke to her, he actually warned Tilly of marrying him, but she just loved and adored Bob, as they say love is blind. Peter was always there for her, many a time Tilly had rung him. He always seemed to calm her down. She often visited his studio, although he was in the band he was a very sensitive caring creative man he loved his craft it was his passion, he was a sculptor, he loved Tilly, and decided to make a sculpture of Tilly's head and shoulders, when he completed it, he invited her to his studio to show her his masterpiece, Tilly was so humbled as to why he would want to do this for her, but she loved it, It clicked when she realised there were a few times when she unexpectedly went round to his studio, seeing him move quickly putting a sheet over something, so she could not see it. Peter always kept the sculpture, as Bob would not have liked this at all. It's wrapped in a cotton sheet, and placed on a shelf at the back of his studio. They had gentle contact with each other every couple of months, but their paths went in different directions, so in the end no contact was made with each other. Tilly sat on the bed reflecting on the band days, the fun they had.

    On a whim Tilly had started dialling Pete's number, she started feeling a bit nervous, she did not even know if this was still his number, he knew nothing of Tillys life, the last she knew of him, was that he got married, to someone he met while in the band, a bit like how Tilly and Bob met, she remembered going to his wedding in Surrey. He had moved back to where he lived before moving to London. The phone was ringing, well she thought at least the number works. Her mouth was dry, she felt butterflies in her tummy, questioning her impulse, on just ringing this number. "Oh My God, what do I say after all these years," just as she was getting a drink of water, a voice said "Hello" ….Tilly could not quite get her words out, as she was swallowing the water, in a muffled voice, she said "Hello" 'is that Peter?' ' Yes,' replied Peter, 'who's that,' he paused…' I recognise that voice, right ok hold on a moment' "I know" its Tilly isn't it.

'Yes it is,' Tilly replied. It's been such a long time now, so much has happened. 'How are you Pete?' 'What's going on in your life, are you still happily married?' 'Unfortunately not,' Pete replied, ' I am divorced. One of the worst times of my life, I found out my wife, well ex wife now' he exclaimed 'was cheating on me, had been for a few years, then she came home and dropped the bombshell, to say I was numb was an understatement, she moved out, took my daughter with her, it has taken me a few years to get back on track again. Now I lead a peaceful life.' 'Oh Pete, I am so sorry to hear that news. Well I am in the same position as you, but have only been divorced for just a year. So it all feels still very raw, but lucky enough my children had left home, so did not have that added stress that you have had to contend with. I cannot believe it, you are such a lovely man, you don't deserve to have that happen to you. Where are you now?' ' I have moved down to Cornwall, well Padstow actually, I just needed a fresh start, I have a daughter, she is all grown up now she went to Uni in Exeter to study dance and theatre. She had a few acting jobs, but mainly theatre work, she has always loved the theatre, now she runs her own dance studio. As we know from the band days, not every band got to get to the big time, I still play in a band, we gig at the local pub in the village most Friday nights, still keeping my hand in playing guitar. I have a small cottage, with a studio on the side where I work on commissions and create my own pieces of work. I still have the sculpture of you, on the shelf waiting to be collected.'

'Hey Tilly less about me, what happened to you and Bob?' ' OMG really, you still have the sculpture, I loved that, such a lovely surprise.' Tilly slightly laughed a bit nervous about knowing how Pete felt years ago. 'Tilly are you ok?' You seemed to have gone a bit quiet' Pete enquired. 'Yes I am fine, I should have listened to you, you warned me not to marry Bob, he turned out to be an abuser, a serial adulterer, gambler and a bordering alcoholic. I lived like that for most of the 35 years I was with him, it has certainly screwed me up mentally.' 'Oh Tilly,' he replied, Pete's voice, gentle as it ever was. 'I am so sorry my darling, I knew he was bad news, but did not realise that bad, when we love someone so much, we just assume we are going to live a happy life, but at least you are free now to heal and move forward with life. So where are you living now?' Well I have gone home to my roots in Bamburgh, practically the other end of the UK to you.' 'Pete, I hope you don't mind me ringing you, I just came across your number in my book, and before I knew it, I was calling your number,' Tilly replied in a quieter voice. 'Don't be silly, I have to say it's been lovely to hear your voice after so many years. We must catch up again, if you are up to it, perhaps we could meet halfway. I am more than happy to come to see you, have not been to Bamburgh for years, it would be lovely to see you and your mum. Pete's voice is a lot chirpier than the beginning of the conversation. 'Pete that would be lovely, I have to say it's been lovely talking to you today. Yes let's keep in contact now, we can have a good catch up, about the old days of fun and mischief,' Tilly laughing down the phone. 'Pete lets catch up next week, get some dates down and find a time that is good for both of us.' 'Yes Tilly, that would be great to speak to you, I'm sure we can get something sorted next week. I have to go now, I am in the middle of doing a Sculpture that I need to complete urgently.' 'No problem Pete, we will talk next week.' 'Bye Pete, take care' Tilly replied. 'Bye Tilly,' replied Pete, 'speak soon.'

CHAPTER 3

Tilly sat on her bed, reflecting over her days living in London with Isla back in the Sixties. I wonder if the pub that Bob played in is still there. Gazing out of her bedroom window, the sun shining down in the garden, Tilly stood up and went downstairs straight into the garden, peering into the garden shed to get out a deckchair, a comfy pillow, and a nice cool drink, she then plonked herself down on the deckchair. Feeling relaxed, Tilly felt that she had accomplished more this week, than in the past year, with sunglasses on, legs stretched out, and feeling the warm sun on her face, her thoughts went back to the pub in North London, scrambling in her mind trying to remember the name, "oh this is so bloody frustrating" Tilly, mumbling to herself.

What is the bloody name of that pub; I can see it, god all those years ago, " Aaha" I know it had Sir in the name, Tilly's head was awash with all these different names that kept popping up in her head, oh it's bound to come to me! Carnaby Street, that's where I really fancy visiting again. We spent so much time there shopping, especially Mary Quant, Biba, Ozzie Clark, spending most of our wages there too !! Oh it has come to me, thank goodness for that. She had delved deep down into the files of her memory, that's it, it was called the The Sir George Robey pub. Well I never realised just how many names have come up from the past, suppose it shows we had a good time, always out, yep, they were good old days. Tilly dozed off for a while, the sun beating down on her. She certainly felt like a lot of emotions had been released this past week.

She heard someone calling 'Tilly Tilly anyone home.' She bolted upright, for a moment actually wondering where she was, she was so relaxed. "Only me" it's Ted the postman.' 'Oh hello Ted, sorry just relaxing while we still have this beautiful sun.' 'Don't blame you, just got a parcel for you.' 'Oh really,' Tilly replied 'I don't remember ordering anything, 'Thanks Ted.' 'Bye Tilly, enjoy your sunbathing.' said Ted. 'I will.' She went into the kitchen, to get a knife to open it up, she looked at the postmark, it said Padstow, how weird she thought that is where Pete lives. She opened it up to see it had been wrapped in lovely floral tissue paper, and in each piece was a photograph from days in the band. They had toured around a bit and even went to Europe a few times. She saw photos of them in France, it was quite an honour to be invited to play at this particular venue, in fact she remembered Bob being very nervous, it was the first big gig they had ever played abroad. Bob had always come across as confident and slightly arrogant, but he had actually told Tilly on this occasion how he was nervous, and hoped his voice would come out, and not a high pitched warbling sound. Tilly had not ever seen Bob so vulnerable. She remembered the gig, like it was yesterday, it was brilliant being out on stage in front of a few thousand people it was just outside of Aaron a town in France, she was in her element, she went back into that time of being so confident, to the emotional mess she felt at the moment, her thoughts on how on earth did I get to the blubbering emotional wreck, how did I let this man who I loved and adored, make me devoid of everything I was, punishing herself and beating herself up mentally. She stood for a second, gained composure, right, that's it, I cannot do this to myself anymore, it happened, I am out of that destructive marriage, I must not dwell on the past but live in the here and now, I need to heal myself , so I can have a happy future. She had booked her counselling session, having regular Aromatherapy massage treatments. She had so much to look forward to, it's like being reborn, new adventures, memories to make wherever her life took her, she wanted to enjoy every opportunity that came up. She perused through the photos, she loved seeing all the different places that they had played gigs at. She was not in contact with any of the other band members, only Pete who she had recently contacted. The last piece of tissue paper was a lovely picture that Pete had drawn of the cottage he lived in, she turned it over to see he had written a note "Hello Tilly can't tell you how lovely it was to hear your voice last week, I found these and thought you may like them. I hope I have done the right thing, and it has not upset you in any way."

    Take care
    Love Pete xxx

Speak soon. Look forward to seeing you. Let's get that date sorted out.

Tilly had goosebumps all over her. I hope I have done the right thing in contacting Pete, I knew he cared about me years ago, and wanted more from me, but I just never saw him that way. Tilly was trying to reason with her intuition, and she told herself. "Tilly, stop all the questioning, you're older now, just enjoy the friendship." Yes she thought, that is exactly what I am going to do, everything happens for a reason. She looked in her diary to find a date to meet up with Pete, that's it, let's pencil that in and hope that Pete can do these dates, I will give him a ring now. As the phone was ringing, her tummy yet again started to have butterflies. What the hell is happening to me, she thought, I must be so out of practice at talking to the opposite sex.! 'Hi Tilly,' Pete answered 'Hi Pete,' 'Just wanted to say thank you for the lovely photos that you sent. What a lovely surprise, I loved seeing them again, and Pete, they did not upset me, just made me realise that although my marriage was a complete mess, I have had many good times in my life. You can so easily get so caught up in all the negative rubbish, it can easily take over.' 'Yes I get you on that one Tilly,' replied Pete 'I was the same, when I was splitting up with the ex wife, fortunately I am well over that now. Thank goodness.'

'Pete, I have got a date in mind if you are able to do it, if not don't worry we can sort out another time. It's 22nd September, is that any good for you?' 'Ok hold on Tilly let me just get my diary, she was hoping that it was ok, while he was checking. Yes that's fine, fits in perfectly, as I need to complete a sculpture I have been working on by 15th September. Right that is in the diary Tilly. Is there a b&b near you I can stay in?' 'Yes there is a really quaint b&b, we used to go there when it was just a pub, many moons ago, not sure if you remembered? I can book it for you, how long do you want to stay?'asked Tilly. 'Yes, I do remember that pub. How about if I come up on Sunday and go back on Wednesday?' Pete added. 'Yes that's fine, my mum is so looking forward to seeing you after all these years. Pete I will book it when I get off the phone, if there are any problems I will let you know.' I will text you the address, I know the owners of the b&b, so don't worry about deposits it will be fine. Anyway I'm sure we will speak before then.' Tilly added. 'I'm sure we will.' replied Pete. 'That's great, although I live in Padstow, sometimes I need a change of scenery.' 'Yep, know the feeling on that one, Isla and I have booked a weekend trip to London, to revisit our old haunts from when we lived there for a short while. Do you remember my friend Isla Pete?' 'Oh vaguely, I think I met her once or twice.' 'Oh it's so good to get away, we all need breaks from our own environment.' 'Absolutely Tilly' laughed. Pete. 'I will text you when I have rang the b&b' Tilly said. 'Ok Tilly no problem, catch up soon, take care.' 'Bye Pete, yes speak soon. Tilly rang the b&b, straight away, and fortunately those dates were available. She was feeling very excited at seeing Pete. She texted Pete straight away, to let him know of the booking and the address. After cooking the evening meal, Tilly felt quite tired and a bit out of sorts, she needed an early night. After settling her mum into bed, she made her favourite drink of hot chocolate, took that to bed, had a little read, and gently nodded off.

Tilly woke up, feeling nauseous, and edgy, hearing the rain, beating down on her bedroom windows, she snuggled down, and pulled the duvet over her. Oooh, this is so lovely she thought it was warm and very cosy. Tilly loved her bed, she always retreated to her bed, if she was feeling poorly, or needing space to sort out her muddled head, especially when she was married, she always had conflict in her head trying to make to decisions about staying or leaving Bob, the children, breaking the family up, the migraines, anxiety, depression, the emptiness and loneliness she felt, the sadness, but she always stayed, then she did not have to face her demons. This had been going on for years, but it became more noticeable, when she had less distractions. Once Sarah and Stanley had grown up, leading their own lives.

"Aahh" this is pure bliss, I cannot remember the last time I had a little lay in. "Tilly", are you awake,' her mum called. Are you up yet?' Tilly had dozed right back off to sleep again, but on hearing her mum's voice, she slowly opened her eyes. 'Er yes, mum sorry, had a bit of a lay in, be down in a minute.' 'Ok pet, what would you like for breakfast?' she replied back. 'Don't worry, I will sort something out when I come down,' Tilly replied. Tilly pulled herself up, sat on the side of the bed, her tummy still feeling very sensitive and still had that nauseous feeling, it must be going to the counsellor today. I have never been anywhere like this before, where I had to share what goes on in my head, but then it has never been the right time to deal with my emotions, they feel stuck inside of me. "Now Tilly, stop being silly, this is so going to help you, so you can feel free yourself from the past, empowered to move forward with confidence, " she said to herself.

Tilly's phone was ringing, it was Isla, 'Hi Isla, how are you? I was going to ring you later, I have my first counselling session today, I was going to let you know how I got on.' 'Tilly, we can do better than that, how about we go to the cafe and have a catch up? I would suggest the beach cafe, but it looks like it will rain most of the day,' Isla replied. 'Great idea, Isla, yes I should be finished by 5pm, that's not too late for you is it Isla? if you have to get dinner for Brian,' enquired Tilly. 'No it's not a problem Tilly, Brian is always busy, out in the garden, playing bowls, fishing, so I can sort something for him when he gets in. I would love us to meet up, see you at the cafe at 5pm.' If it's raining and you get there before me, I will meet you inside. replied Tilly.' 'Great Tilly, See you later.' replied Isla.

Tilly did not like this apprehension she was feeling, I wished I had booked an earlier appointment, at least I would have had my appointment by now, she smiled to herself. Tilly was getting herself ready to see the counsellor, she wanted to look smart, she did not want Lucy thinking she was a complete mess in all areas of her life. Tilly set off to the therapy centre, she was feeling even more nervous than ever, right….. Tilly, calm down, take deep breaths, you are safe, it will be fine…she loved talking to herself, it gave her the confidence to do things that were outside of her comfort zone. She arrived at the door of Aromasense, pulling her umbrella towards her as she rang the buzzer. ' Hello Sophie, it's Tilly Fellowes. I have come for my counselling session, the buzzer went and Tilly walked in, 'Hello Tilly nice to see you again,' said Sophie, 'Take a seat, Lucy won't be long. Not long to wait until your next massage, are you looking forward to having another one?' Sophie enquired as she could see that Tilly was feeling agitated waiting for her counselling session. 'Oh yes' replied Tilly. 'I can't wait, I found it so relaxing and loved the aroma of the oils. Think you will be seeing a lot of me, with the massages and counselling,' Tilly laughed as she spoke to Sophie. 'No problem, this is a therapy centre, where we have many different therapies, sometimes in life we need a few therapies at one time, they compliment each other.' Sophie smiled as she replied. Tilly had hardly sat down, when Lucy appeared, Tilly was rummaging around in her handbag trying to distract herself from the nervous feeling she was experiencing.

'Tilly, are you ok?' Lucy enquired. 'Yes sorry, ' said Tilly, stuffing in all the bits of rubbish that she had pulled out back into her bag. She got her coat and followed Lucy to her therapy room. Lucy opened the door for Tilly, Tilly, please take a seat, the cosy chair in the corner by the window. Tilly walked across the room to the chair, feeling a bit lightheaded, she sat down holding her handbag, so tight to her, it was as if she was guarding the Crown Jewels. 'Tilly, are you ok? You seem a little on edge, would you like some water?' 'Yes please, I feel a bit lightheaded and nauseous and..' before she said the last word she was sobbing. 'Tilly, when we are releasing problems from the past that we have suppressed for many years, it's amazing how our subconscious mind seems to know before we do, what needs to be released. The light headedness and nausea is all the suppressed anxiety, fear of the unknown to you, the power of the mind and body are something else, it always lets you know what is needed for you, But you have been resistant to letting the past go. Tilly take a few sips of water, just try to relax, this is your first appointment, so it is really making sure, we are right for each other, it's very important that you feel comfortable with me. I always like to make sure that I can help you to have a fulfilling life, free from the past hurts you have endured.' 'Thank you Lucy, I am feeling slightly more relaxed and comfortable, hope you don't mind me saying, you have a very relaxing and calming voice.' 'Thank you Tilly, that is a very kind thing to say. Are you ready now?' 'Yes, sorry Lucy that I got upset before we even started.' Replied Tilly in a quiet voice. 'Tilly, please no need to say sorry, you have done nothing wrong, your emotions got the better of you, that's all, when we are holding in anxiety and fear through worry and apprehension of not knowing what is expected of you, it's quite normal. Everybody responds differently to each situation, you are clearly a very sensitive woman?' 'Yes I am, not sure if that is good or bad sometimes.'

'So Tilly, I will need to take some details from you, then when we have completed the consultation form, I would like you to tell me why you are here, and what you are seeking from having counselling, is that ok?' 'Yes of course.' Lucy proceeded with taking her details. ' So tell me in your own time, what has brought you to having counselling?' 'Well er,' Tilly started to speak, then paused. 'I don't know where to start, there is so much going on in my head.' 'So how about we look at where you are now, and the situation that got you to feeling the need to have counselling, would that help you Tilly?' 'Yes, that would help, thank you. So I got divorced last year after 35 years of marriage. I have found it very hard to come to terms with feeling guilty at splitting up my family, as I made the decision to divorce. I could not stand it anymore, the abuse, the gambling, the drinking, all the affairs throughout our marriage. I tried really hard to keep everything together, so as my family would not be broken, but in trying I became broken and lost,' Tilly said, the tears tumbling down her face again. 'Its ok Tilly, take a deep breath, I do understand, the human body and mind can only take so much abuse, then we become suppressed, depressed, anxious and fearful, abuse has a catastrophic effect on the psyche, whether mental, physical, emotional, they all are destructive and lead to certain behavioural patterns. Then we create strategies, to get us through all the pain and hurt. So Tilly please carry on.' 'We were fine in the band days, well actually I did see the red flags, but I loved and adored him so much, I ignored them, looking back he used to control what I wore when we first met, I thought he was because he loved and cared about me, but it got worse especially when we were going on stage, he would make me wear clothes I would not normally wear.

It really started to get worse, when my son was born, it was as if he was jealous, as I could not give him so much attention, he definitely was someone who needed attention all the time, that's when he became abusive, blaming me for everything not going right in his business, or just things in the house, that went wrong. He came home late most nights from going to the pub after work, by this time the band had folded and he had started his own business. I knew he was stressed around money, but he was always spending or borrowing money. He has spent hundreds of thousands of pounds throughout our life together, doing exactly what he wanted to do. It just got worse, where I was treading on eggshells, and feeling afraid of him putting the key in the door. I was never sure what type of mood he would be in. It really all depended on whether someone had upset him, if that was the case he would take it out on me. I had never really seen that side of him. I knew he had controlling ways, but not the abusive side.

Once I had Sarah, things got much worse, he went out early in the morning. I was lucky if I saw him by 9pm that night. By this time it was a ritual, most evenings he would come home, quite drunk. I do have to say that he was a hard worker, and always provided a home for us all, but it was never a happy home. I always thought that I would be happy with him, and we would be happy together.' 'Tilly, you are doing really well, please continue.' Tilly continued, to speak, 'he seemed to want to spoil every occasion, Christmas, birthdays and holidays, it was not an easy life with him, but the more he was abusive to me, the more I gave to make things better, to prove to him that I was a good mother and wife. He started going away, some weekends regarding work, when the children were young. I later found out he was lying to me, and had actually booked a hotel for the weekend taking the woman he was having an affair with for over 3 years, in fact Sarah was one when that affair started. I did find out later that he had in fact done this quite a few times within our marriage with different women he was seeing .' 'Oh Tilly I am so sorry to hear this, but I need to ask, how was your relationship with your father?' 'Well not good really,' Tilly replied 'my father was very controlling, could be abusive to, I never really felt loved, he never cuddled me, I saw my mother controlled, and she had to stay at home, I have to say that I have had a similar situations in my own marriage, I stayed at home, because that is where he wanted me to be. I have worked out why now, so that it was safe for him to have affairs, if he knew I was at home. I was also very unwell after I had Sarah, I had postnatal depression, suffered panic attacks, I had Agoraphobia, I did not go out for over 4 years, unless someone was with me, my mum was my rock, she would come and stay to support me, but my ex husband disliked her, she saw straight through him, he did not like that. The responsibility of my children, my mental health, I remember,' Tilly started sobbing, 'one day, ringing the health visitor, to get my children looked after, as I felt they deserved a better mum than me, I looked on the floor, where they were playing, Stanley must have been nearly three and Sarah just over a year old both happily playing in front of me, they are so precious to me, I love them with all my heart, and always will, but I felt so unworthy of being a mum, as I felt I was not giving them the best they deserved. I was lucky the health visitor came round to see me, she was very supportive, but I couldn't be truthful to her about my ex-husband's drinking and abuse, so I just blamed it on the post natal depression. It felt like a betrayal to him. I was so scared of him, I was also ashamed to have to admit such things, but I also knew if I did tell, it would have been me ending up being put in some hospital for mental health, and maybe never ever being their mum after all.' Tilly could not stop crying. Speaking through her tears.

'Tilly, let's take a minute for you to compose yourself. I cannot believe how open you have been today, especially as you have never been to see a counsellor before.' Lucy said. 'I'm surprised too, I really thought I would struggle to even say one word,' replied Tilly. 'This is what is coming up in your thought processes, this is how you move forward Tilly. I also want you to know, none of this is your fault. In the beginning he showed you love, made you feel good about yourself, he had charisma, was charming, appeared to be confident, and outgoing, you lacked love in your life, so it felt good for a man to love you, you probably felt safe, even though you were confident in yourself, that is your type of personality, but the one thing you needed more than anything was to be loved, and made to feel special, I think most human beings need that, men included, it's the normal function of being a human being. Tilly, you see what happens, when we have a childhood that is not loving and caring, but only fear, anxiety and control. For a little girl, your daddy is the first man you love, for a little boy, it would be his mother, so for you, you were used to being put aside, and to add to that you are sensitive, so things will go deeper, and hurt even deeper, so when you met Bob, he showed you love, affection, cuddles, but when the other side of him starting coming through as time went on, It was familiar to you, to be shouted at, controlled, abused, made to feel guilty that you had always done something wrong. The ages of one to seven are pivotal to how we form relationships, if we grow up in an environment that is full of anger, abuse, shouting, control, that is the way you would perceive life, you are not going to know any other way. When we are older, whether friendships, or relationships, but relationships are the main ones, what we see in our environment from these ages determines how we react when older. By then we have created strategies for coping in life, strategies are the barriers to stop anyone hurting you, it's called survival. You saw your mother being controlled, and shouted at, so when you started having romantic relationships, you had no comparison, of what is the right way for someone to treat you properly, if you had a loving relationship with your father, and a happy environment of feeling safe, you may not have met someone like Bob, or, if you did then you might have stayed with him for six months or so, but in your psyche, there would be a feeling of unease, because you would know that your father never treated you this way, so you would have ended the relationship. Tilly that's why you are always apologising, because you have always been made to feel you are always in the wrong from a very young age. Yes there are times when we need to apologise, and that is when we have hurt someone's feelings, when we know we have done something wrong to someone else, we all have those times, we would not be human otherwise we only need to apologise when we have done something wrong, nothing else. So please Tilly please don't feel guilty, I feel you reached the end of the road, you were brave and courageous, that you had enough strength inside of you to make those decisions, abusive and controlling relationships are hard to get out of, but from that decision, you are sitting here, with freedom, to make your own choices in life, and becoming an empowered woman. You have more strength then you give yourself credit for. Tilly it will take time to heal, to rid yourself of the guilt and everything you have been carrying for years.' said Lucy in a strong positive voice.

'All what you have said makes perfect sense, I now need to work on myself to release the pain and hurt and recognise myself and the empowered woman that lives inside of me. You know Lucy I like the word empowered' she said smiling at Lucy. 'Yes it is a good word. Tilly, how do you feel? We must end the session today. Would you like us to continue the counselling sessions,' Lucy enquired. 'Oh yes Lucy definitely, I want to rebook. I feel I understand how you explain things, and feel so much better. In fact I feel lighter, for speaking today, I feel more relaxed now, so no nerves or anxiety, now I have got through my first session.' Tilly replied, trying to find her purse in her handbag, ready to pay Sophie. 'That's good' said Lucy, I will always work with what you bring to each session, but I also look at what has been spoken about today. If I feel we need to delve deeper to get to the root of the problem I will ask certain questions. Is that ok for you Tilly?' Are you happy to do six sessions, one every week, then we can go from there and see how things are with you.' looking at Tilly to make sure that she was composed. 'Yes that is perfect, thank you Lucy.' So let's go down and get you booked in, Sophie will be able to sort out some dates and times with you.' Lucy said, as they both stood up together. 'Thank you so much I have found it helpful already.' 'Glad it has been helpful Tilly, life can throw us some difficult curve balls, but it is our strength and having faith and trust in ourselves, that we can overcome such times, it helps us to grow and evolve and to become the person we were born to be. When we are through the other side of the storm, that's when we realise how far we have come. Tilly that will happen to you. All storms pass eventually, and we come out the other side, happier, looking forward to a new chapter of life.

'They both walked down to the reception, 'Sophie could you please book Tilly in for one session a week for six weeks,' asked Lucy. 'Oh Tilly if something comes up and you cannot make it, just ring reception and they will rebook for you. Ok Tilly see you next week, have a good week.' 'You too Lucy.' 'So Tilly,' Sophie enquired, is Wednesday a good day for you at 4pm.' 'Yes, that's fine. So I have booked you in for the next six week's same day and same time.' Sophie handed over the appointment card with the dates. 'Have a good week Tilly.' 'You too Sophie, thank you, bye.' 'bye.' Tilly left aromasense, feeling on a high, feeling lighter, with a much better understanding of herself, realising that if you suffered abuse and control when you were a child, then how would know any different when you are are an adult, and more then anything, its is not your fault that you encounter abusive relationships when you are older, but if you do, it is to help you find who truly are, what your needs and desires are, and be strong enough to make the decision to leave the relationship, whether married, or in a partnership. you are ready to heal your emotions, and the codependency to have a happy healthy balanced relationship, that is where love, communication, trust is reciprocal. It will take time, but we can regain our power moving forward to a better life that you so deserve. You can look back and see how much you have grown and evolved.

Tilly walked down to the cafe to meet Isla, Tilly was running a bit late. Seeing Isla sitting by the window, as she walked past, waving to her, to attract her attention. Isla got up to greet Tilly. It had been a few weeks since they had seen each other. 'Oh it's so cosy in this cafe, such a warm welcoming feeling when you come through the door, even on a dreary rainy day. Oh lets get a hot drink, what do you fancy Isla?'' I fancy a latte Coffee, and a piece of that chocolate cake, it's so inviting, I cannot pass that up, what about you Tilly?' Mmm I fancy hot chocolate, and a piece of that chocolate cake too.' The waitress came over to take their order, it was the same one as before. 'Hello ladies, nice to see you back here, what can I get you?' We would like one latte coffee , a hot chocolate and two pieces of that chocolate cake,' Isla replied, scanning the rest of the homemade cakes on the counter to make sure she had picked the right cake. 'Right Oh,' said the waitress, ' won't be long.' 'Thank you,' said Isla. Isla looked at Tilly, her eyes still red and puffy from the counselling session. 'You ok Tilly?' Isla enquired, looking into Tilly's eyes. 'Yes I am now Isla, goodness I feel I've been on the fast spin of a washing machine, completely rung out, it is quite heavy mentally, trying to recall the past without getting upset.' 'I know Tilly, but did you find it helpful, all that hurt and pain needs to come to the surface,' Isla replied, being mindful not to prod too deeply. 'Yes very, Lucy the counsellor is lovely, she really has helped me already, she seemed to work differently to what I had expected from counselling. I have booked for a few weeks ahead, I don't know where it all came from, Isla, my head was spinning, the anxiety feeling, nauseous, feeling light headed, by the time I got there I was a complete bloody mess' 'Well, you have done the first session, it could become more painful, but the deeper you can go the better is for you to move forward in your life. I have always found meditation very helpful, whenever I have been in situations that have been uncomfortable, 'Here we go ladies, ' said the waitress balancing the drinks and cakes as she carefully walked over to the table. one latte coffee, one hot chocolate and two pieces of chocolate cake. I have given you both a bit extra, we are closing soon, so the cake has to be eaten, could not have gone to nicer ladies than you…. Enjoy.' 'Thank you, they both replied at the same time, looking at the delicious cake that was sitting in front of them with the thick chocolate fondant hanging over the moist cake, where it had been cut. 'Just what we need on a rainy day,' said Tilly, 'chocolate cake, it looks lovely, all the chocolate flakes on the top, oh, it's so moist, the cream in the middle, with the chocolate flakes, I don't want this to end,' as she spoke with a mouthful of cake, Tilly continued, 'Oh, the meditation sounds interesting Isla, would you be able to help me to meditate? My head is always going round and round, I do feel I need to calm my mind. Also just lately I have been drawn to crystals, I really like holding them and touching them. I went to town the other week, and there was a shop, they sold crystals, candles, incense, tarot cards in fact everything you could think of. I felt drawn to the rose quartz, the aventurine' Tilly said.'Why am I not surprised at that' Isla piped up 'rose quartz is for unconditional love, kindness and healing, you are working on loving yourself more and empowering yourself, the adventurine is for the heart chakra, calming the nervous system, which you are now opening up to heal from your past, that chakra would have an energy block.'.

'Oh really Isla, I did buy them to keep them with me all the time. The lady in the shop said to either put them in my knickers or in my bra. I decided to go with the bra option, I did not fancy walking with crystals jiggling around in the knicker area' Tilly said laughing, and the thought of the crystals clanging around as you walk.' 'No, not a good look either Tilly, said Isla, if they were to fall on the floor, how the bloody hell do you explain that one,' they were nearly choking on the cake laughing so much. They had to try and compose themselves. 'Isla, I would love it if you could help me meditate, there were other crystals that I was drawn to, maybe we can go to the shop one day.' 'You know, I would love that. There are lots of these shops in London too so we can have a mooch when we are there. I love the energy of these shops, it makes me feel peaceful and calm,' replied Isla. 'Yes I know, that's exactly how I felt when I was in the shop.' replied Tilly feeling excited that her spiritual journey was beginning to open up. 'Did you want to come to my house to meditate or what do you think is best Isla?. 'I was thinking maybe, would you like to come to me. I have meditation music, a lot of tarot and oracle cards, crystals, candles and incense sticks which I use every day. I have a room which I use to meditate, I would love to share that with you Tilly.' 'Oh Isla, I would really love that, how exciting,' Tilly was smiling from ear to ear. '

Look !!! I am completely starting a new path into my spiritual side.' 'Tilly, you have always had that beautiful spiritual soulful side, it has just got hidden under the fear and anxiety, you are free from that now, your head is emotionally clear from your marriage, you are ready to find that part of you, that's the exciting part'…'you really think so Isla,' 'yes I really think so my beautiful friend.' 'Oh Isla why I think of it, I have managed to find a hotel near Hyde Park, The Millennium Hotel, I got us a twin room so we can share the costs, it works out to about £141 each is that ok? We are in easy reach to get to North London, Oxford Street etc.' said Tilly. 'That sounds brilliant Tilly, thank you for sorting it out.' 'Hey Isla, I would love to go back to the pub, where we first listened to the live music, it's The Sir George Robey. Do you remember that pub Isla? 'Oh yes I do, very well, it was the most frequented of them all. I wonder why?' Isla smiled as she replied remembering that Tilly wanted to go there every week to see Bob singing. "What do you mean Isla!!!' Tilly looked at Isla laughing, knowing exactly what she meant. The good old days where she first saw Bob playing at the pub. 'Now, going back to the hotel, that sounds good to me Tilly, let me know when you want payment. I am so looking forward to our break away.' said Isla. 'Me too, replied Tilly, I think we pay just a few days before we arrive, so when I pay, I will let you know. I have my family coming up this weekend, I can't wait to see Sarah and Stanley, and the grandchildren, giving them all a big hug and lots of kisses. We are going to have such a fun time, can't remember a time when we were all together under one roof. Mum is so excited about seeing them all together.' 'Oh that sounds wonderful, nothing more precious than family time.' replied Isla. 'So what day can you do next week? Tilly continued, would next Friday work for you Isla? Yes that is good, Brian is out all day playing bowls, so he won't be home until late, I will cook us a nice lunch, then we can talk about all things Spiritual all afternoon, if that is what you would like?' 'Perfect Isla.'Replied Tilly so excited to try meditation.

Tilly paused, 'please don't think that I am prying into your life, but you seem to spend an awful lot of time on your own, Isla, is everything ok in your marriage ?' 'Yes, I suppose so, I think I have just got used to being on my own. Brian really did not want to come back from Italy, I don't blame him, but he seems to punish me, "mmm" Isla putting her hand on her head, her eyes looking directly up trying to search for an appropriate word. 'Maybe that's not the right word, it's like, I asked to come back, so I could be near my family and grandchildren, we had spent a lot of years in Italy. I love it now that my daughters are only thirty to forty mins away now instead of a plane journey. But since we have been back, he has joined every club going, he plays bowls, golf, goes fishing, meets up with friends at the pub, we have certainly drifted apart since we came back, I did say to him, that we could go on holiday back to where we lived, don't get me wrong Tilly I loved living out there, but I missed my family and seeing the grandchildren grow up, its sad we don't do anything together anymore,' Isla said in a low sad voice. ' Isla, that is so sad, I don't always understand a man's mentality sometimes. If only they were to talk about their emotions more, we would have a better communication and understanding of how they are feeling. Do you have any idea why he is acting like this? It's not like you asked to come back, because you miss the shops, it is your family, have you tried talking to him about this situation.' Tilly asked. 'Oh yes many times, it just falls on deaf ears, I think we have drifted so far apart now, there has not been any intimacy for a few years now, not even a cuddle, it's not like I want sex every night, I don't think I could manage every night anyway but just a loving snuggle would do. Anyway sex is just the by-product of intimacy, if it gets to that fine, if it does not, then that's the way it's supposed to be, and moving back here has widened the gap between us. We actually have separate bedrooms now, it is what it is Tilly, I just get on with my life, meeting up with you is a dream come true, and we still have the special friendship from when we were little girls.' 'Oh bring on the sisterhood, where would we be without our besties in our lives, we can support one another.' Just as Tilly finished talking the waitress came over. 'Sorry ladies, I am going to have to close soon, can I make your bill for you.' she enquired as she scooped up the plates and cups. 'Yes of course, sorry when we get chatting we never stop.'Isla replied laughing. Within minutes the waitress came over with the bill. Tilly and Isla settled up and left the cafe. 'Thank you Isla for inviting me to your home next week, I am really looking forward to that.' 'No problem Til's I will ring you in the week to give you my address, it's my pleasure. It will be nice to share my passion with someone. Tilly have a wonderful time with your family this weekend.' 'I will,' replied Tilly, they gave each a hug, knowing that they had the support of each other. 'Take care Isla, speak soon.' 'Bye Tilly.' as they glanced around giving each other a wave as Isla disappeared round the corner to her car.

When Tilly got home, her mum was watching one of her 1940's movies. 'This takes me back to my dancing days,' she said, ' nothing like a bit of Ginger Rogers and Fred Astaire, to make your feet dance, even if the rest of me cannot move that quick anymore,' Edith said laughing. 'Yes Mum. I remember seeing you dance many times indoors, and you didn't even know I was watching you.' Tilly replied laughing, Edith still laughing. 'How did you get on pet? ' said Edith. 'Really well Mum, Lucy is lovely, I think I am going to feel a lot like myself after this counselling. Mum, I suppose we need to think about food, and for me to sort out the sleeping arrangements for when the family arrives on Friday. I will sort out the shopping and get it tomorrow, is there anything you fancy Mum?' 'Oh, I cannot wait to see them all. Yes ok, I will have a think.' replied Edith. 'Would they like a good old fashioned beef cobbler?' Edith enquired, looking up at Tilly with delight at the thought of it. One thing still remained the same: Edith loved her food. 'Don't see why not, that's easily done.' Tilly continued, 'I have not cooked for this amount of people for a few years now. Sarah said she will help out, better get loads of eggs, bacon, black pudding, they all love a cooked breakfast. I am going to book the cafe for lunch on Sunday if you fancy coming with us Mum ?' 'Oh yes pet, that would be grand, have not been out in a long time for lunch' Edith replied 'That's good, it will do you good to get out, I will get that booked tomorrow.' Tilly said.

Friday had arrived. Tilly was already feeling exhausted, making up beds, kitchen brimming over with food, treats for the children, chocolate for Stanley, Sarah's choccy biscuits to dunk in her tea. Sarah rang to say they were on their way, a few minutes later Stanley rang to let his mum know they were on their way. Looks like they will all be here around 3ish. Tilly was so excited she kept plumping up the cushions, checking the bedrooms, then checking the kitchen to make sure she had enough food for everyone, then getting panicky that maybe there was not enough food. Edith could hear Tilly banging and crashing about. 'Tilly, are you alright, you seem to have a problem of not being able to keep still' Edith laughing, as she spoke. 'Yes Mum, just worried in case I don't have enough food.' 'Tilly, you are joking you could feed Bamburgh, with what you have out there. Now come and sit down, or you will be too stressed and tired, to enjoy their visit. I am going to make you a cuppa,' Edith said in an authoritative voice. 'Yes, you are right Mum, I do feel really tired, I just want everything to be perfect for them, you know what I'm like,' 'I know pet, but they just want to be with you, nothing else, it always works out, you know that.' Tilly sat down and closed her eyes to relax her overstretched brain. By the time Edith had made the cup of tea, Tilly had fallen asleep so Edith put her cup of tea on the coffee table. Edith looked at her daughter knowing how tired she was, and glad she was resting. Edith was also glad she was staying with her, she loved the company of her daughter, and the life Tilly had brought back to the home. Giving Edith memories of bringing up her family long ago. It was not always how she wanted it but her home seemed very quiet when her children flew the nest, until Tilly asked if she could stay with her mum after her divorce.

CHAPTER 4

The doorbell rang, it was Sarah and her family, there were tears and hugs all round, the grandchildren seemed to have grown so much since Tilly last saw them. Sarah had tears in her eyes, and Martin, Sarah's husband was trying to squeeze past, with the cases and bags, the granddaughters waiting patiently for their turn to give their nanna big hugs and kisses, it seemed like pandamonium. Not long after Stanley turned up, with his family, Stanley gave his mum a big hug and a kiss on the cheek, and continued through to the lounge as he was also carrying the luggage for the weekend break, where he was greeted by his sister and her family, they too had not seen each other for a while. Tilly stood in the doorway of the lounge, with tears in her eyes, this was the first time since she had got divorced that she had seen her children on her own, no Bob by her side. She had spoken to them all on the phone and occasionally had spoken to her grandchildren. She could not help it, memories came flooding back to the years gone by, when they were all a family, Sarah caught her eye and enquired if she was ok, Edith was in her element, with all her great grandchildren gathered around her, playing with them, chatting to them, tickling them, all had questions they wanted to ask her, Edith also had lots of questions to ask them, about their schools, friends, their hobbies, favourite foods. Unfortunately Edith never really saw much of her grandchildren, let alone her great grandchildren, as she lived in Northumberland, and her grandchildren lived about a five hour drive away, and having busy lives, it was difficult.

Tilly asked them all if they would like a drink and something to eat, there was a resounding yes from everyone, she made her way into the kitchen, the children had filtered out into the garden to play, the cases and bags had been deposited into the designated bedrooms. Sarah went into the kitchen, and put her arms around her mum. 'Are you ok Mum? only I saw you were very tearful standing in the doorway of the lounge.' 'Yes I'm fine Sarah, thank you for asking, I guess, this is the first time that we have all been together, and your dad is not here with us.' 'Don't be silly, you made the right decision, it is going to bring up memories from the past, but let's face it, dad never really treated you well, Stanley and I saw that. Yes, we were sad that you and dad split up, but you cannot live with all that control and abuse, and what about all those affairs if Martin ever did that to me, his bits would be pickled and on a shelf never to be used again. You are being hard on yourself, Stanley is as disgusted with dad as I am. I know Stanley does not say much, or show much emotion, but he loves you, we both do, and hope you find your true love one day. You have started counselling, so let's hope it helps you to not to feel so guilty, it's not necessary.' 'Thank you my darling, I have been feeling very guilty. You have made me feel a bit better.' 'Ok, we have all come up to see you, have some fun, visit the beach, the kids can't wait to splash in the sea, paddle and make sandcastles with you, so let's get drinks and food sorted, then how about we go for a walk to the beach.' 'Sounds like a good plan Sarah.' Tilly said, wiping her tears away, knowing Sarah was right, they had come to spend time with their mum. Edith had fallen asleep, all the great grandchildren had worn out poor Edith. Martin and Stanley happily sat in the garden chatting about football, having a beer in the garden, while Frances, Stanley's wife, was looking after the children, Frances called through the kitchen window. 'Are we sitting out here, if so I will get the seating organised.' 'Yes' Sarah replied, 'nearly done,' Tilly continued as she was getting everything organised in the kitchen. 'Could you give us a hand Frances,' she came through to the kitchen, loading up the trays to be taken outside. 'Oh what about Nan, Mum. Would she like something to eat as well?' 'I can hear snoring coming from the lounge. I hazard a guess that your nan's asleep, worn out by all the excitement of the day, best leave her. I will sort out food for her when she wakes up.' 'Sarah, everything is out here now, so shall we get the children sorted with food and drinks,' asked Frances, trying to collect all the children together' 'Yes, good idea, I will be out in five minutes Frances.'

Tilly was feeling more relaxed now that her family was fed and watered, they were all in the garden, Tilly looked out of the window, down the garden, seeing her grandchildren playing. Seeing both Sarah and Stanley in happy marriages, just made her so happy. Tilly was pleased that Sarah had taken some of the good bits of her mum, and left the bad bits behind, making sure she did not have a marriage like her. Sarah knew from a little girl that something did not feel right between her mum and dad. Tilly was proud of her children and how they had made good choices in their lives and had good solid relationships. 'Come on Mum,' called Sarah, as she was enjoying the food that her mum had prepared. 'This food is lovely, come and have something to eat and drink.' 'I really could do with something to eat and drink.' Tilly replied to her daughter, filling her plate with the delicious food. Sarah called out to Martin, 'do you fancy a walk to the beach?' 'How about you Stanley, do you fancy a walk down to the beach?' Both replied back 'yes,' followed by the children begging to go now, ok, 'how about in fifteen minutes,' they all cheered a resounding "yes" They arrived at the beach, with buckets and spades, ball games and whatever else anyone could carry. The children were so excited to be playing with each other. Although they were cousins, they did not see each other regularly. Tilly quickly got stuck in, helping to make sandcastles, with little Amelia who was two and Stanley's daughter, and Hallie who was seven and Sarah's daughter. Sarah and Frances decided to play a beach game, while Stanley and Martin took the rest of the children to the sea to have a paddle in the water, which as Stanley put it, was bloody freezing. 'So Shall we have fish and chips a bit later? While we are here, it would be nice to eat them by the sea,' Asked Tilly. 'Yes lets,' Frances said. The children and the adults were having a great time. The twin boys, who were Stanley's sons, William and John, were thoroughly enjoying their dad digging holes in the sand, while they sat waiting to be put water in the holes to fill them up. The time had passed so quickly, looking at her watch, Tilly called Sarah and Frances over to ask what they would all like from the fish and chip cafe. 'Shall we go together Tilly?' asked Frances. 'Yes perfect' said Tilly trying to remember what everyone had said they wanted. Sarah had found a couple of benches so they could all sit and eat, while Stanley and Martin had got the children sorted, wiping all the sand off their feet and hands. In the twins case, it was all over. They all finally sat and enjoyed their fish and chips. Tilly was thoroughly enjoying having the family around her, she felt content and happy. 'Oh this is lovely' said Sarah, just what the doctor ordered, and the lovely warm weather too.' Frances replied, 'I totally agree with Sarah, we all need to go by sea sometimes, it's so refreshing, kids happy, fish and chips, what more could we want. Tilly how lucky you were to be brought up here when you were a child, I can see why you left Kent to come back here.' 'Yes I know Frances, I had the best childhood up here. My mum has lived here most of her life, once she married my father.' Tilly replied, reminiscing in her head of how lucky she was to be born living by the sea. 'Oh I could quite happily live by the sea,' Frances replied, 'such a wonderful lifestyle for the children.' 'Well you never know,' Said Tilly, 'life has so many twists and turns, creating new chapters, you never know this could be part of the tapestry of your life, thinking back to her life with Bob, never ever thinking she would be divorced living back with her mum, and spending time on this beach with her family and grandchildren, due to the twists and turns she had encountered on her life's journey.

"Very deep Mother," said Sarah laughing, Tilly laughed back, "mmm," 'yes it is a bit, but that's how I see life now, the tapestry can have many changes, with lots of loose stitches, but in the end, they all get sewn together, completing the circle of life.' Sarah looked at her mum, she could see the sadness and stress she had been through, Tilly had gathered everyone together to go back home. Tilly stayed at the back watching her family walk in front, she just wanted to reflect on her own tapestry, where it is now, and what would be the next chapter for her. "Mum" "Mum", Sarah called, look at all the shops, and how they have changed over the last few years. As Sarah stopped and peered into the dress shop, a dress caught her eye. ' We need to come here tomorrow, why don't we have a girly day, you Frances, and me, the men can look after the kids.' 'Good idea, 'Tilly said, 'yes that would be lovely, there is a little village, not far from here, they also have a lovely shop, with lots of beautiful items of clothes, shoes, jewellery and bags, they also have a lovely coffee shop, in the square, where we could get some lunch.' Yes,

Frances agreed, 'that would be lovely, might as well make the most of our time together.' Right then, Sarah replied, 'done, we are going on a girly day out,' she said with a big smile. Tilly was excited at spending some time with her daughter and daughter in law. When they got home, Edith was in her favourite chair, looking at old photos she had come across a few weeks ago. She had a few tears in her eyes. When she looked up, her great grandchildren all descended upon her. Edith reached her arms out to greet them. 'You ok Mum,' Tilly enquired looking quizzically at her mum, 'Yes pet,' seeing you all here, and finding these photos, has brought back many happy memories of the good old days.'

Martin and Stanley found themselves chatting again with a beer in their hands, oblivious that the children needed to get ready for bed. The children were still excited from being at the beach, it was far too early for them to settle down and sleep, they were all giggling and playing together. Sarah called over to the men, laughing as she said, 'you better make the most of this, you are both looking after the kids tomorrow, we are having a girly day out.'both looking over, nearly choking on the beer they were about to swallow, Stanley piped up laughing. 'Yes that's fine Sarah, you can safely leave the kids in our care, looking at Martin. Peace had now reigned in the house, as all the children were asleep. Edith had gone to bed early, she was exhausted, not used to having lots of people around her, but equally enjoyed every minute of it. Tilly came in with a tray of coffees and some treats to eat. By the way, I have booked Sunday lunch at the cafe, they do lovely food there, it's my treat. Thanks mum, Stanley and Sarah, both said together this is so lovely we are all together, think we need to meet up more often, when time permits of course.

Tilly went to sleep very quickly, it only felt like she had a few hours sleep, as she could feel her grandchildren jumping on her bed. Three of them had snuggled beside her, she was in her element, she loved her grandchildren with all her heart. The twin boys could be a bit of a handful, they were jumping up and down falling off the side of the bed, clambering back on again, but the older girls were just happy snuggling and Amelia just wanted her morning "bot bot" as she called it. Hallie, Sarah's older daughter, loved looking after Amelia, her cousin, like a little mum. As Sarah was awake, she got up and made Amelia her bottle, they all followed her down stairs to have their breakfast. Sarah and Frances had arrived in the kitchen, so Tilly went back to bed, to collect her thoughts, she looked at the clock and realised she could have another hour snuggled in bed, she was tired but happy, she had a girly day with Sarah and Frances to look forward to. Tilly woke up at 8.30am, and thought how quiet it was downstairs, when she got up, she put her dressing gown on and went down in the lounge, the TV was on the children's channel they all sat there glued to tales of Horrid Henry and The Little Princess.

'Bye Martin,' we are going now, called Sarah. 'Bye Stanley' called Frances, see you later. 'Bye,' said Martin and Stanley, 'have a good day, enjoy your retail therapy.' The front door closed, they got into Tilly's car, first stop, the dress shop in the village, Sarah could not wait to try that dress on. They parked up and went to the little boutique. The dress was there on its hanger, just waiting for Sarah to try the dress on that she had seen in the window. Within five minutes Sarah appeared from the dressing room, with the dress on. 'Well, what do you think Mum?' 'Oh Sarah it looks lovely on you,' Frances also glanced round, whilst looking at a nice handbag, 'That dress looks lovely on you Sarah,' replied Frances, who still had the handbag in her hands, inspecting it to see if it was the right colour for her. 'Why are you trying to flatten your tummy Sarah, there's nothing of you?' Tilly had been watching Sarah, looking at her body shape in the mirror which was placed just outside the dressing room area, flattening her tummy, looking at the shape of her bum in the dress. 'Oh' replied Sarah, trying desperately to pat her stomach flat. 'Hey Sarah, there is nothing wrong with you , you have had children. Most women's bodies go a bit out of shape, but you have had life in your tummy, you have grown two beautiful girls.' replied Tilly, still looking at Sarah feeling insecure about trying a dress on that was more fitted then she would normally wear. We spend most of our lives as younger women, complaining about our weight, the boobs, bum and tum syndrome could be bigger or smaller, longer legs the list is endless, then when you get older, you find old pictures of yourself, looking slim and gorgeous, then all those wasted years worrying about things, that were already ok. 'Please Sarah, you look lovely.'

As Tilly was watching her daughter still looking at every angle of her body in the dress. It took her back to the times when she felt exactly the same, the difference was Martin loved her for who she was, and had never made any comments about her body after giving him two gorgeous daughters, but for Tilly it was a different story, Bob was always mocking her when she was pregnant, and afterwards as well, making Tilly feel very insecure, lacking in confidence, and hating her body, and never feeling good enough. Especially as she loved clothes and was on stage in a band. It created anxiety in her when buying clothes, that she started just wearing baggy clothes, to hide her body. As Sarah came out of the dressing room holding the dress in her hand with a smile on her face. It's my treat Sarah, I want to buy this dress for you, and Frances if you see something you like today, I would like to treat you as well. 'Thanks Mum,' Sarah replied. 'Thank you Tilly, that is kind of you.' 'Your welcome, you have both given me five beautiful grandchildren, they are the best gifts you could have given me. I am very lucky and blessed.'

Tilly paid for the dress, they left the shop, Sarah holding number 1 bag of the day. They all got into Tilly's car. They arrived at the village of Warenford, 'Oh this is a pretty village,' said Frances, 'it didn't take long to get here either.' Tilly parked the car and they started their venture around the village. Although it was a village, there were quite a considerable amount of shops to look at, Tilly took them straight to the boutique she had been talking about, they had a wonderful range of clothes, and accessories, as they went through the door, they were greeted by a shop assistant, who just let them browse. Frances was looking at handbags, Sarah was drawn to the shoes to match her dress, and Tilly was looking for some outfits, for when she was going away to London for the weekend. After an hour and half of perusing, all the clothes, handbags, shoes, scarves, and other accessories were all laid on the counter, ready to be packed and paid for. Frances had picked a lovely brown leather slouch shoulder bag that Tilly had treated her to. Frances had also found a nice jumper, Sarah had matched some sandals for her new dress, and well Tilly had, jacket, jeans, skirts and a few tops. Sarah had come to the counter, 'Mum look at you with your new clothes lovely to see you treating yourself' Sarah said with a broad smile. 'Sarah, I am off to London for the weekend with Isla.' 'There you go ladies, all packed and ready. Thank you for your custom,' said the shop assistant. As the shop assistant was giving Tilly her receipt, she thanked her for all her help. Just as they were leaving they saw Frances trying on a jacket, 'hold on she said, I just need to pay for this.' trying to juggle the bags she already had in her hand. Another purchase was made. They all left the shop with more bags. 'Well we have had a good day of retail therapy,' said Tilly, Sarah and Frances were excited with their new purchases. 'Yes it's been lovely, thank you Tilly for my handbag, I love these shops, they seem to have different things in the smaller shops.' Replied Frances. 'So anyone feeling a bit peckish, and in need of a drink, there is a lovely little coffee shop a few minutes away?' Enquired Tilly. 'Yes that sounds good,' replied Sarah, feeling rather parched and needing a drink. 'What a pretty square,' said Frances, 'with all these lovely shops, such a pleasure to visit, looks like a chocolate box picture, wonder what shopping would have been like three hundred years ago?' 'Well, one thing for sure, we would not have had the lovely clothes we have all bought today,' Sarah said laughing. 'Very true,' said Frances.

'Here we are, it's looking quite busy, but let's see if there is room,' said Tilly trying to push the door open with all her bags. Luckily enough there was a table for four which was perfect given the extra seat that all the bags could sit on that spare chair. They had a mix of sandwiches, scones with fresh cream and jam and pots of tea, they were chatting about the things they had bought, and just enjoying being women, who needed a break from the normal, and a break from their kids. 'So Mum, what's this about London?' Sarah enquired. 'I'm so proud of you, getting on with your life, and new clothes too.' 'Well, Isla and I bumped into each other on the beach, we had not seen each other for quite a few years, we have been best friends since primary school. When we were younger, we both went to London for six months to live and work. We are going back to some of the old haunts, and yes some retail therapy too.' She laughed. 'Oh that sounds brilliant, good for you.' 'I have so enjoyed myself,' said Frances. 'Yes, it's been so lovely to see you and my lovely daughter, spending some time together. I do miss those days Sarah.' Tilly sat and listened to Sarah and Frances chatting, realising that if she had not made that decision to divorce she would not be sat here, with Sarah and Frances, spending quality time with all of her family. They paid the bill, and set off round the rest of the shops, Tilly was feeling rather tired, and the girls were ready to go home to the smell of the beef cobbler that Tilly had prepared before they went out. They walked in with loads of bags, Stanley and Martin, looked at each other, 'looks like you had a good day' Stanley said. "We had a lovely day, shopping, chatting, and afternoon tea. How have the children been, have they been good? Tilly enquired. 'Yes they have been so good, we took them down the beach, they had a good run around, when we came home, they all fell asleep for an hour or so,' replied Martin. 'Ok,'Tilly said from the kitchen, 'dinner will be ready in twenty minutes. Do you all want the beef cobbler with mash, dumplings and fresh vegetables?' 'Sounds good to us,' they all replied. 'Ok Mum, Frances and I will get the kids sorted out ready for dinner.'

It was 10pm everyone was in bed asleep, although Tilly was tired, she could not sleep, she was reflecting on how the weekend would have been with Bob there as well, then she realised she was wasting too much energy on a man who had had a series of affairs, abused and controlled her. Oh why do I keep going back into the past, Tilly was so deep in thought. I was so unhappy, and yet I am thinking about the happy family scenario that never was, the fantasy that has always been playing in my head for years. Time to delete this programme in my head, and look forward to all the new chapters and adventures that are awaiting me. As Tilly opened her eyes, the sun was again peeping through the clouds. What a wonderful weekend, Tilly stretched, as she put her slippers and dressing gown on. Edith and Sarah were in the kitchen, making some toast. 'Morning Mum , did you sleep well?' Sarah enquired 'Morning Sarah, yes, I did, just going to make a coffee and wake up a bit.' "How lovely the sun is out today again, we have been so lucky with the weather, " said Edith. "Yes we have been lucky with the weather,' Sarah said to her nan as she was spreading marmalade on her toast. 'I am so looking forward to going out with you all for Sunday lunch, it has been so lovely spending time with you all' said Edith. 'Yes, Nan, it's been so lovely spending time with you, we will definitely come and see more of you, we can book into the b&b, mum looks happy but tired, you look happy but exhausted, all these energetic children around you.' Sarah replied. 'I won't hear of it, you staying at the b&b, you are always welcome here, this is just what your mum and I needed Sarah.' Tilly was in the lounge having a cup of coffee before everyone got up. 'Your mum is doing ok, she gets a bit stressed sometimes, but that is because she wanted everything to be perfect for you all. The divorce has taken its toll on her, your mum has to grieve as well, it's important, it's the ending of a long term marriage,' looking at Sarah who seemed rather worried too. 'Yes I know Nan , I have been concerned about her, we managed to have a little chat, while I have been here, I know she loved dad, but she was always anxious, and seemed to have lost her soul, and the twinkle in her eye, she was very depressed, I know it was the hardest thing for her to make such decisions, but Stanley and I are grown up married with our own families, I want mum to be happy Nan, that's all.' 'I know Sarah. Can I ask, do you see your dad at all?' 'Yes, sometimes, but he seems very preoccupied with his new family, and is not really interested in me or Stanley, or his grandchildren. I think he puts on an act to the outside world, that he is a loving caring loving dad and granddad but inside does not seem that bothered. I was quite close to dad, when I was a little girl. It does hurt sometimes.' Sarah said. 'I know Sarah,' said Edith.

'I have felt very left out Nan' said Sarah. 'Dad's new partner has a son and daughter, he seems more interested in them then me, then blames me for not seeing him, and complaining about not seeing his granddaughters, but does not bother to ring or to even find out if we are ok, and when I ring him, he's always busy and its always about him. I do feel I have to work hard just to get some response from my own dad. I don't understand his mentality, I am his flesh and blood, he can be very controlling and manipulative, I saw it for myself when mum and dad were together. I am sorry nan, did not mean to speak to you about this, I just want mum to be happy, I see the sadness in her eyes. Still, I have told her not to feel guilty about getting divorced, it was for the best.' 'Now Sarah no need to apologise, your mum will be fine, she is doing all the right things to help her have a happy life. So dry your eyes pet, let's have a cuddle, and let's enjoy your last day here.' said Edith who had a few tears in her eyes too, as she gave Sarah a big cuddle. Tilly came into the kitchen. 'Are you two ok over there?' 'Yes we are fine, said Edith 'We were just having a chat that's all, putting the worlds to rights, isn't that so, Sarah?' 'Yes we were indeed Nan.' 'What do you want for breakfast? Said Tilly 'looks like the others are having a lie in, I have given all the children their breakfast, they are watching their programmes on the TV.' 'How about I make breakfast for Nan and you and me?' Said Sarah 'Nan and I have only had a bit of toast, before it gets busy again. You look knackered mum, sit down, I will make you a cuppa and make breakfast, speaking as she was looking in the fridge to get out the bacon and eggs.' All three of them enjoyed their breakfast before the others had arrived downstairs.

'Goodness, look at the time, where does the time go,' said Tilly, 'it's 11.30am, the Sunday roast is booked for 1pm.' Tilly said to her mum. 'Don't panic pet, look, everyone is dressed, the kids are dressed, I am dressed, you're dressed, in fact everyone is dressed. I think as long as we are all dressed we will be fine.' As they walked into the cafe, the waitress greeted them and showed them to the tables that they put together so they could all eat together. Tilly spoke to the waitress, we seemed to have taken up most of the cafe. 'Now don't you worry yourself about that.' said the waitress 'We love seeing families coming together on a Sunday, that's how it used to be, just take a seat, get yourself comfy, and we will bring over the menus' 'Thank you, said Tilly.' 'Right here we are, the menus and children's menus, will be back when you are ready to order.' The drinks had arrived, shortly followed by all the Sunday roasts, a lot of laughter and chatting, the children, colouring in on the placemats, to keep them occupied. 'Oh this has been lovely,' said Edith, as she spoke, 'I have thoroughly enjoyed this weekend.' 'Yes, thank you all for coming up here,' added Tilly. 'It has just been wonderful, time passes so quickly.' They all put their glasses together, "ching" "ching" all the glasses being raised, even the grandchildren raised theirs too, all her grandchildren said, we love you Nanna, and will miss you, we will come and visit you soon, we love you Nanny Edith. 'Thank you my little darlings, I love you all too.' said Edith; proud to be a great nan of five gorgeous children. Everyone was feeling very full from the yummy roast dinner, followed by a variety of delicious desserts. I think we need to walk this off, said Martin, how about we have a last stroll down to the beach, I love it here, the beach is beautiful.' They all joined in agreeing with Martin, the children excited at going to the beach again. 'Mum, 'said Tilly, 'do you want to go home or come with us?' 'Would you mind if I went home? I am feeling tired, would you take me home Tilly.' 'Yes of course Mum.' Tilly drove her mum back home, then walked down to the beach, to meet up with the rest of the family. Tilly found herself a bench, "Ahh "Tilly sighed, this weekend, has been everything I hoped it would be, she was feeling very blessed, with her life, as she was watching Stanley and Sarah, with their partners, chasing their children on the beach, dipping in an out of the sea, the sun gradually lowering towards the horizon, the beautiful sunset of the pink and purple hues with some red now spreading across the clouds creating a magnificent spectrum of colour on the sea too. 'Ok,' called Sarah, 'time to go back to Nanny Edith.' All the children started moaning and groaning, saying that they did not want to leave. 'We love the beach, we love being here,' they all declared. 'I'm sorry kids, but we have to get packed, so we get an early start to miss the traffic' Sarah said. Stanley backed her up. 'Yes come on kids, we can come back and be all together again soon,' 'really!' said Hallie, the eldest granddaughter. They were making a bee line to their nanna, as fast as their little legs could carry them, even little Amelia, age two. "Nanna" "Nanna" they all cuddled up to her, 'we are going to miss you,' they all said in unison. 'When can we come up again?' 'I will sort out a date with your mummies and daddies, you wait and see, it won't be too long, I can even come down to you, how about that,' replied Tilly. 'Yes we all want to see you,' said Lyla, 'right, that's a date with my grandchildren.' said Tilly.

Back home it was hectic, the kids ready for bed, then the packing, getting everything together. Tilly was in the kitchen, and both Stanley and Sarah came out and put their arms around their mum. 'It's been lovely Mum, thank you for a lovely weekend,' Sarah said, giving her mum a big kiss on her cheek.' 'It's been a pleasure, I have loved every minute of it, let's not leave it so long next time, I know I have had a lot of change and am trying to work through the divorce,' Tilly was now shedding tears. 'I cannot tell you how much I love you both,' wiping tears from her face. 'Hey Mum, you are doing well, it's not your fault, it's dads loss. He chose that way of life mum, he was just somebody who did what he wanted to do, without even considering the hurt that he caused you over the years I could never treat Frances like that, or emotionally mess with my kids' heads,' "Stanley," Mum is upset, she never wanted her life to work out like this,' Sarah said. 'I know Sarah, but it's just how I feel, 'replied Stanley. Tilly paused…. Sarah quickly filled in the gap, 'right group hug, let's just be happy, we all have each other, that's all that counts, yes, all agreed' Sarah said with a smile.

That time had arrived, Tilly did not want them to go, but they both had their lives down south, Sarah and her family, lived in Buckinghamshire, and Stanley lived in Hertfordshire. It was manic, all the bags, suitcases, toys. Stanley and Martin in and out the house, Sarah and Frances making sure nothing was left behind. Eventually everything was packed in the boots of their cars. 'Right, kids in the car, say goodbye to Nanna,' Sarah requested. They hugged their nanna so tight and gave lots of kisses and hugs. Stanley was calling out to Frances, to make sure everything was packed. The twins were queuing up to say goodbye, little Amelia, was swept up in her nanna's arms,

Amelia, giving her nanna kisses too. Stanley and Frances, Sarah and Martin, each gave Tilly the biggest hug, and said their goodbyes. As soon as the cars drove off and disappeared around the corner, Tilly could not control her tears, already it felt quiet, she loved the hustle and bustle of everyone around her. She walked back indoors, smiling and crying at the same time, 'Oh Mum, how lovely has this weekend been.' 'I know Tilly, I have thoroughly enjoyed it, hope they visit again soon' with a big grin on her face. 'Oh they will definitely be visiting again' Tilly replied

CHAPTER 5

Tilly came down the stairs quite quickly feeling very flustered. 'I can hear my phone ringing but cannot remember where I put it, 'said Tilly. 'I thought I heard it coming from the kitchen,' Edith replied. 'Ok I will look in there, I was going in there anyway to have some breakfast, would you like anything Mum?' 'No pet, I am fine thank you' replied Edith. Tilly went into the kitchen, as she started moving things to put away after the family weekend, she caught sight of her phone, it was under the tea towel. "Phew" she thought. Tilly picked up the phone, to see missed calls from Sarah, Frances, Peter and Isla, right let's get some breakfast first, then I can ring them back. Sarah and Frances had rang to say thank you for the lovely weekend, and when could they all descend on her again. That made Tilly happy knowing that her family were happy to come back, even though it was chaotic, Tilly enjoyed every second of them being together. The phone was ringing, it was Isla trying to get through to Tilly.

'Hey Isla, you ok? I was just about to ring you.' 'Yes I'm good Tilly, how was your weekend? I was thinking about you.' ' Isla, I could not have wanted for more, we all had a wonderful time, it was just great, having everybody together, the grandchildren were all good, we had lots of cuddles, and kisses, so yes it was great, will fill you in when I see you on Friday.' Tilly replied. 'Oh Tilly, I am so pleased for you, glad it all went well. I rang to give you my address, have you got a pen handy?' enquired Isla 'Yes, sorry I missed your call, I heard my phone ringing, but could not find it,' Tilly replied laughing. 'Not surprising really, my head feels like cotton wool today. Right Isla, I have a pen in hand.' 'Ok, I will give you my address, I can't wait for us to meet up. Its Lavender Cottage, Howling Lane, Alnwick, NE66 1DN.' 'Right that is written down, thanks Isla, what a lovely name for a cottage.' 'Yes, that was the name when we moved here, just as well really, I love the aroma of lavender essential oil, it's so relaxing.' 'Yes, I remember Charlotte, using lavender in my aromatherapy blend, it smelt wonderful.' Tilly replied 'By the way, Isla we have our appointments next week, it comes round so quickly, can't wait for another massage.'

'Yes I know Tilly, I have that date firmly in my diary, looking forward to that too. So see you Friday. Tilly thought I would cook us an Italian lunch on Friday. Do you like Italian food Til's?' 'Yes, I love Italian food, shall I get to you for Midday Isla. Is that ok for you?' 'Perfect' Replied Isla, feeling excited. see you then Tilly, lots of love, bye.' 'Love you to Isla, Bye.'

Next on the list was Pete, she waited to ring him last, as Tilly was still feeling all jittery, about him coming up to stay, all sorts of thoughts were going through her head, "OMG" what if he tries to kiss me, what if he holds my hand, what if he wants more than a kiss, I feel panicky, I have not had proper intimacy for a few years now. I could not stand Bob near me in bed, knowing he had been having affairs. I felt useless, no self worth, low self esteem, I practically slept on the edge of the bed, making sure that my bum or any part of my body was not touching him, all these thoughts, bringing up my lack of self confidence with men. Right Tilly Fellowes ``enough" she put that thought in her head, you are and have always projected the worst case scenario that could possibly happen. Pete is coming up to see me and for us to spend some time together, as friends that's all, so just enjoy his friendship. Tilly pondered on those thoughts, "Mmm" yes, that's the way forward just enjoy, dont project into the future, it never normally happens anyway. Deep down Tilly was feeling excited about seeing Pete. They always got on really well, maybe part of her subconscious, was longing to be cuddled and kissed, but she feared the intimacy, so this was the trigger point which caused Tilly to go into panic mode, she feared being hurt again, her heart had been broken, she was trying to fix it, so intimacy at this stage would send her emotions into overdrive. 'Hello Pete, sorry I missed your call, I heard my phone ringing but couldn't find the place where I had left it.' Pete started laughing, 'Hi Tilly, lovely to hear from you, don't worry, I am always doing that, it must be an age thing.' 'Yes, maybe' Tilly replied laughing. 'You ok Tilly?' enquired Pete, 'you seem a little hesitant, do you still want me to come and visit you and your mum next Sunday?' 'Yes of course, sorry Pete, if I came across like that, it's just we have not seen each other for quite a few years, and feel a bit nervous that's all "sorry" should not have said that Pete, just voicing how I feel, I guess.' 'Hey Tilly, that's ok, I feel the same, so don't worry, no apologies needed. We have always got on with each other, and been there for each other, so to meet up again can make you feel a bit nervous. To be honest, I feel a bit like you. I'm sure we will be fine, don't you?' 'Yes, I agree, glad you said how you feel Pete, my nervousness has now gone down from 8 to 4,' Tilly said with a slight laugh. Pete laughed, and paused. 'I am looking forward to seeing you, we have a lot of catching up to do and a lot to chat about. I am setting off in the early hours of Sunday morning, so should be with you by 11am. That's why I decided to come up on Sunday, to miss the weekday traffic. I can check in and come to you, if that suits you,' replied Pete. 'Yes that sounds good to me, Pete, do you remember where the b&b is?' asked Tilly. 'Yes sure, I remember, I will ring you when I am near to the b&b then we can sort out a time to meet up. I might have a nap Tilly if that is ok? as it's a long drive' Pete replied. 'Yes no problem, of course,' Tilly replied. 'Great' said Pete, 'so looking forward to seeing you next Sunday, take care Tilly.' 'That's good, at least we have sorted out the details, looking forward to seeing you too. Take care Pete, bye.' 'Bye Tilly take care.' Tilly felt a little bit more relaxed "wow" where were my thoughts going before that call, well at least he feels like me, so not so worried now.

Tilly was busy getting the bedrooms back to normal, getting all the bed linen and towels together and any other dirty laundry that was hanging around. Thank god I am not seeing Pete this week, I would have been so tired, she thought to herself. Right what's next on my agenda, I know, a well deserved cuppa I think. She took all the laundry down stairs, put the kettle on, while she was loading the washing machine. 'Mum, would you like a nice cup of tea?' . 'Oh yes pet, that would be nice. I do feel a bit parched,' she replied in a jokey voice. 'Ok, coming right up Mum. Tilly took the cups of tea and some biscuits into the lounge, she gave her mum her cup of tea, and biscuits, then sat down with a big sigh. 'Oh Mum, I need a sit down, I have got everything sorted out upstairs, all back to normal, I just spoke to Pete, he is coming up next Sunday. I'm so looking forward to seeing him,' Tilly said with a big smile on her face, 'we used to get on so well back in the band days.' 'Thanks pet, sorry I couldn't help you but I...' Tilly broke in, 'Mum I would not expect you to, so just enjoy your cuppa.' Edith continued, 'So what time is Peter due up here?' 'Oh around 11am to Midday, but he is having a nap, before I see him, as he would have had a long drive.' replied Tilly, dunking another biscuit into her lovely cup of tea.

'I think that it will be good for you to have some male company Tilly, you can easily get out of the habit of being in mens company when you are single, having had a bad marriage, you need to begin to feel comfortable. He is lovely, I used to like Peter, thought he was very caring, and could tell he always had eyes for you that were as clear as glass.' 'Yes I know Mum. when I was upstairs, I felt a bit panicky, as I have not seen him for years,' Tilly said in a quiet voice. 'Tilly, you have always read to much into things, and far into the future, just enjoy his company, you will find once you see each other, that connection, will just fall into place, he is coming a long way to see you, you said he's been divorced years ago, maybe he seeks to spend some time with a woman, who he knows and trusts.' 'Yes you are right Mum, just my silly thoughts going on in my head. Right, ok, this is not getting the baby washed, I need to sort out the kitchen, get the laundry out, and get some bread and milk. I need a little walk to ground myself.' 'Ok pet, I will let you get on, but I would like to help with dinner tonight, and give you a bit of a break.' Ok mum, how about we cook dinner together, just like I used to, when I was a little girl.' Edith smiled back, remembering all those years ago, where did time go she thought to herself, 'Tilly that would be lovely.' replied Edith.

It was Wednesday 17th September, Tillys second counselling session was today, she was nowhere as nervous as the first time she went. She was going back over her first session, wondering what Lucy was going to ask today, and how she'd react. Tilly pressed the buzzer, the door opened. 'Hi Sophie, me again,' looking at Sophie's big smile. 'Good to see you Tilly, how have you been?' 'Yes, I am good, thank you.' 'Tilly, take a seat, Lucy will be with you shortly.' Within seconds, Lucy appeared, 'Hello Tilly, are you ready for your counselling session?' Tilly followed Lucy to the room. 'So how are you Tilly?' 'Yes I am fine thank you, I certainly don't feel like last week thank goodness.' replied Tilly, feeling at ease as she spoke. 'It's ok Tilly, it's quite normal. So how have you been over this past week? Has anything come up from the past that has caused you any problems? You also mentioned last week, about how guilty you felt.' 'Well, I had my family come and stay with me for the weekend, we have not been together for quite a while, it did bring back memories. I had not discussed with my children, how I was feeling about the divorce, its strange, there were a few times, I had wished Bob my ex husband, was there to complete our family, to me, that's how it should have been, but I very quickly pulled myself together, and remembered all the hurt and pain he had caused over the years, not just to me, but to our children, I did shed some tears, my daughter Sarah, saw that, and came out to the Kitchen, we did have a brief chat, I told her how guilty I felt, but Sarah was not sad, she said she had seen it over the years, and that is was great that I could be myself, and get on with my life, my son said the same thing, and to never feel guilty.' 'So how did that make you feel, that both your children do not hold any grudges?' enquired Lucy. 'I actually felt relieved straight away, that they both understood, they said they were both married, had their own families, and just wanted me to be happy. Funny thing is, I don't feel so guilty either, since we had that chat.' "We all had such a fun weekend, it showed me how far I have moved forward, and my emotional strength has come back, and not to take on the guilt. I had to hold myself together for the children over the years, trying to fix everything, I felt guilty for actually breaking up the family,' Tilly replied in a husky voice, trying to hold back the tears. 'It's ok Tilly, please if you want to cry and release all this pain, please do, this is a safe space for you to do that.' 'So Tilly...... last week you spoke about the abuse and how he would mess up every holiday, birthdays, Christmas, so what happened that made you feel you were treading on eggshells, feeling nervous, and anxious when did this abuse start?' asked Lucy.

Tilly took a long pause. 'Tilly, I know this is painful and you may wonder why you are being asked for this information, but in order for you to find you again, you have to realise how the abuse has affected your mental and emotional well being, take your time I do understand.' Lucy spoke in a soft voice. Tilly started to speak in a slow voice. 'It got worse, after I had Sarah. 'I had postnatal depression really bad, sometimes I felt so much responsibility and everything just kept piling up in my head, feelings of not being good enough, as a wife and a mum, I was never the same person after I had Sarah, I guess, deep down I knew there were cracks, in my marriage, especially after I had my daughter. The panic attacks, anxiety, fear, were building so much, I think I was trying so hard to hold it all together. Bob never knew how I felt, I kept it to myself, pretending everything was ok, but inside I was falling apart, I actually felt suicidal sometimes. Lucy, I just want you to know, that how I was feeling had nothing to do with my daughter being born, it's just how it was, I love my daughter very much, in fact I feel I missed out a lot when she was a baby and a young girl time I cannot get back, due to my mental health.' 'Tilly, you don't have to explain that to me, I know how much you love your children and grandchildren the way you speak about them,' Lucy added. 'Then one day, when I went out with Bob, we went out for the evening to a restaurant with his friends. I just had to run out of the restaurant. I needed fresh air. I felt so anxious and panicky, I thought I was going to faint, my heart was beating hard, lightheaded and hot. I could not hold it all together anymore. I did not want to go back inside, but forced myself to. Bob was not happy. When we got into the car on the way home, he told me how embarrassed he was of me, that I had shown him up in front of his friends. Unfortunately my mental health just got worse, that everytime we went out, I had so much fear before I even stepped out the front door, he would issue a warning to me, that I was not allowed to leave the restaurant, or anywhere we went, otherwise I would regret it when we got home, many a time, he shouted at me, the physical abuse, of being punched, kicked and pushed around, how useless, fat an ugly I was, a bad mum, and a bad wife, the pressure I felt was overwhelming, the anxiety just rose inside of me, this then turned into agoraphobia, which led to issues with food, it seemed to control my life. I remember one day looking in the cupboard and there was only one potato left, I had such a panic attack, I always had to have two of everything or more. I could not face going out, but I did push myself to go to the little shop to buy some potatoes. This is the pathetic person I had turned into. My children were in their early teens and they did not know how bad my mental state was. This completely took hold of my life. I could not see a way out.' 'Tilly,' said Lucy,' 'you are not pathetic at all, the mind is the most powerful part of the body. It governs everything about how we think, how we behave, how we create strategies for survival, which then becomes a behavioural pattern. These patterns go so deep, they become embedded, when that happens the mind uses the new pattern and translates that into normal for you, before we realise it, we have created even more patterns, which are the layers to your survival especially in these types of relationships, so for you food became one of those patterns. When we have no control in our life, we can use food, exercise, addictions to drugs and drink etc, as a control mechanism, as it's the only thing we have control of.' 'Yes, I can sort of see where that has come from now.'

'My mum was a great support, but my father just used to say to me, 'you need to pull yourself together. I remember, one night Bob told me how bored he was of staying in night after night. I told him that we had children now, and that life was different now we had a family, then his face changed to one of anger. You would have thought that I had just given him a prison sentence, so I just turned to him and said, that he could go out anytime, and I would look after the children, that night I knew I had given him a verbal agreement to do just as he pleased, and after that conversation, that's exactly what he done, he went out drinking in the pub, that was part of a normal life for me by now. That's when the gambling started, and the affairs just kept going on. By this time I was a complete mess, my physical health was now suffering as well as my mental state. I had also got pregnant, and knew I could not look after another baby, so made one of the most heartbreaking decisions of all time, to have a termination, I remember him driving me to some place miles away from where we lived, he dropped me off, left me, and then he came and picked me up later in the day. He never asked how I was, then when we were driving home, he told me that he was going out that night, and not to expect him to stay in and look after me. I had only the termination ten days before Christmas when I found out on Boxing Day that he had been seeing a barmaid at his local pub for nearly 3 years, this meant Sarah was not even 1 year old when he started this affair. This was who he had been seeing the day I had my pregnancy termination. My heart was completely broken. How could I love and adore someone so much, and feel like this? How can your husband be so callous and uncaring about you? I don't feel I have ever really recovered or healed from that painful day, it was the worst Christmas I had ever experienced. Boxing day was spent with my in-laws, and his family. It was devastating. They had come home from the pub, when a fight ensued in the lounge. I was in the dining room with my mother in law, and sister in law, and my sister in laws babies were in the lounge where the fight was, I walked into the lounge to see what was going on, when I overheard my brother in law, the youngest brother, say to Bob, "I don't know how you can do that to Tilly", Bob and his elder brother, were still fighting, I was concerned for the babies. My father in law took me outside, and told me that Bob had been having an affair, I felt numb, my world fell apart, and my poor children, how could he do such a thing, I came in and saw Bob in the hallway, the first thing I did was to cuddle him, but my heart literally broke into a thousand pieces, I felt numb, my whole world as I knew it fell apart in a split second.' 'Tilly you are so brave to tell your story, I feel for you and what you have been through.' 'Please may I continue Lucy' said Tilly 'I feel I need to release all of this, I have held onto all of this for so many years?' 'Yes of course, Tilly, the more you verbalise the quicker you can heal from this chapter of your life.' So Christmas, as you can see, were never good times. I had to pretend to my children that everything was ok, so on Christmas eve, I would put my excited children to bed, waiting for Father Christmas to visit them. then wait for Bob to come in a dreadful drunken state, never ever knowing what damage he would cause.

There was one Christmas eve, when he came home and I was not at home, he obviously went back out again, when we got in, I went to check the food for Christmas, none of it was not in the kitchen, Stanley looked out of the patio doors, to see something laying on the grass, when we went out there, it was the food lying there on the grass. We all stood there crying, as we knew what would happen when he came home. I had everyone round to dinner the next day, I got the children to bed, and waited for the key in the door to turn, my stomach was churning, as I was trying to get everything ready for Christmas day. On another Christmas, he had bought me a leather jacket and some lovely jumpers. I opened them up, excited as they were just what I wanted. Within minutes, he came into the lounge from the kitchen with a bread knife, and in front of the children stood and ripped them all up with the knife. He put them in the back of the car, Then smirked and said 'well you can not wear them now can you, you don't deserve them anyway' then drove off to the pub. It got harder as the children got older, trying to hide the other side that went on, but I think they already knew things did not seem right to them, but I have never discussed anything with them, I tried to keep it all hidden, and to protect my children, so they never really knew what went on with their dad, I guess I was protecting him as well, nobody really knew the extent of what went on. Lucy, so many things happened like that. He would cause arguments when we went on holiday, birthdays, I don't feel he ever wanted a family life.

He had numerous affairs during our marriage, at least 30 to my knowledge. Then when the children got older, I always strived to work and earn money.' 'Tilly, sorry to stop you but you have mentioned that Bob had over 30 affairs, you said that as if that is a normal occurance in a marriage, did you not think that actually marriage is for two people and no more?' 'Yes I suppose so, but it became part of my life to always be looking for signs to see if he was having a affair, my intuition was always right, I could tell by his behaviour towards me, he was very abusive, he would get dressed up and go out, never telling me where he was going, and to be honest, I was fearful of him. I realise now that I became very co-dependent on him. He was a pathological liar, in the end I never knew whether it was a lie or the truth.' 'Tilly,' Lucy said ' this is a man who has serious issues, an abuser, gaslighting you, pathological liar, he has a personality disorder. He thought he was entitled to do whatever he wanted, he had groomed and manipulated you so well, you did not know who you were anymore. You have paid a very heavy price indeed, and still hold all that fear within you, I would say he still has those traits, but maybe mellowed a bit.' Replied Lucy ' He never ever wanted me to succeed, he hated that,' said Tilly. 'One time I decided to sell clothes via parties, I held the first one in our home. I did really well, when he came home, he asked me how much I had taken, he was very money orientated. I told him, I was so excited, that it went well. I started taking the clothes upstairs, and putting them on the rails, when he started throwing them back down the stairs, and then pushed me down on top of them. I just could never understand why he was so nasty to me, that happened a few times. The more he treated me badly the more I gave to him to prove I was a good wife and mum. We did split up a few times, but I always went back, it was like I was under his control, or spell, he always said things would change but they never did. Then when we got back together, he would then turn it on me, and blame me for everything, the affairs, when he went bankrupt, why his life was not as it should be, but it was all of his own doing.' Tears were falling uncontrollably from Tilly's face.

'Tilly, I think we need to stop here, you need some time to ground yourself, I can see how your marriage to Bob and his behaviour has destroyed the sense of who you are as a woman. You are right Tilly, your marriage was all about abuse and control, gaslighting, making you feel you were going crazy. Tilly I cannot diagnose your ex husband, but have you heard of narcissism,' enquired. Lucy. 'Yes I have come across the word, but have never really understood what it means.' replied Tilly who was interested in what Lucy was about to say. 'Ok Tilly, well there are 9 levels of narcissism, 8-9 are the sociopaths, and psychopaths, I feel Bob may have been a 6-7, there are also different types of narcissism, the overt one, I would say this is your ex husband but there is also the covert narcissist, these are the undercover, silent ones, very hard to read and are really hard to detect. They all want the same outcome, to break you down, so they can control you. It is done in such a way you don't even realise it is happening until you are broken. gaslighting you, playing tricks with your mind, stonewalling, these ones are not who they seem, the mask is firmly on. You see Tilly with narcissism, they actually hate themselves, and are the most insecure people, they normally gravitate to someone who is strong and confident, who has a gentle, caring compassionate heart, like yourself, these types of people want to please the person they love, they have mostly suffered some abuse or neglect themselves when they were a child, but not everyone has to have gone through this in their life as a child, but are just caring souls, who are sensitive and empathic.

The type of narcissist we are talking about is the overt one, they only look out for themselves, they have friends in high social places, as it makes them look good, they have delusions of grandeur, they love any bit of attention, good or bad, they don't care, as long a they are getting attention, and gravitate to people who have a vulnerability about them, they can smell a sensitive and empath a mile away, they are a bit like vampires, but instead of sucking blood, they suck the energy lifeforce out of someone. Sensitives and Empaths are like a moth to the flame for a narcissist. The sensitive likes to please, which is the primary reason a narcissist is with one, so the sensitive person is happy to give and give, whilst the narcissist can never be sensitive or empathic, that is why they despise themselves, so when they have broken you they feel so much better, and some can actually mirror you, so they become you. It's quite scary Tilly, that's why it takes such a long while to heal, and why you lose yourself, this goes for all narcissists they just have different ways of how they manipulate. '

'So Bob started by putting pressure on you, to make you feel insecure, he abused you by making negative remarks to you, his behaviour towards you. Then he watched you fall apart or cry, this then makes them feel good about themselves, because they have brought you down. This is very mentally disturbing, as you begin to lose all sense of reality, your mind is confused. Their persona is totally fake. They are normally very charismatic, very charming, they have their flying monkeys who are people they get on side, whom they have conned into thinking they are the best thing ever, the flying monkeys are also groomed, and would never hear anything bad said about the narcissist, as they believe everything they have been told. The narcissist will give them gifts, help them out, support them, so if someone were to say something bad, they would automatically stand up for the narcissist in all areas. it's like you said earlier Tilly, you felt you were under a spell, that's exactly it.

There are different types of narcissism, for Bob he needed to have more affairs, as it boosted his ego, in fact they are on the superego level, which is a dangerous ego to have, as it supersedes everything else that is going through their minds. He knew he could get sex, which was his primary object and stayed with them until they either worked him out, or he got bored, or when a new source of energy appeared. I can assure you Bob, never had any feelings for these woman, it was just for pure self gratification, then he would come home and take it out on you, blaming you for the state of the marriage, blaming you because he knew he was incapable of love, you became lost, anxious panic attacks, fear, are all part of the tricks of the mind, you were also suffering post natal depression, in the end he broke you, probably more then once. They like status, money, and being seen with influential people, it makes them feel good, they are pathological liars, they believe their own lies. Tilly does this resonate with you at all.' Lucy said looking at Tilly for a response 'Yes it does Lucy, I knew he was a controller, but always felt as the years went by, there was something else, but just could not put my finger on it. You have solved the last piece of the jigsaw puzzle. He was very good at lying, he used to take them away for weekends, telling me he was away working. The first time it happened to my knowledge was with the barmaid he had been seeing for 3 years. He would ring me from the hotel, telling me that he was working hard and that he hoped there would be a nice roast dinner for when he got home. Of course that is exactly what I did. Then one day I found a receipt for a hotel, nowhere near the area he said he was. I later found out that he had done this on several occasions, with some of the women he was having affairs with. Oh Lucy, I feel such a fool, how did I let this happen to me, he did not love me, I know that now, when he left and our marriage had finally come to an end, he had to come back to get some things, wiping her tears from her eyes, he had completely wiped out 35 years of our life together as if it had never existed, bloody, bastard man, sorry for swearing.' 'Tilly, it's fine, it's the anger you feel inside, it is totally unjust to be made to feel totally disempowered, but that's their goal, so you then become co dependent on them, as I said you can be who you are here, don't feel a fool, narcissists, always get their way through lies and deceit, they know exactly how to manipulate everyone they want to charm, whether its a woman or a man they know how to con someone. Always remember Tilly, he will be no different with his new partner, He will treat her exactly the same, once he has cast his narcissist spell on her by moulding and grooming her. Just be thankful you are now out of that marriage and free to find the life you want. How do you feel, Tilly?' 'I feel this session has helped me a great deal, of understanding myself, and how I got psychologically messed up. No wonder I could not go out, I blamed myself for everything, he certainly did a good job on me.' Tilly replied feeling a lot calmer now, but exhausted.

'Tilly I want you to remember how powerful you are now, you ended this marriage, not him, regardless, of him seeing other woman, they take the chance that they can have a home life, with extra marital affairs on the side, it forms part of their life, they are so complacent to think they have done such a good job of grooming and moulding you, that you will never ever succeed without them. How wrong was your husband to assume that of you. You took control, made the decision to divorce, and told him. That it takes a lot of courage and strength to do that after so many years, although you are out of your marriage, Lucy continued 'you still need to heal from this so you can have a new healthy relationship should one enter your life. I feel you are coming through this, but need you to understand where this has come from. Before next week I would like you to look at your own childhood, and how your father made you feel. There is a close connection as to why you ended up with Bob. Tilly we have come to the end of the session. Are you ok?' 'Oh Lucy, I feel so much lighter, I will see what I can find on healing from abuse and narcissism, as I am someone who likes to find things out for myself.' replied Tilly feeling a lot more positive. 'Yes that is a good idea Tilly, I think maybe keep saying to yourself that you are an empowered woman in her own right, Tilly I really want you to concentrate on where you are at this present time, and move forward, towards your new life.' Lucy replied, seeing Tilly feeling more empowered than when she walked into the room.

'Yes of course, I feel I don't need to relive every single detail of my past, for me it's about understanding me and clearing the past, letting go, and stepping into a new life, whatever is out there for me. And yes Lucy, everytime I have a wobble, I will say to myself,

"I AM AN EMPOWERED WOMAN, I OWN WHO I AM, WHO IS STRONG AND READY FOR A NEW LIFE"

Thank you Lucy, finally I can put a name to the monster that took over me completely, and finally put it to rest.' 'See you next week Tilly, have a good week, enjoy..' 'Yes, thank you Lucy, you too.'

Tilly stepped into the little high street, the sun seemed to peer from behind the clouds, she took it as an omen of what was to come in her life. Feeling happy, safe and secure, was top of her list, and not forgetting love. Tilly gathered herself together, smiling as she was letting go of one of the biggest test and challenging situations she had faced in her life. Tilly started humming one of the songs she used to sing before she met Bob, as she was humming "you make me feel like a natural woman", she realised she had not sung or even hummed a tune for a long time. She knew she was healing, as she was humming that song, out of nowhere Pete kept coming into her mind.

CHAPTER 6

Tilly walked through the door into the lounge, she plonked herself down, kicked off her shoes and took a few deep breaths. 'Well, by your movements, Tilly, am I led to believe that it went well today, but draining?' Edith asked inquisitively. 'Yes mum, it was, but I have only been twice and already I am getting a sense of how the past has led to me being a submissive wife, as I have never have thought, that would happen to me, I have always been very independent, had a strong sense of knowing who I am. But I have to say it was very interesting. I like the fact that Lucy explains why this happened, how it happened, his type of personality, it all makes sense. I have spent years knowing something was not right by his behaviour, but I have always blamed myself for everything going wrong. Bob always blamed me so eventually I believed what was said to me, and all the other damning things he said and done. It really has messed with my mental health, but I know I can come through this, so yes Mum, it was a very positive session.'

'Oh that good pet, I think you need a good ol 'cup of tea, somehow, it always seems to put things right again, you relax Tilly, I will make you a cup of tea.' ' Mum, that would be good, I do need a good strong cup of tea, and yes I do feel rather tired.' Edith bought in the teas, and a few treats, that were left over from the weekend. 'There we go pet, enjoy, there was some of your favourite cake left over from the weekend.' 'Oh thanks Mum, I forgot we had some of that yummy cake left.'

Tilly sat quietly while Edith watched one of her quiz games. She loved to try and guess the answers, everytime she got one right, she was always pleased with herself, and thinking, I may be getting old, but my marbles are all still intact. Tilly was sipping her tea, trying to absorb her counselling session today. It's weird she thought, now that she had spoken about all that went on, it did not seem to be buzzing around her head anymore, she thought that she would ask Lucy why that is next week. She thought how interesting the counselling was, how when you are comfortable with someone, who is not emotionally close to you, you can speak out and say what you want. Tilly looked across at her mum, smiling at the host on the TV, when a funny question came up on the screen, and everyone had a fit of giggles, seeing her mum joining in giggling along with them, she knew she could never tell her mum the full extent of abuse that she had suffered over the years, in her marriage. She is too old to have that landed on her lap, she is peaceful and happy and I am not about to disrupt her life. She had never had this much information running through her head, since she was in her twenties, rehearsing and remembering all the words and lyrics to her songs for when she played at gigs, solo and when she was in the band. Tilly had finished her tea, the quiz show had finished.

'So Mum, what have you been up to this afternoon?' 'Well pet, I was going to tell you. Adele actually rang today.' 'Oh, how is she?' Tilly asked. 'Well, yes she seems ok.' replied Edith, quietly hoping that Adele would come for Christmas. She has lived on the Orkney Islands for over 20 years. She really does enjoy the solitary life, away from the madding crowd, is how Adele would put it.' 'Is she going to pay us a visit?' Asked Tilly. 'She is going to try and get down, she has not had a Christmas at home here for a few years now, but it all depends on the weather for getting off the Island, so we shall see.' replied Edith, who understood Adele, and the choices she had made in her life. 'It's sad really,' Tilly continued, 'we don't seem to keep in contact like we should as sisters.

'Adele loves her freedom up in Scotland,' Edith said, especially being on an Island, she has made lots of friends who all share the same way of life. She works on the farm near her, and the hotel on the Island. They rely on the holidaymakers to bring money onto the Island. Her daughter Isabelle, lives in Peru, and leads a similar life to her mum. You know Tilly, Adele has never met anyone else after her divorce, she prefers it that way.' 'Oh I don't think I could handle not seeing Sarah and Stanley and my grandchildren, it would really affect me, especially if they lived abroad.' 'What about Edward? Do you hear from him at all?' 'Yes, he is in more regular contact than Adele, but being out in Australia, he has made his life out there with his family. I do get calls and talk to my grandchildren, but it's not quite the same. I have only really met them 3 times, I do feel really sad about that, but that's how it is Tilly, you are the only one who has remained close to me, I know when you lived down south, it was not easy to visit regularly but at least I did see you and my grandchildren. You never know where your children will end up, and how their lives will turn out, but I believe when your children are grown up, they must find their own path and lead their own lives, Edith said in a quiet voice.' 'Mum'....'Yes Tilly'……. 'Why is our family so fractured? I worry that now Bob and I are divorced that Sarah and Stanley will drift apart and become part of Bob's new family. You and dad were not divorced and our family are not at all close, I to feel sad, that there is not much contact from Adele, and Edward, well I never ever seem to have contact now, when we should all be in contact, and still be a family unit, wherever we are living in the world,' Tilly said in a sad voice, waiting for some assurance from her mum. 'It is something that has gone through my mind over the years, said Edith 'Adele has always been independent, she never let her dad get one over on her, she stood her ground, much to your fathers disgust, that he could not control her, she loved the boys, and god knows how she never came home pregnant, it's a miracle that it did not happen, I did try talking to her. Adele was a wild child, and wanted to be a free spirit, free from responsibility. But she did like work, and found jobs that got her wages, and then spent it and was all gone by the end of the weekend. She then found herself a partner, and had her daughter Isabelle. Found out her partner was a controller, she left, took Isabelle, and headed to Scotland. Adele and your dad, have very strong personalities, and they would lock horns, you must remember some of those days Tilly?' said Edith 'Yes I do mum' ……..replied Tilly clearly remembering those times.

'I used to go out or go to my room,' replied Tilly. ' I just felt with Adele, she wanted to escape the family, Edith continued. 'I think she met her partner, hoping he would support her financially, and to get away from Dad. Her partner was not what he appeared to be,' Edith replied. She had visited Scotland on various occasions as she had friends up there, so it seemed natural that is where she would head to, and has remained there ever since. She has become nomadic in her ways, and does not like many people around her. Tilly please don't take it personally,' said Edith 'I know you have tried to keep in contact with her, and she hardly ever replies to your letters or phone calls. I am not saying I agree with her, after all she does have a sister and a brother, but one thing I have learnt in life, is that life very rarely turns out quite as we plan. Some people do live the plan they had in their head, but most people's lives, take unexpected twist and turns, and takes us of the road we had planned in our head, That is what has happened to Adele, had she stayed and had a happy relationship, maybe her life would have been different, but I firmly believe that there is a destiny in our lives, we are always where we are supposed to be. When we encounter tough times, they are the times, when we need to grow and evolve, become stronger, then the path ahead clears, making way for opportunities to unfold, heading us towards a new direction, but it's only when you get older, that you look back and can see the journey, and where you are now. Of course we have choices, I chose to stay with your dad, to be honest, back in those days, once married, it was for life, good or bad, then when the children grew up some woman left the home, and made a life for themselves, but very few. Fortunately today, women have gained some control on how they want their lives to be, whether married or not. Like you Tilly, you made that decision, because your mental health was suffering, now you are free to go in whichever direction your life takes you.'

Edward well, he is very much like your dad, motivated and driven, needs to be in charge of situations, don't forget Tilly, he left at 18, to travel to explore and to experience different ways of life, he has worked his way up in the TV industry, he leads a very high life. I feel with Edward he is so far removed from his roots, he has forgotten where his roots are. Tilly it is what it is, life chooses its path, not always us.' Edith replied, wishing she also saw and heard from her son and daughter. 'So what you are saying mum, that the family is fractured, because of dad's behaviour to us all, including yourself. I have had some contact with Edward,' Tilly added, 'but not a lot. I feel sad that I have a brother and a sister, nieces and nephews who don't know me or my children and their cousins.' 'Tilly, sometimes this happens when abuse goes on in homes, not just abuse, but abandonment, and neglect. When you are a child, it unfortunately stays with you. Each child handles it differently, some go on to have some kind of therapy, to help clear the past hurts and wounds from childhood, and go on to have a more stable life, after clearing the emotional pain.' said Edith, deep in thought.'

'Tilly, you have always been here when your dad was alive, but Adele has chosen to lead an isolated life and Edward lives a celebrity lifestyle in Australia, each person carries their own trauma, and wounds. You are starting to heal yours now, which is healthy, and means you are not running away from the past, but facing it, Adele has locked herself up, but I bet there is an angry fire that burns deep inside of her, which will never be released. Edward being similar to your dad is a man who does not show emotions, he is locked up too, but that's because it feels safer to keep it inside. He probably doesn't even think he has some traits like his father. I don't feel his family has ever suffered abuse from him, but he does like to control, but not the same way as your father. But Tilly, my darling daughter, you married Bob, who was like your father, and Bob has brought these feelings to the surface, they have been triggered so you can heal. You have achieved much in your life. Don't be sad Tilly, not everyone has a life like the Waltons, in fact there are very few families that do.'

Tilly looked aghast at her mum, 'so when did you get so much wisdom and truth?' exclaimed Tilly. 'Well' said Edith, 'underneath this old lady, lay chapters of my life, things, that have happened to me and my friends, you learn as you get older, you see things very differently, I have always been very sensitive, and had a strong intuition that has guided me through many a rough terrain. I have always managed to come out the other side, stronger than I was ever before, the experience began. Tilly you and I are similar, that's why we get on, you too, will come through the storm and into the sunlight.' 'Well you are working well today mum, you are like my wise old owl' Tilly laughed. 'Hey less of the old now, inside my head is a twenty year old, out dancing with the girls, having fun, plenty of energy, but the body keeps saying NO: you can't do those things anymore.' Edith said sadly. 'You know Mum, you are right, it does make sense, I promise not to take it all personally anymore.' said Tilly knowing that her sensitivity always got the better of her. She now realised that she needed to work out in her head, was it worth using her energies on these negative feelings that always seem to bring her down especially by people she loved, she now realises it's not her, and not everybody thinks like she does. Mum was right, she thought. 'Mum, changing the subject, did you remember that I am off to Isla's on Friday, I should be back in the early evening.' 'Yes I did remember.' Edith replied, glad that Tilly had met up with her best friend.

Friday had arrived so quickly. Looking at the time Tilly was stressing about where the time goes, she needed to leave to visit Isla in half an hour, but she was still trying to get some financial things sorted out from her divorce, she was also having problems even though she was divorced, trying to get Bob to sort out the rest of the financial affairs, which was a nightmare, mainly because he did not want to give Tilly her the full settlement which he agreed on in the beginning. He kept changing his mind, just to be bloody minded. She had recently heard from the solicitors to let her know the final settlement should be on its way to her in the next few weeks, she had to reply to the solicitors to ok the final settlement. Oh well, Tilly sighed, thinking that this will have to wait now, I need to get going to see Isla. Tilly came down the stairs, grabbed her coat and bag. Tilly came into the lounge to make sure her mum was ok, before leaving home. 'Right, I'm off now. Bye Mum, see you later.' 'Enjoy yourself,' said Edith. Give my love to Isla.' Ok, yes will do, bye Mum. Tilly set out in her car, she roughly knew where Isla lived, but had not driven to that village for a few years. As Tilly was enjoying the drive, along the country lanes, she then got stuck behind a tractor that was stacked so high with hay that had been cut and made into big round bales ready for winter. The odd wisps of hay blowing off the tractor, gently flicking on her windscreen. Tilly was looking at the lush green pastures, and a rainbow in the distance, where it had been raining, and now the sun was peeking out in between the darkened clouds. Tilly realised how much she had missed not living up in her native land. Although Kent had green pastures and fields, where she lived it was mainly a town. 'Ahh, I think I am nearly there,' Tilly thought to herself. She saw this beautiful cottage on the left hand side, oh yes this is it, how beautiful, the garden is full of lavender, lemon verbena, with the scented pink roses, that merged gently with the lavender and lemon, creating a gorgeous fragrance as you walked up the gravel and paved pathway. As she reached the door, there were a variety of herbs, peonies and a patch of garden with wildflowers, gently blowing in the wind, delicate colours of pale blue, and pink , with daisies scattered in between.

Tilly had her flowers in her hand, ready for Isla. As she approached the door, it opened up immediately. Isla was ready and waiting. 'Hello my lovely friend,' she flung her arms around Tilly, and Tilly reciprocated the same back, they gave each other a kiss on the cheek. 'Hello Isla, your cottage is beautiful, I just love your garden, it smells just divine,' she said laughing, it's like a chocolate box cottage. 'Thank you Tilly, it has taken a few years to get to this, but I love the garden, and finding new things to plant every year. Come on in, it is so nice to see you.' Tilly handed Isla some flowers. 'Oh Tilly, they are gorgeous, thank you.' 'It's so lovely for you to invite me. I have been looking forward to this all week.' replied Tilly taking off her coat. 'Aww Thank you Tilly, Let me just get a vase to put them in.' replied Isla. 'Oh Isla, It smells delicious, very Italian, 'said Tilly. 'Yes it is spaghetti bolognaise, that's my favourite.' Replied Isla. 'When I lived in Italy, I learnt some secret ingredients from the local women, and what they used to add to the sauce. I have used it ever since, in fact I learnt a lot about Italian cooking whilst living out there. The Italians love their food. Brian and I would be invited out to dinner many times to join their families. Isla said whilst stirring the bolognaise. 'Sounds delightful, such a sociable way to live,' added Tilly.

'Yes definitely, they are very family orientated, I loved that side of Italy, something that sadly lacks in the uk unfortunately. It is a beautiful country to live in.' Said Isla, checking the spaghetti was cooked al dente. 'Hey Tilly, maybe we can go back sometime to where I lived, you would love it.' 'Oh Isla I would really love to do that.' Tilly replied excitedly.' 'Tilly lunch is served.' Tilly pulled her chair out and sat down. The table was laid out beautifully, with fresh lavender in a delicate cream vase, with a small amount of lemon verbena , freshly picked from the garden. A blue checked tablecloth, with a basket of garlic bread, a lovely white linen tablecloth, serviettes with sprigs of lavender tied around the middle with white ribbon, lovely wine glasses, and bottles of red and white wine. 'Buon Appetito'……..

'Red or white Tilly, what do you fancy?' 'Oh a nice glass of white , Thank you Isla, this looks lovely, can't wait to taste the spaghetti bolognaise , It smells sooo gorgeous.' 'So how have you been Tilly?' enquired Isla 'how did your counselling go this week' 'Yes it went really well, I do feel a lot lighter. I feel like a big weight has been lifted from my shoulders, especially the guilt at what I have put Stanley and Sarah through. It certainly feels a lot clearer now. Lucy is a very good counsellor, she explains a lot of things so I can understand how it has manifested mentally, and how to release the demons of the past.' Tilly really wanted to share with Isla, just what she had been through, but knew today was not the right time or place, she already had a feeling that Isla was able to read between the lines and knew that there was more to my marriage. 'Oh that's good Tilly, sounds like you are beginning to heal, that's brilliant.' 'So how have you been, Isla?' enquired Tilly, 'Yes ok, still the same really, I do feel lonely sometimes, I am glad that I shared it with you, it's amazing when you start talking, like a road has opened up, that was blocked off. It has made me think more about my relationship with Brian, about my life and my future. I love where I live, love my home, but sometimes it is not enough, especially now the girls are grown up.'

Isla, carried on eating her meal in deep thought. Tilly could pick up that Isla seemed a lot more unhappy then when she last saw her, and deep down knew that she had felt like that for years, she could see that Isla was trying to stay upbeat. They carried on with their chit chat over lunch, glasses being refilled, chatting about their families, grandchildren, and the things they wanted to see and do when they revisit some of their old haunts in London for the weekend which was only a few weeks away. 'It's so good Tilly that we are friends, it means a lot to me,' Isla said. Tilly sat pondering whether to tell Isla about Petes arrival on Sunday, without another thought, the words started tumbling out of her mouth. 'Isla can I tell you something?' 'Yes of course Tilly, what is it ?' 'Well…… do you remember Pete from the band days?' 'Yes I do, I only met him a few times, wasn't he the sculptor?' Isla replied. 'Yes that's right,' replied Tilly, Isla continued, actually I always liked him, he seemed a very gentle and sensitive man, nice looking too if I remember.

'Well Isla, he is coming up for a visit this Sunday. And staying until next Wednesday. I feel excited, but a bit nervous as well.' 'Why is that, Tilly?' 'Well I have not seen him for years, we were always good friends, he really helped and supported me when things with Bob were very Rocky, I always felt he wanted more, but I have never seen him in that way.' 'Tilly, relax and enjoy his friendship, how did you get in contact again?' 'Well, I was sorting out some boxes that I had brought with me, when I moved to mums. I started sifting through the boxes, I opened one and I found an old diary with names and numbers in the back. I saw Petes number and rang it. I was not sure if it was still his number, but when he answered I knew it was him. It was lovely to speak with him again, and he mentioned meeting up. I was thinking, would you like to have lunch with us? Maybe on Tuesday if you are free, he is going back Wednesday, I'm sure he would like to see you again too.' 'Yes, Tilly I would love that. Hey, just enjoy yourself, nice to have male company every so often,' 'You're right Isla, I will do just that, my mum said exactly the same thing.' 'Well there you go,' Isla replied laughing,' 'so shall we go and do some meditation and use some crystals?' 'Oh yes Isla, I have been looking forward to this.' ' Tilly, shall we go upstairs to my little sanctuary.'

'Ahh, you have essential oils burning Isla.' 'Yes, I have put some frankincense in the burner, it helps with meditation.' replied Isla As Tilly walked in, the walls were a pale lemon colour, with cream curtains with a little lavender motif on them, spiritual quotes hanging on the walls, Tilly could feel the peace as she walked in. 'Isla, this is so tranquil, I love the colours.' Isla had everything ready for Tilly, the track was all set up, the crystals were glistening like the jewels that they are, all with their unique healing properties with the lighting that shone on them, there were tarot cards, oracle cards, crystal wands, it was so magical. Tilly made herself comfortable as Isla explained to her about meditation. 'Isla I have never meditated before, so if I fidget it's not you, I am not used to being that still, I feel quite tense at the moment.' 'Tilly,' said Isla,' don't worry, I will know when you have had enough, it takes quite a while to learn to switch off and be still for a long while, so don't worry, don't get frustrated, if you can't clear your mind, just go with it.' 'Ok, thanks Isla. Those cards look inviting, can I look at them too,' Tilly enquired trying to work out which ones she wanted to look at first. 'Yes of course,' replied Isla, 'I want you to enjoy this room like I do, just go with what you want, and I will go with that. So Tilly, get comfortable in the chair, let your body relax as you listen to the music, take a few deep breaths, try and breath from your tummy area, not your chest if you can't, don't worry, I just want you to relax, feel your feet being grounded to mother earth, feel your legs, and arms getting heavier, as you relax even more, now move that feeling up into your stomach, chest, and then to the your head clearing your mind as much as you can, if thoughts come in just let them go as quickly as they come in, see them as if a bird has just flown through, and let them take the thoughts away with them as they fly out. Just go with your breathing, inhale, peace and harmony, when you exhale, release the pent up tension and stress you may be feeling. Isla looked across to Tilly, to see her body relaxed and her breathing was slowing down, the more her breathing was slowing down, the more she let herself go. Isla too closed her eyes and relaxed with Tilly, both were in their own worlds just enjoying the peace and silence. Isla glanced over to Tilly to make sure she was ok, as this was her first time. Isla had opened her eyes to see that they had in fact been meditating for over 15 minutes, Tilly was still in deep meditation, so Isla gently brought Tilly back to the room, when Tilly opened her eyes, she felt so peaceful. 'Wow, Isla, that was so lovely and peaceful. I really enjoyed that experience, it felt very natural. I found myself in space, surrounded by beautiful stars, the galaxies, with billions of stars all clustered together, with a beautiful background of the merging colours from the galaxies. The moon was so bright, it was a full round circle, the energy I got just from the power of the moon and how it radiates its light. I have always loved the moon, it was as if I was weightless, and just bumming around in space, if you pardon the expression.' Tilly and Isla were laughing, 'I would love to try that again.' replied Tilly 'There you see Tilly, when something feels natural, it's your intuition and your soul bringing you back home to your spiritual energy, that has been blocked for years, having said that, when we are in emotionally charged situations, like you were with Bob, it will be blocked, because you have had too many emotional issues, buzzing around in your head you are unable to connect with your true spiritual self, Tilly did you know that you was meditating for 15 minutes.' 'Really!! Isla, I'm impressed with myself,' smiling within, that she had just sat for 15 mins not moving a muscle.

'Can I have a look at the crystals now?' 'Yes of course, look to see what crystals you are drawn to, then we can look at the cards.' 'Isla, can we do this again? I feel like I have come home today, I feel like I have had an energy shift today, it feels so good.' 'Yes of course Tilly, I have thoroughly enjoyed today, it's been lovely to share with you different ways of helping yourself, and connecting with your higher self.' 'Isla, I am definitely going to start meditation at home, might even get my mum in on it.' 'It's so peaceful Tilly, meditation can clear your mind, lower your blood pressure, eases stress and anxiety, it brings clarity of mind, and can help with health issues. I would say it's a perfect way to keep yourself in a good place, mentally, emotionally and spiritually.' Said Isla, and she was watching Tilly run her hands over the crystals, she could feel the energy resonating off them. 'Oh Isla, I love them all, the colours, the intricate markings on each crystal, making the crystals unique and special in their own way. I feel very drawn to these, I am always drawn to Pink, but this one has a smoky look to it, and this, a gorgeous Turquoise colour, with beautiful White fine lines running through the crystal, you have so many Isla, they are all lovely in their own way. I know it goes deeper than just the colour, as each crystal holds its own property, for which we need to work with, should we feel drawn to it.'

'So Isla, what do I need to learn from what I have picked today?' Tilly said with eagerness. She handed the crystals to Isla. 'Tilly the Pink crystal is called Morganite, this crystal is used for emotional healing It can also help with opening channels to your higher consciousness, to a better connection. This crystal will also help you through your emotional healing journey, with you starting to release your past hurts. When you feel you are having a bit of a down day, just hold this over your heart chakra, feeling the energy coming from the crystal. Ahh, the blue crystal, is called Larimar, again you have chosen a crystal that goes with what you have been searching for, which is peace, relaxation and communication, so today, you have peace, and relaxation through meditation, and opening up to communication of your higher self. Maybe this can also be for help with communication when Pete comes up to stay. Tilly, keep the crystals with you, you picked them for a reason. So do you fancy a look at some of the cards, Tilly?' 'Yes, please Isla.'

Tilly was looking at them all arrayed on the table in front of her, some colourful, some not so colourful, others that have a gold gilded edge to them. 'Isla you have a lot of tarot and oracle cards, I don't know what pack to choose'…'Tilly, just sit quietly for a few minutes, then when you feel ready, see what pack you are drawn to, pick a tarot deck and an oracle deck.' Tilly picked up the cosmic tarot deck, and the wisdom oracle deck. She picked up the cards, as she wanted to get the feel of holding these cards in her hands, then started shuffling them. She went for the cosmic tarot cards first. 'This is so therapeutic just shuffling the cards Isla, how weird is that.' 'Tilly just keep shuffling these cards until you feel ready to pick out four cards, and put them on the table.

Then pick up the oracle cards, shuffle them the same as before, then pick out just one card from this pack.' Tilly shuffled, and within minutes there were five cards on the table. 'Right ok, lets see what you have picked out,' Tilly looked intently as the cards were turned over, leaving just the oracle card to be looked at.'

'So you have the queen of pentacles, king of wands and eight of wands and the devil card. So we have a bit of fire here, with the wands, and the queen of pentacles. This is a lady who is grounded and financially stable, who is in charge of how she views her life and what she wants to create, and also can be very business minded. The king of wands is a fire sign, so this man has an energy around him, a presence about him, a strong character. This is what I am picking up, the eight of wands is news of communication coming towards you, and moving forward.' 'Isla could that be Pete?' 'I know I never saw him in that way, but that was years ago,' Tilly looked on as Isla looked at the cards. I am not sure if this is Pete, his energy is a more gentle energy, do you know Petes birthday at all?' 'Yes I do know, it's July 12th, he is a cancerian.' 'Mmm, perhaps, he could have some fire element in his chart, as he owns his own business, and he is creative, he is a good communicator, so there is some balance between the fire and water element, but I feel there another man is on the horizon, the devil card has also shown up, so Tilly, be aware of falling for the wrong type of man, he will have a lot of issues around him, the devil card can be a manipulator, charming. Sometimes the universe puts this type of man on our pathway again to see whether we are strong enough to see through their lies of deceit and abuse, to let them go completely, helping us with the healing process. Tilly I really feel you are going to have a man in your life, you will hear, via a message being given to you about a man, this message will be significant to your life, it could be a relationship where you are needing to learn more about yourself. I just feel the devil card sitting there plays an important part of your life moving forward. Just let your life unfold, you are on a healing journey at the moment, it's important you don't draw another narcissist into your life, it's easy done, especially when they turn on the charm. How do you feel about that, Tilly?' 'Well, I don't know at the moment, I feel a bit shell shocked. I do hope I will have the relationship that I have yearned for and to feel loved by a man. I have never ever felt that in my life, thought Bob was my soulmate,' 'Yes, Isla broke in, he was, but he was in your life, as a soulmate, who was there to help you to evolve and grow spiritually, that is where the emotional pain has come in, it is a very painful journey, that's why certain soulmates come into our lives Tilly, because of the connection, and intensity in the beginning, its feeling of never being able to let them go, even when you are not being treated properly. I think Bob had some narcissistic traits Tilly, but look where you are now, free to make your own choices, no control. Tilly we have more than one Soulmate, some last forever, others end when the karma is finished between them. I know that's tough, but that is how it works.

You have had many past lives with Bob, some good some bad, in this lifetime you needed to grow and evolve, so Bob came down here at the same time as you, so he could help you. You will thank him one day, when you are with the right man in your life, who can give you the emotional love and support that you lacked with Bob. So let's see what the oracle card has to say. Tilly, this is a lovely card ,"Poised" this is of someone who is ready to move forward in her life, she is poised to take flight, your wings have been unclipped, your arms stretched out, holding onto your glorious wings, shimmering with a golden hue, ready to take flight, and set your life in motion, just like a beautiful butterfly. Tilly you have had positive cards today, your guides wanted you to know that nothing is in vain, even the bad emotional days can reset you. When you have had the strength to leave a controlling and abusive relationship, that takes guts and determination, and you have done a lot of work on yourself, you have not stayed where you were made to self doubt yourself. Tilly, I can see that you have had enough for today,' Isla said, seeing Tilly with tears running down her face. Isla went over and gave her bestest friend a hug. ' How did you know about my marriage, Isla? I have never told you the full story of what went on? crying in between words. 'Tilly, I just felt there was more to your marriage, I could tell by how vulnerable and broken you were, when you had your counselling, I never asked, as I did not feel it was right to pry into your life, sometimes, it can be very painful to bring it all up again, if you are not completely healed from the trauma.' 'Isla, I really wanted to tell you, but did not know how. It seems crazy to say to someone that you have been in a marriage for 35 years, being abused on all levels and lots of affairs, and you still stayed and put up with it. I felt really embarrassed.' 'Tilly I am not here to judge you, we were and still are best friends. You can talk to me anytime, I have opened up about Brian and me. You are the first person I have ever shared this with. I trust you Tilly, I know you would give me good advice, as I can for you should you need that. It's ok to cry Tilly, you have been through a lot over the years, it's your soul singing, that's how I see it.' Isla smiled as she said 'and healing too.'

'Thank you Isla, I have to say I am so glad that you know now, the full extent of my marriage breakup, in time if things come up I will share with you.' Tilly had a lovely cup of Chamomile tea to calm her down. 'I feel so much better now Isla, thank you.'
So today, ……..
I have meditated, and loved it !!!!
I have connected to my higher self, and loved it !!!!
I relaxed, and loved it !!!
I have found peace, and love it !!!
I have been told that I have a new man coming into my life, and loved it !!!
And am poised to take flight on a journey of self discovery, and loved it !!!!
All in all, I call that a proactive day.
And even more important, I have to love myself,
Know I am enough, to trust and have faith in me.
Then the right man will appear who will love me
with his heart and soul.

'Tilly, we can make time to meet up regularly, if you like, next time you can use the cards on me, see what comes through,' said Isla. Tilly shook with excitement,' I cannot believe how tingly I feel inside, it's like I have come alive.' Tilly replied.

'That's good, replied Isla, giving Tilly the crystals that she picked, Isla continued 'you can use your meditation now, through doing that as regular as you can, you will soon see a big difference in your life,' ' Isla, I will definitely be visiting that new age shop again, if you fancy coming with me Isla. I love tarot cards, crystals, everything that is spiritual, I will be buying cards, crystals, some essential oils, and incense. Goodness,my mum, will think I've joined some hippy commune with Adele on the Orkney Isles,' Tilly said laughing. 'Yes I would like to come with you, it always does my soul the power of good. When I step into those shops, we can make an arrangement for a few weeks, don't forget we may find one when we are in London, replied Isla. 'Oh yes.' replied Tilly.

'Tilly you have always had this side to you, but you was not in the right place to open up to it properly, anybody who is creative in any genre has a spiritual energy about them, so you are a singer, and play guitar and piano, you can write songs, I like arts and crafts, we are using that to create. Spiritual energy runs through your blood, guiding towards knowing who you are, and then to be able to be true to yourself, you are having counselling to help you, you are doing everything right, this side of you has wanted to emerge and experience this today to give you confidence to find your purpose in life, who knows you may go back into singing, or teach children. Don't forget Tilly, your mum is a very spiritual person herself.'' Yes you're not wrong there, my mum has been talking to me, and her wisdom is just coming through all the time, though she is shocked at what she is saying.'

Tilly got her coat and bag, 'Isla thank you for today, for the lovely meal, and helping and guiding me to see my spiritual path unfolding.' 'Tilly, I have loved sharing my passion with you, we will be sharing a passion that is equal to us, many many more times in our life' replied Isla. They gave each other a hug, a kiss on the cheek, 'I can't wait to come and read some cards for you.' 'Neither can I,' replied Isla. 'I will text you about lunch on Tuesday. l will text Pete, when I get home so he knows what's going on, maybe I will book the Swan, we can have a nice lunch there.' Tilly replied, feeling excited about Pete coming up to stay at the weekend.' 'Sounds good to me Til's, and don't forget, just enjoy Pete's friendship, but if you want some fun, don't feel bad, at least one of us will have some longed for intimacy,' Isla said winking one eye. 'I will, let's just see how it goes, bye Isla,' 'bye Tilly see you Tuesday.' 'Oh don't forget, we have our aromatherapy treatments on friday,' Tilly shouted across to Isla, 'Oh yes, I forgot about that, good job you reminded me Tilly. We can have another cheeky catch up, we can never get enough of those.' replied Isla, waving goodbye to Tilly as she indicated to pull out on her journey back home. Reflecting on the day, she was so happy, she was growing in confidence, and knowing that her life was on the up. Nothing ever stays the same, life changes all the time, it never stops, that's one thing in life, that is a certainty.

CHAPTER 7

As soon as Tilly arrived home, she text Pete to see if he was ok for Isla to join them for lunch on Tuesday. It was not long after she sent the text, that Pete replied with a yes, and would look forward to having lunch not with just one beautiful lady but two. Tilly replied saying that he was indeed lucky to be in the presence of two lovely women, ending the text with a smiley face. She could feel herself relaxing now knowing that she could enjoy Pete's company and not feel so tense or anxious. She had not been in a man's company for a long while, she even pushed the boat out, adding a kiss at the end of the text to Pete. How brave am I getting she thought, sending kisses now, she then thought about that action, "Oh No", what have I done, I should have left it with a smile, not a kiss. One thing Tilly has learned to do, is to go back into the rational mind and process her thoughts. It has taken time for Tilly to get used to this way of thinking, to stop and rationalise how her anxiety builds up, when she over thinks a situation. After being married for all those years. Tilly knew that this was the start of a new chapter in her life, even though at times seemed so uncomfortable, she can now recognise those overwhelming feelings when they come up. She has had to learn to sit with those feelings so they do not overpower her anymore, and to not fight the feelings, with adding other thoughts to the mix. She now knows how to deal with them, which has given her a new found confidence in herself. These feelings are from her past, abuse and gaslighting are insidious, they can make you feel overwhelmed, when you constantly keep doubting yourself.

'Tilly,' called to her mum. 'Are we cooking dinner together tonight, as we never got round to it the other night?' 'Yes of course, what fine fayre are we cooking then?' continued Tilly. 'Well, I thought we could make something I used to make you when you were a wee girl, that is pan haggerty. I know you used to love that with fresh crusty bread and butter.' replied Edith. 'Mmmm.... I can smell that already Mum.' 'So if you want to start to chop the carrots and onions Tilly, I will start slicing the potatoes, and start the bacon cooking in the pan.' Tilly got to work straight away peeling and slicing the carrots and the onions, the smell of the bacon gently frying on the stove wafting all around the kitchen. Edith had sliced the potatoes, and was adding them to the sizzling bacon that was cooking. She had set aside some bacon to add to the layers of the vegetables, the onions and carrots were added to the pan. 'Mum, that just smells delicious, I forgot how much I used to love this meal. You used to cook this for us when we all came in from school starving hungry.' By now the stock was being added and Edith was about to put the lid on the saucepan. 'Mum shall I add some black pepper before you put the lid on?' 'Oh yes pet, silly me, I forgot about that' Edith replied smiling. The black pepper was added, and the lid was put on. The fresh crusty bread was taken out of the bread bin. Tilly could not help herself, she cut the crust off, and put a good generous helping of butter and savoured every mouthful she took. 'Oh yummy, that's good, wiping away the butter around her mouth.' 'Yes, I can see that Tilly, it did not touch the sides' Edith said laughing. 'So pet you carry on cutting the bread if there is enough left!! I am going to put this into a dish and add the grated cheese on top, and put it in the oven until it has melted and crispy on the top.' ' Mum, you have made a good choice for dinner tonight, we need to have this again, the smell "well" I can't wait to start eating.' 'Shall I make some tea?' 'Yes, good idea pet, then we can sit at the table and enjoy our meal.' Tilly got the placemats out, laid the table while her mum brought in the pan haggerty and the crusty bread. They both sat down to enjoy eating their meal together.

'How did your afternoon go with Isla?' 'Yes, although I had not been to that village for a while, it soon became familiar to me. Isla lives in the most beautiful cottage, it looks like a chocolate box cottage, with trailing roses around the door. lavender and a wonderful mix of herbs as you walk along the path to her front door, the aroma is just gorgeous. In the corner is a mix of cottage country wildflowers. Her garden is just the same, but she has trained wisteria to grow over her pergola. It's so relaxing. Isla cooked us a lovely Italian spaghetti bolognaise, with homemade ice cream for dessert, it had pistachios and a lovely mild coffee taste. Yes, we had a really lovely time. Isla helped me to meditate, which I totally got lost in . She showed me all the crystals she has, her tarot and oracle cards, it's like walking into a magical room, full of goodies. We are going to try and meet up regularly and meditate, but I am going to start meditating regularly myself. I found it so relaxing, such a good feeling, to let go of the thoughts that come into my head on a regular basis. Isla also gave me two crystals that I picked out. I am going to go to that little shop in Warenford that I found, and get some cards, crystals, relaxing cd's to meditate too, with some incense to burn as well.' 'Oh pet you seem very into it all, I did not know Isla was interested in tarot cards, does she read them?'

'Yes, she does, she saw in the cards of a man coming into my life, it would be through a message, very intriguing. I cannot for the life of me see how that will happen, but, interesting to see what happens there.' 'Oh pet, you never know! I used to dabble with the tarot cards, never did anything with them, but some things did happen that I saw in the cards. I quite like the idea of meditating, could we do it together, Tilly?' 'Yes of course, it makes it more interesting and spiritual, then we can talk about our meditation after. That's what Isla and I did, it's fascinating mum, I think I have always had gut feelings about things, especially when I was a singer, and when gigs were offered to me, shame, I did not follow the signs from Bob that I felt back then. I do feel other people's emotional pain as well, and just sense things, maybe now I am not with Bob this side of me may emerge. Isla said that she always thought I was that way inclined, when we were younger, but I have never really been aware of the feelings of a spiritual nature, or intuition.' 'Oh Tilly, I look forward to that. Yes, I am going to the shop next week, so once I have got the cd's we can start.' Tilly said with a smile, 'I might even bring back other goodies as well, you never know.' 'I know you Tilly, that is most definitely going to happen.' Edith smiled back at her daughter, looking at how much her daughter was was changing, getting stronger, more confident, trying new things, so different to the day when she first arrived, very thin, and gaunt her face pallor looked grey, her eyes was sunken in, and sad, Edith was so worried about her, but look at her now, she has a new life that she is starting to rebuild, the fun side of her is shining through, I am so proud of her and how she has got the help she needed and has worked on that to find who she is, this is just the beginning.' 'You ok Mum? you looked like you were deep in thought there.' 'Yes of course pet,' 'can't a mum look at her daughter and be proud of her.' 'Well, yes I guess so, thank you Mum, that means a lot to me. Shall we get the table cleared, and get the washing up done and put away,' Tilly continued. 'I need to sort out my clothes and what I am going to wear when Pete comes up,' glancing over her shoulder, taking the plates and bits out to the kitchen, as her mum trundled along behind her, with the few bits she could manage, with a cheeky glint in her eye.'That's my girl, you have always loved your clothes and how you look. I know you are on the mend, when the clothes come out of the wardrobe, for a modelling session.' Edith grinned at her. 'I really can feel a change inside that the feelings and emotions have now shifted within me.' as she made her way upstairs into her cosy bedroom.

Mmm, Tilly holding her head, right where do I start, she sifted through her wardrobe. Her jewellery and a good selection of shoes, appeared, and spread on the floor, dresses, skirts, tops gradually making there way out of the wardrobe and onto the bed, and hanging up over wardrobe doors, "where do I start," she thought, why am I doing this, why do I feel the need to make this much effort," Tilly was thinking in her head. "MUM," Tilly called down to her mum, 'help!! I need some help up here. I have all these blimmin clothes out, but cannot make my mind up, could you help me please?' 'Yes pet, will be up in a minute' Edith called back to Tilly. By the time Edith appeared, Tilly had a selection of clothes on. 'Goodness pet, you seem to have more out of the wardrobe than in it. Ok, I am going to sit on this bit of the bed, then we can sort out your outfits.' ' Mum, why am I doing all this for Pete? He's coming up for three days, that's all.' 'Well pet, let's get this straight, you are doing this for you, not Pete, it's been ages since something nice has happened to you, something to dress up for, to look smart but casual. Pete has put a bit of a spark back into you. This in turn has taken you back to who you really are, the Tilly I knew, loved dressing up, loved going out, loved playing to an audience singing. Unfortunately, you have got so lost within your marriage, unhappy, more worried about what Bob was doing, then looking at yourself, which is what Bob wanted all along, as long as he got your attention, whether it was positive or negative, it did not matter. So Tilly my darling, let's get you sorted, this is good for the soul. So how about your new jeans, the Blue and yellow top with the ditsy pattern, and that lovely Cream jacket that you bought, and do I spy a lovely Lemon scarf hanging over the wardrobe handle, and a nice pair of flat loafers, try that on Tilly.'

Tilly gathered all the clothes up and put them on, 'I like that, casual but smart.' Edith knew a lot about clothes, she used to make all her own clothes, and the childrens clothes when they were small. She was trained to a very high level, a dressmaker and a tailor, she also showed Tilly how to sew. She was asked a few times to make clothes for the gentry who lived at Bamburgh Castle, where Wilfred her husband had worked as head gardener. 'That looks lovely Tilly, so maybe that could be Monday's outfit. When he comes up on Sunday, he may be tired and just wants to sit and chat with you, so just wear something nice but that you are comfortable wearing.'

'I was thinking of the Tickled Trout on Monday for lunch, and have booked The Swann Inn in Seahouses for lunch on Tuesday. Isla is coming on that day, she knew Pete from the band days, and then just see where we go from there.' 'Oh very nice Tilly, it's lovely there, been there a few times. 'Right, so we had better get this outfit sorted out. Tilly I can see a nice dress you have hanging up in that wardrobe, like a shirt dress hanging up with a belt around the middle, looks like a viscose material in a Lavender colour can you see it?' 'What that old thing, I don't even know why I bought it in the first place.' 'Ok Tilly so how about you try it on, it does not look that old to me, it looks brand new, actually I can see the tag still on the dress, looking at Tilly straight in the eyes, Edith knew her daughter well. One of the things Tilly used to do was to buy clothes, never wearing them, tags still intact. 'Ok I will give it a go, I bought it a couple of years ago, as I liked the colour.' Tilly took off the jeans, top and

flats, and put the Lavender dress on, 'Tilly, that looks lovely on you, very elegant, you could wear a nice delicate necklace with earrings, 'Do you feel comfortable wearing it?' 'Yes I do actually, before you came up, I must have tried so many clothes on, and got in a right muddle.' 'So,' Edith replied, ' how about you put that dress to the side with the accessories, you can always change your mind, but at least you have a few outfits set aside.' 'I have to say mum, I thoroughly enjoyed a modelling session with the clothes, ' Tilly laughed.
'Right pet, I will leave it to you now, I am feeling tired and need my bed.' 'Ok,' said Tilly, 'have a good night's sleep'…. nite nite.' 'Nite Tilly, you too pet, see you in the morning.'

Sunday had arrived, and she had already heard from Pete, he was a couple of hours away, she had asked him what he wanted to do, Pete replied that he just wanted to chill out and have a long overdue catchup. They arranged for Pete to come round after he had a nap at the b&b and to freshen up, to see Tilly and Edith and enjoy a lovely roast dinner together. Pete texted Tilly to say he had arrived and would be round to hers for about 1.30pm. Tillys nerves were coming to the surface, her tummy was feeling weird, she felt a bit nauseous, she kept finding something to fiddle with checking she had everything ready and prepared for dinner. "I have just got to calm down", she thought to herself. I should be smiling and happy. I have looked forward to seeing Pete, but I never ever seem to feel excited, just fearful. I have been so good keeping my nerves at bay, but they have let loose on me today. I cannot seem to gather them up and put them in the right place, right this calls for a bit of mindfulness." Tilly went to her bedroom, sat quietly on the bed, she had a couple of hours, so she had plenty of time to get the nerves under control and in check. She quickly ransacked her handbag for the crystals that Isla had given her, then one fell out of her hand, and rolled under the bed, " Oh bloody hell, that's all I need," as she got on her hands and knees, something she could no longer readily do now, as age was the culprit. She put her hand flat under the bed, "I can feel the escaped crystal." She gently pulled it out to her, clasping the two crystals together in her hand, she gained her composure, as she heaved herself up, feeling as if her knees were still on the carpet.

She sat on the bed to clear her mind, she took some rescue remedy, as this always helped. "Tilly," she started talking to herself, "deep breaths in and out, inhaling peace and calm, and when exhaling, let go of the tension and stress that I have built up in my mind." After a few minutes Tilly started to feel a lot calmer, her mind was emptying all the negative thoughts, then the thoughts she had over the last few weeks, decided to join in. "Right" Tilly said to herself again, "deep breath," she was now holding the crystals gently in her hands instead of the clenching she was doing earlier. Tilly could feel the calmness coming over her. I really need to do this meditation and mindfulness regularly and not when I am anxious, it does help the mind and body to calm down and feel relaxed. Tilly was beginning to realise how much pressure she puts on herself, the anxiety that builds up. I need to speak with Lucy on Wednesday when I see her, she always helps me to understand, so I can work through the situation. It is weird how every week, there is a new layer to be revealed in my healing process." Tilly loved holding conversations with herself, it was as if she was giving herself self counselling. Tilly went downstairs to do the last minute preparations.

There was a knock at the door !!!! "That must be Pete," looking in the mirror in the hallway, "do I look alright, do I look panicky, stressed, no I am calm I am ready to open the door." 'Hello Pete,' 'hello Tilly, long time no see.' As Pete walked through the door, they gave each other the biggest hug. 'It's so lovely to see you.' Pete said, 'you have not changed at all Tilly' 'Yes it's good to see you too Pete, you have not changed much either. Come on in, there is a lady in that room, who has been looking forward to seeing you.' 'Right, let's go and see the other lovely lady of the house.' Pete walked into the lounge, and saw Edith sitting in her chair with a rug covering her legs, to keep her warm. 'Hello Edith, you are looking good, how are you doing?' 'Yes, I am ok, pet, I can't grumble the normal aches and pains as you get older. I do suffer with arthritis, which slows me down, but at least I am alive. That's all that matters.' Pete bent down to give Edith a hug and a big kiss on the cheek. 'Aww, it's so lovely to see you Pete, it's been years since I have seen you, you look well, how are you?' 'Yes I am good thanks Edith, getting a bit older, needed a nap before I came here, as I was knackered from driving up from Cornwall, a few aches and pains like yourself. I never thought I would ever speak to Tilly again, let alone come up and see you both. It was a lovely surprise to hear from Tilly.' 'Well Pete, lucky your number was still in my little black book, even more then that, you still had the same number. You never know what's around the corner.' Tilly laughed as she spoke to Pete. 'You are always welcome at my home Pete.' 'Aww thanks Edith, that means a lot to me, doesn't seem as if much has changed up here, still a beautiful village.' Pete replied. 'Yes fortunately, still much the same, the shops have changed owners a few times. A lot happened when the big supermarkets opened up in the big towns, a lot of people started shopping there, but we are a village, and we all support the local shops as best we can.' Edith replied. 'Sorry to interrupt,' Tilly said, would you both like a cup of tea, and some cake?' 'Yes please,' they both replied at the same time. 'Good to know that cake is still in the line up. I always remember cake was a necessary pleasure, good to see that has not changed.' Pete said laughing. 'No pet, me and Tilly love our tea and cake, it puts the world to rights, and that will never stop.' replied Edith. 'Oh Pete, would you like a sandwich too, as you have not eaten. I am still going to cook a roast dinner tonight, then we can sit and chat and be relaxed.' 'Tilly, that would be lovely, please could I have a sandwich too?' Edith asked. 'Yes of course, are you both happy to have cheese and pickle. and of course cake?' Tilly replied smiling, 'That would be lovely,' Pete said. 'Sit down Pete, and make yourself at home,' said Edith.

'Thank you Edith,' as he sat down on the comfy sofa. Tilly brought in the sandwiches, cake and pot of tea, the posh cups and saucers made an appearance, these were reserved for when guests came. Tilly sat next to Pete on the sofa, so she could pour the tea, and hand over the sandwiches. They all found themselves chatting and laughing, and talking about the band days, how life has changed, the world, everything you can imagine came up for conversation. Tilly glanced over at the clock, on the mantelpiece. 'Goodness, it's 4 o'clock already, where has that time gone? I am going to make a start on tonight's dinner.' Edith had already dozed off in her chair, all this excitement, and chatting has made her tired, with a gentle snoring coming from her. Tilly and Pete, glanced over at each other smiling. 'So Pete, are you ok just chilling here while I start the dinner? You can put something on the tv if you want to, or just relax.' 'Thanks Tilly, I will find something to put on tv and yes I am already relaxed.' Tilly disappeared into the kitchen, she felt a lot calmer, now he was here, she cut the potatoes, par boiling them so they would cook crispy on the outside and soft and fluffy on the inside. The beef was being prepared to go into the oven, served with fresh cabbage, broccoli, leeks in cheese sauce, peas and yorkshire puddings, her specialty, with a lovely thick beef gravy poured over the roast Beef. "I do hope my roast dinner turns out ok," panicking slightly, at the thought of her yorkshire puddings coming out as flat as a pancake. "Right, she thought to herself, pull yourself together, you have been making these puddings for over 40 years." Everything was now prepared, and the dinner was starting to come together. Tilly went back into the lounge, to find that not only Edith was still gently snoring, but Pete had fallen asleep as well, mouth slightly open, but not snoring. Tilly was secretly quite happy, they were both having a snooze, so she could put her feet up, the potatoes were parboiled, ready to go into the oven. Tilly had now dozed off, and woke up, as she could smell the beef gently cooking in the oven. As she opened her eyes, Pete was just looking at her, with a gentle smile, she felt slightly embarrassed. 'You know Tilly, seeing you asleep like that took me back to the band days, when we were touring, we had to sleep in the most uncomfortable coaches, and seeing you asleep back then, exactly as you are now.' Tilly, made a bit of a dash to the kitchen, "I didn't mean to doze off. I hope the beef is ok and not overcooked,' she was over thinking the worst possible scenario. The smell of the beef woke Edith up too, 'that beef smells delicious murmured Edith,' 'it certainly does,' Pete added. Pete could hear the sizzling of the fat being poured over the potatoes, then heard Tilly ask if anyone was thirsty as she put the potatoes in the oven.

Pete called back, 'yes please could I have a black coffee with no sugar,' Edith added 'a nice cup of strong tea.' Within seconds

Pete came to the kitchen. 'Hey Tilly, let me make us a drink, you have been out here, preparing and cooking dinner.' 'That would be good Pete thanks,' she could feel Pete brushing past her to get the cups, fill the kettle, reaching in the cupboard for tea bags and the coffee. Actually she was quite enjoying feeling Pete brushing up to her, it was as if something inside of her had come alive. Tilly was questioning her feelings. Maybe this time, we are supposed to be together, how I found his number, rang it, it was still the same number, he has travelled all the way up here to see me. Well only time will tell, I have not felt anything like this in years, it's such a nice feeling, and Pete is so lovely, she thought smiling to herself. Think I could get used to this, blushing as she had a few thoughts rushing through her head. 'You alright Tilly, you seemed to have been in another world for the last few minutes.' 'Er, yes Pete,' as Tilly was putting the thoughts she had way to the back of her mind. 'Just thinking how nice it is to see you.' Pete had made the tea and coffee and took it back to the lounge. Pete and Edith, had put a good film on the telly to watch, Tilly was dipping in and out of watching the film, as she was still concerned that the yorkshire puddings could fall flat. Tilly was near to dishing up. 'Tilly, would you like me to help you lay the table?' Pete asked. 'Yes please,' answered Tilly. Everything is in the kitchen, if you want to come and collect them,' secretly hoping that Pete would brush past her again.

He came into the kitchen and somehow, Tilly, had managed to be in the exact position that Pete needed to be to get the cutlery and tablecloth out, she felt his hands around her waist to move her to the side, she could feel herself, feeling rather hot. What the hell am I doing, Tilly thought to herself, it's a Sunday afternoon, mum is in the the lounge, I am waited with baited breath, that my yorkshire puddings will rise, and I am thinking about sex, I need to get my head straight, this could lead to all sorts, and it could ruin the friendship. 'Right, Til's, she thought, let's get this dinner dished up, otherwise, it could all go wrong. Pete came back into the kitchen. 'Is there anything else you want me to do, I have laid the table, hope it's to your satisfaction,' he enquired, 'have to say Tilly that smells delicious,' 'actually Pete, could you stir the gravy in the pan? I just want to finish dishing up.' 'No problem Tilly,' as Pete began to stir the gravy, Edith decided to join them in the kitchen, 'ok mum, you go and sit down and I will bring your dinner in for you.' Pete took his plate, alongside Tilly, as they both went into the dining room, Tilly had put a nice bottle of Chardonnay that had been cooling in the fridge on the table. They all sat down to enjoy the roast beef that Tilly had cooked. Ecstatic, that her yorkshires had risen, amidst the tingling and thoughts. 'Shall I pour,' asked Pete. 'Yes please go ahead,' 'Mum, would you like a little wine.' 'Yes please pet, don't normally drink Pete, just a small amount thank you.' Pete poured the wine, as they were all enjoying being together after so many years of not seeing each other.

Pete was the first to finish. 'Tilly, I can't remember when I last had a home cooked roast dinner. That was delicious.' 'I'm glad you enjoyed your dinner, hope you have room for apple crumble and custard, ' Tilly replied. 'Oh yes, Pete said, I can always find room for a pudding.' They had all finished the meal, including the pudding, sitting around the table feeling like stuffed whales. 'Pete, what do you fancy doing tonight?' 'Do you want to go out for a drink, or go back to the pub where you are staying?' 'To be honest, I don't mind just staying here for a few hours to relax and catch up, we certainly have a lot of that to do.' 'Yes of course Pete, we can stay in, I have got some beer in, and a few more bottles of the chardonnay wine we can open and enjoy.' 'Sounds good to me.' Pete and Tilly, were sitting in the lounge listening to music, reminiscing from the band days, Edith had gone to bed, and left them to catch up and enjoy the evening.

'You know Pete, I really envy you, still playing guitar in a band. I often wonder what I would be doing now, if I was still singing, maybe not in a band, but I gave up, about a year before Stanley was born.' 'Why was that Tilly?' 'Well' said Tilly, 'when the band parted ways, Bob decided he did not want to play anymore gigs, or get involved with another band. I did a few gigs on my own, like I used to, and he got very jealous of that and made his feelings quite clear that he did not want me singing without him being involved, so I just gave it up to keep the peace.' 'Oh what a shame Tilly, you are a great singer. You never lose your singing voice. I knew Bob was very protective over you, everyone in the band knew that, but having known Bob for years, I knew he had certain traits about him, I saw that with previous girlfriends he had long before you came along. He always seemed so confident to the outside world, but I got to see the insecurities he had, when we were a band. He was lead singer and lead guitarist. So he was the front man, which he loved, but I could feel the pressure coming from him.' 'Yes unfortunately,' Tilly replied 'Bob was more than that, it became more apparent when Stanley was born, and got worse when I had Sarah. I knew he was over protective, but there was a lot of jealousy, especially when I was singing in the band. He used to choose my clothes, he would choose frumpy clothes, but every so often I would argue, and get away with wearing what I wanted to wear.' 'Yes,' said Pete, 'we did hear raised voices coming from your dressing room.' 'The thing is Pete, I saw it as love, that he cared about me, but it got worse over time, where it became more physical and emotional abuse, he really was a controller, it affected me on every level of my being, I did see the red flags, but did not take any notice, but then you do know a lot, as it was you I used to come to, when I could not cope. I will always thank you for that Pete.' 'I know Tilly, I knew Bob was wrong for you, but you know they say love is blind, when we love someone with our heart and soul.' 'So how come you got divorced then Pete?' 'Well, actually not too dissimilar to you Tilly. Fortunately Maria was not as bad as Bob, but she made my life a misery. With all her demands, she spoke so badly of me to other people, I only found this out after we split up. I was so upset, but at least I eventually knew why our friends or people treated me like I was someone to be wary of. She was only with me for money, and hated it when I took a sculpting commission on, especially if it was a woman, her insecurities really came through.'

'Pete, I am so sorry to hear that, as I said before, you are such a lovely person to be around, how on earth did we get it so wrong with our marriages,' Tilly said with a heavy heart. 'Because Tilly, we are easy targets. We care, nurture, are empathic and give way too much out, get nothing in return apart from abuse, then we continue to still give more, until we are broken, if anything Tilly they have taught so much about ourselves and who we are now, and what we want in our life.' Pete looked at Tilly seeing she had tears in her eyes. 'Yes Pete, I totally understand what you are saying, looks like we were both married to similar types of people, but one thing is for sure, we are not broken now, are we?' They found themselves looking into each other's eyes, and could gently feel the softness of their lips being drawn together, both reaching out for comfort, from the cold, unemotional marriages they found themselves in the past. Tilly pulled away from Pete. 'I'm so sorry Pete, I don't know what I was thinking to do that…'.'It's not your fault Tilly, please don't apologise, I think we both needed some physical contact to feel a closeness to each other, we have been friends for years, in fact very close friends.' 'Yes I get that Pete, having not had any intimacy for a good few years, it felt lovely, a nice warm feeling, but it was not for the right reasons Pete, I'm sorry,' Tilly explained. 'Tilly it's not your fault, I have only had a few relationships in the last few years, and the women I attracted were very controlling and demanding like my first wife. I have to say it has put me off relationships. I alway seem to attract the wrong type of women, but it felt good to feel some warmth and comfort,' Pete explained to Tilly. 'How about we just act like the grown up adults that we are, we enjoyed the feeling, and both needed some comfort, but this is not the right time. We are friends and will be now forever,' said Tilly. 'Agreed,' said Pete, ' I don't want to lose your friendship, that means the world to me.'said Pete. 'Me too,' said Tilly, gently holding Petes hand. I don't want to spoil the friendship, I have not had any other relationships since my divorce, to be honest, I am still healing from the abuse, so let's pour another wine.' 'Actually Tilly, would you mind if we skipped the drink? I am feeling rather tired, and I think the driving has caught up with me. Shall I ring you in the morning? 'let's see what we fancy doing, and what you would like to do.' 'Yes of course Pete,' she said in a low voice. 'Pete I have not offended you, have I?' 'No of course not, come here, we can at least give each other a hug and a kiss on the cheek, I think that is a safer bet don't you. Hey Tilly don't get upset, these things happen, and Tilly please dont think there is anything wrong with you, I know how sensitive you are and totally understand. I have been there too, but in a different way. You are a beautiful soul inside and out, attractive, funny and the voice of an angel, you are free now to attract what you rightly deserve, and that is the love of a good man.' Pete said smiling. 'Thank you Pete, you have always been so understanding of my tears, you know, you're not so bad yourself.' Pete went over to Tilly to put his arms around her waist. 'What an idiot Bob was, I thought he was the luckiest man in the world when I watched him marry you. How on earth could he have so mistreated you so badly.' 'I know' Tilly said, 'but it is the same for you, Maria treated you badly, you did not deserve that, You are a lovely kind caring man with a good heart.' 'Well,' said Pete, 'time to put the past behind for both of us. You are starting a new chapter in your life, and I for one am happy to be part of that new chapter.' 'Likewise,' said Tilly. 'See you tomorrow for our next adventure in beautiful Northumberland.' 'Bye Tilly' 'Bye Pete, see you tomorrow.'

Tilly closed the door, and just leant against the door, "bloody hell, holy shit, how did that happen, she thought, "I did not expect that, I had to pull away, otherwise it could have ended up as a lot more than a kiss. I did enjoy the brief kiss that we had, but I will have to be careful here, as I have not slept with anyone apart from Bob, I have only had a few boyfriends when I was younger where you kissed, and if you liked them, let them touch your boob, but that's about it. I could literally fall for Pete, he has such pure energy, which I could feel, and I was worried about my yorkshire puds rising, something else was rising too." As her thoughts ran amok, she could feel her cheeks blushing, "well it's quite a compliment I suppose, that Pete was ready for action. I have to say I enjoyed the feeling of being wanted, he is a good kisser too, But I just don't feel the chemistry, and I am still healing. It's not fair to get involved with Pete, if we did have a relationship and it ended, we would lose the friendship we have. But at least it has switched the pilot light on in me, that flame went out years ago." She laughed to herself. "What the bloody hell is going on in my head, just get yourself ready for bed, and look forward to tomorrow. 'Tilly,' called her mum, 'are you awake pet it's 9am.' Tilly slowly came to, from her slumbers, her brain had not woken up either. Am I dreaming or is my mum calling out to me? Tilly heard her mum again, nope, I am definitely not dreaming. 'Yes mum, I am awake now, will be down in five minutes, once I am fully awake enough to slide out of the bed.' 'Ok pet, there's a cuppa down here for you' 'Thanks mum.' Tilly rubbing her eyes, and hearing the rain beating against her bedroom window, made her feel all cosy and warm, she nestled back down snuggling under the duvet, listening to the rain, and collecting her thoughts from the night before, she dozed off again, this time being woken up by her phone ringing, she picked it up and answered without looking who it was.

'Hello,' said Tilly in a sleepy voice. 'Hi Mum, you ok, you sounded like you were asleep? 'Hi Sarah, yes, that's because I was,' she started to laugh. 'What's the time? I must have dozed off back to sleep.' Well Mum, it's nearly 9.30am, what have you been up to, you are normally an early bird.' 'Oh Sarah, someone I had known back in the days of the band, came to visit me, I found his number and contacted him. It was lovely to see him, he is staying for a few days, he lives in Cornwall now.' "HE" Sarah said loudly, 'is he staying at nan's house?' 'No, Sarah, he is staying at the local b&b. I would not ask your nan to let him stay here, although your nan does know him, she probably would have let him stay here, but anyway' Tilly continued 'we are meeting up again today, not sure what we will be doing yet,' replied Tilly. 'Mum, you sound very tired, like you had a really really late night,' Sarah replied laughing. 'Hey Sarah, what are you trying to say?' 'Yes I went to bed a lot later than I usually do, but we had a lot of catching up to do,' Tilly replied, and added 'we are friends.' 'Oh ok, Just nice to hear that you are enjoying yourself.' 'So how are you, Martin and my gorgeous granddaughters?' 'Yes Martin and I are fine,' Sarah replied, He's a bit stressed through work, and the kids are all well. They keep asking when they can see you again. I spoke to Martin and Stanley about maybe coming up for Christmas, do you think nan would be up for us all staying again?' 'OMG you are joking aren't you, your nan would love you all here again, especially for Christmas. I will speak to her about it but I know for sure she will say yes. Sarah, you have made my day, I was thinking maybe I could come and visit you in the October half term. Is that doable, for you Sarah?' 'I don't see why not, there is a bed in the spare room, you are always welcome here.' 'Sarah, I will get back to you in the week, I can sort some dates out with you, I am going to London with Isla the weekend before, and let Stanley know about Christmas will you?' Tilly replied. 'Yes ok, take care, speak soon, love you.' 'Love you too Sarah, give hugs and kisses to those beautiful granddaughters of mine. Yes will do, Bye Mum' 'Bye Sarah.'

Not a second longer, the phone rang again, Tilly still had not yet made it out of bed. It was Pete ringing, 'Hi Pete, how are you this morning?' 'Good morning Tilly, yes fine, good, ta. Just finished breakfast, what about you, are you washed, dressed and having your breakfast?' 'Well, Er, actually no, to all those questions,' she said in a low voice, 'I have not even made it out of the bed yet,' laughing as she was speaking. 'I dozed off back to sleep, then Sarah rang me, and we had a chat. The cup of tea that mum made me will be stone cold by now.' 'Ok, no problem, I can have a mooch about, get a newspaper and read in the pub, just give me a ring when you are ready.' ' That's great Pete, speak soon, I am aiming for about 12.30pm.' That's fine Tilly, I have a few things to sort out regarding work. See you soon bye,' 'bye Pete.' Tilly sprung out of bed, as fast as her body would let her, she had a fresh cuppa, and breakfast. 'Morning pet, you must have had a late night?' 'Did you have a nice time catching up.' 'Yes, It was really nice to spend time with him, he is such a good man and has not changed at all. Mum, Sarah rang, she has asked if they can all come up for Christmas this year, but thought it best to ask you first, they want to stay here?' 'Well pet, what you think is the answer is to that, it's a big YES, I can't think of anything better than having you all together here,' as a broad smile appeared on her face. 'Thanks Mum, it will be lovely to have my family together for Christmas and have a happy one for once.' 'You don't have to thank me pet, I am so lucky and blessed with you and my grandchildren, and great grandchildren.' 'Right mum, now I need to get in the shower, get dressed, and get myself together. I am not used to rushing around like that anymore, my body was well out of its comfort zone. Thank god we sorted out those outfits mum,' she replied laughing. Tilly put her makeup on, did her hair, got dressed, got her handbag to make sure she had everything she needed. She had a quick look in the mirror to make sure she looked ok. Yes I feel comfortable and casual, then rang Pete to let him know she was now ready. She waited in the lounge for Pete to turn up, taking a few deep breaths, and relax after the manic morning of getting up late.

Within minutes Pete was at the door, Tilly went to greet him, Tilly and Pete both shouted out goodbye to Edith, 'see you later.' 'Ok you two, have a good time.' 'We will.' they said together. They got in the car, 'Pete, what do you fancy doing?' 'I really don't mind, is there a pub where we can have lunch?' 'Yes, there is, it's called the tickled trout. It's not that far away, how does that sound?' 'Yes perfect,' said Pete. I would like to have a wander around the castle too, would you mind Tilly?' ' No of course not, actually I have not even been there myself since I have been back, yes it would be nice to do that.' 'Tilly you look lovely, it's great to be seeing you again.' 'You scrub up well too,' said Tilly, as they both laughed together, as Tilly put her seat belt on. 'Tilly I can't remember where the pub is?' Don't worry Pete, I will direct you.' They arrived at the pub, and were shown to a table that was tucked away in the corner. It was quite a quaint little pub, dating back to the 15th century, it was like stepping back into the 15th century too. The wooden front doors were the original doors, the beams, and open fireplace with a lovely roaring fire, giving out a warm glow, small windows with tiny curtains. 'There you are sir, I have brought over two menus , for you to peruse, there are also today's specials on the board. Can I get you both a drink?' asked the waiter. 'Yes please, Tilly, what do you fancy to drink?' 'Can I have a glass of wine, chardonnay please?' 'And I will have a pint of Northumberland ale please.' 'Thank you sir, I will bring your drinks over shortly, while you look at the menu.' 'Thank you, said Pete. 'how do you feel today Tilly? 'Actually I feel ok, although my head felt a bit fragile when I woke up, I had a bit too much wine. How about you?' Tilly continued, 'are you ok? Probing to see if Pete would say anything about last night. 'Yes I am all good Tilly, and I know what's going on in your head, I can feel it,' Pete smiled as he spoke. 'Tilly blushed, and averted her eyes to the door, so as not to look at Pete in the eyes.'Tilly it's alright, don't feel embarrassed, these things happen as I said last night. I can't say I did not enjoy the brief kiss we had, but I do understand and to be honest I want to be part of your life now, but as friends. Come on Tilly, look me in the eyes, we have to move on from this, if we ended up having sex, a completely different scenario, but we didn't.' Tilly turned her head and looked Pete in the eyes. 'Yes I know it just feels a bit weird that's all, we women are wired differently to you men, we dwell on it, all the emotions come up in our heads, you men just take it for what it is.'

'So let's put this behind us and enjoy our meal together. 'So Pete,' Tilly continued, 'talking about embarrassing moments, have you had many over the years?' 'Oh yes,' said Pete, 'I remember when I was first divorced, and trying out the dating scene, I encountered a few frisky women. "Really"!!!!! Said Tilly. 'Yes Really' Pete replied. 'Oh do tell, I like a good laugh.' Tilly continued. 'Well, there was this occasion, when I met someone online, we had been messaging and talking for a few weeks, I had seen a picture of her, she seemed really nice and pleasant, anyway we agreed to meet up and have a drink, I worked out quite quickly, to only meet to have a drink or coffee on the first meeting. These tips may help you Tilly. If you book for dinner, if you don't get on with someone, or the conversation dries up, and you are just on your starters, it's not easy to spend another couple of hours, main meal and dessert, just looking at someone hoping that one of you may speak, ' he said laughing. 'And you know that they are not your type, by the way that goes both ways too, you can't just get up and walk out, especially if they are just about to put another Strawberry in their mouth, you have to stay.' Tilly was laughing so much, she forgot how funny Pete was. He had a great sense of humour. 'So anyway, where was I, Oh yes, so we decided to meet up, at one of the pubs in town, so anyways, I got there waiting outside patiently, then this lady approaches me, 'Hi Pete she called out to me,' I was taken aback she was nothing like the picture she sent over, please Tilly, I am not being horrible, her dress looked like it had not been washed or ironed, for a long while, wellie boots on, a great big shopping bag full of everything. I was just hoping she did not have overnight clothes in that bag, and she was expecting me to cook eggs and bacon in the morning.' 'You are funny, can't believe this happened to you.' said Tilly. 'The story goes on,' said Pete, so I replied to her and asked her if she was Carole. Yes she replied, but how can you say to someone, you don't look anything like the picture, being the gentleman that I am. Smiling at Tilly. So we walked to the pub, she tried to link my arm, to say there was no attraction, or spark of chemistry was an understatement, I was trying to move my arm close to my body, so she could not link her arm with me. Her wellie boots were two sizes too big for her, they were making a squeaky noise with every footstep, her coat had buttons missing and that was 2 sizes to small for her, so we got to the pub, and I got her a drink, we started talking, then I realised it was not the same voice. I became very intrigued so I was talking to her about some of the things we had spoken about, but she could not recount everything. I felt embarrassed. I know you should not judge someone for how they look, but this was off the scale. In the end, I had to ask what this was all about. I said she looked nothing like her picture, or her voice, without any embarrassment whatsoever, she told me it was a friend of hers, she had used her picture, and she was the person I was talking to, no wonder she never bloody remembered anything, she was sometimes listening in. Her friend wanted to help her get a date, so they decided to do it this way, the only thing she remembered was to make out that she was her friend, she said her real name was Mandy, I did feel sad for her, but I could not handle it anymore and left the pub and left her in there. The other date, we met for coffee, and sitting at the table, she started playing footsie with me, then just as I was taking a mouthful of coffee, I felt her hand land on my crotch, Well !!!! the coffee left my mouth as soon as it had gone in, spraying out everywhere, I could not believe what was happening to me, just sitting in the bloody cafe, she again showed no embarrassment either, I left as fast as I could, again just leaving her sitting at the table, I didn't even want to know what possessed her to grab my crown jewels, I am quite a private person, and I do like to get to know someone before we get to the intimacy part. That was the last thing I would have expected to happen. Pete was laughing so much, and Tilly was crying with laughter, tears running down her cheeks, holding her stomach, 'Bloody hell Pete, what a situation to be in, but that is so funny, er…..out of interest are you still on dating sites?' Tilly smiled. 'I have occasionally, when I have felt a bit lonely. but really that is the wrong time to go on dating sites. I have met some lovely ladies, but unfortunately they were not for me. I think when you are older, you are not in such a rush to meet someone, and get married within six months. To give that type of commitment, you have to first make sure, there is compatibility, trust, love, and enjoy each other's company,' replied Pete. 'Yes, I totally agree,' said Tilly.' I have not yet encountered any dating sites, or dates as yet, I am not ready yet to go on any site. Not sure if I ever will, I still think it's nice to meet someone who has crossed your path, you can feel the attraction and chemistry instantly.' As they finished talking, the waiter brought over the meals they had ordered. They both sat and enjoyed their lunch together, raising a glass to their friendship with each other again. ' Pete, when we have finished lunch, do you still fancy having a walk around Bamburgh Castle, and maybe a walk on the beach? I know it's a bit blowy.' 'Yes, that sounds good' said Pete. 'I have not been to the castle for years, it holds so many memories for me as a little girl. Glad you fancy a walk on the beach. I can always visit the beach in all weathers.' 'Yes me too,' replied Pete. They ate their meals, had a few drinks, Pete paid the bill, Tilly offered to pay but Pete would not have accepted that, as he wanted to treat Tilly. Pete helped Tilly with her jacket and they both headed out to Bamburgh Castle. Tilly was thinking about what Pete had told her about the dating sites, it certainly made her aware of some of the pitfalls of dating online. But she now had a heads up on some of the dos and don'ts, and grabbing some man's crotch whilst they are drinking their coffee was something definitely not on her agenda, I really don't need to be sprayed by someone's coffee, through shock. Smiling as she was thinking of that scenario. 'What are you smiling at,' Pete said, 'I have not seen that wicked smile since the band days. 'nothing Pete, just smiling and enjoying your company that's all,' she replied, thinking inside, that she did not want to give Pete the idea especially after our brief kiss that I would grab his crotch, trying to keep her laughter intact. 'Nearly there,' said Tilly.

'It is still a beautiful place, you are so lucky to be born up here Tilly. I was born in good old Sutton in Surrey having said that, there was always some live music in some pub going on most nights along with discos and just places to meet and socialise. That's how I got to play guitar, the man who was teaching me, know a few bands and one of them was looking for a guitarist, I went for the audition, and they asked me to join the band, it was a progressive rock band, we played a lot of gigs, I was only sixteen, but it gave me a lot of confidence, then I met Bob, at one of the gigs, he saw me play and said he was starting a new band, The Blue Fairground, and would I be interested. I think we are all where we are meant to be, until life wants us to shift to another direction, which fascinates me.' 'Ok Tilly, where do I park?' Pete asked. 'Just over there is fine by the entrance to the castle.' Tilly replied. Pete parked up, and they wandered around the castle grounds and gardens, and into the castle. It was only open a few hours every day, especially out of season, they had got there with an hour to spare. Pete got lost in the architecture of the building, one of his favourite ways of sculpting was to find unusual angles in the architecture. He always carried his camera in the car, so it was always at hand. When wandering around, He managed to take some good angles. Tilly was also interested, she had never viewed the castle in this way before. Unfortunately they could not finish as the doors were about to close. 'Great,' said Pete, 'I have some really good pictures, I can use for my sculpting.' They left and
went to the beach. It was quite wild and exhilarating. The waves of the North Sea can be very powerful and forceful, as they crash to the seashore. The wind was blowing, in fact they were the only two people on the beach. Tilly linked Petes arm and cheekily asked him if this was ok, or was he going to keep his arm tight to his coat, he did not reply, but took her hand and slipped it through his arm, they walked side by side taking in the fresh sea air after a short while Tilly asked if they could go back as she was freezing. They both walked back to the car. 'Do you want to come back to mine?' asked Tilly, 'Yes that would be lovely, I can see your mum again.' 'Mum would love that, you can stay for tea, and we can relax.' 'Now that sounds like a plan to me,'

replied Pete. 'Ok home we go, and get warmed up.' 'Thank you Tilly, I have enjoyed today.' 'So have I Pete it's been really lovely, spending time with you. Thank you for treating me.' 'Why would I not treat you my dear Tilly.' ' I think that visit to the castle has taken you back to the 1500's,' Tilly said laughing.

    They sat in silence on the way home, Tilly realising that this is normal, being treated like a person, not being controlled or made to feel so insecure about herself. I do hope that I am lucky enough to have this in my life, it's so refreshing, so easy no anxiety. If only she sighed, if only I could see Pete in another way, on a relationship level, but unfortunately I can't. I do love him and will always want him to be part of my life, but as friends we work well, deep down I think Pete feels the same as me, we are both older now, more wiser, and both know what we want. He will make some lovely woman happy, he deserves to be happy and loved. Pete had to beep his horn, as a dog shot out into the road, which brought Tilly back to reality with a jolt, 'You alright Pete?' Yes fine, I think a dog got spooked, 'we are home now' replied Pete.

CHAPTER 8

'Hi Mum, guess who I have with me? he can't stay away from you.' Pete and Tilly both standing in the hallway laughing. Pete walked into the lounge. 'Edith, how lovely to see you again," Pete said as he walked towards her, his arms opened wide and placed a kiss on her cheeks as he hugged her. 'Lovely to see you again Pete.' 'Mum, Petes staying for a few hours, so I will cook dinner for us all.' 'Pete, is Ham Egg and chips ok for you?' Yes that's perfect, I still feel a bit full from lunch.' 'I will make us all a cuppa. Mum, would you like some biscuits?' Tilly said as she walked into the kitchen. 'Yes please pet, could I have my favourite dunking biscuits.?' They all sat down watching the drama that was on the TV. It was Hercule Poirot, Edith loved watching him, she found him fascinating with his Belgium accent. They were all drinking their tea, and dunking their digestive biscuits, whilst trying to decipher who the murderer was, trying to work out what had happened and who was there, they were right little sleuths. Tilly, a bit later went into the kitchen to cook the dinner. When she came back Pete was asleep on the sofa, Edith still watching the TV, she looked at Tilly when she walked in pointing to Pete who was asleep. 'He must feel very comfortable here, he is relaxing well,' Edith said in a sartorial way but laughing at the same time. 'Mum, it's the North Sea air that has knocked him out,' laughing as she spoke. 'Yes but he does live in Cornwall, 'Edith said. 'Yes mum, he does, as I said it's the North Sea air, it knocks everybody out,' she replied smiling . Think I need to give him a nudge.

'Dinner is nearly ready. Pete, wake up,' Tilly gently spoke in a soft voice, and placed her hand on his shoulder to awaken him. Pete started to stir, opening his eyes to see Tilly bending over him. 'Oh wow, that was some power nap,' Pete said, as he was coming too. 'It sure was Pete.' replied Edith 'We heard you,' laughing as she spoke. Pete felt a bit embarrassed. 'Oh sorry I hope I didn't disturb you watching Hercule Poirot? This sofa is so comfy, I just felt the need to doze off.' 'Hey, no worries Pete, only joking, how can I talk, when I just nod off,' said Edith. 'Well, if you put it like that, I don't feel so bad,' Pete replied laughing. Tilly was in the background laying the table, all was ready, knives and forks neatly placed, the coastal placemats in position on the table, the condiments out, including Tomato and Brown sauce. 'Right you two, dinner is ready'….. They all sat down to eat their dinner, tucking into their ham egg and chips, which appeared to disappear quite quickly. They all helped to clear up, and watched some quiz show that was on. A little later Edith went to bed, leaving Tilly and Pete to have another catch up.

'How about we play some music tonight Pete, and have a little dance, like we used to when we were playing at a gig, when the DJ came on to give us a break, while Bob was invariably sitting in the corner somewhere moping because he was not getting any attention?' 'Hey Til's, I would like that, let's see if we can remember any of the words. Actually I have my guitar in the boot of my car, shall I go and get it?' 'It won't wake your mum up will it?' Pete, you seem to have everything in the boot of that car.' Tilly laughed. 'No, mum is a heavy sleeper. That would be good, going back to those days,' Tilly replied. 'Great I will go and get it.' Within minutes Pete was back with his guitar, he just sat whilst tuning up his guitar, he then started playing some of the tunes, when they were in the band together. Tilly was joining in singing, but her voice kept wavering, as she started to feel emotional, trying to sing and hide the tears that were building up and ready to tumble down her cheeks and bounce off onto her lap. Pete looked over at Tilly, he could see she was feeling emotional. 'Tilly are you ok?' 'I can stop if you want me to, what's wrong?' 'Pete, I don't know to be honest, I seem to feel like this sometimes. I guess seeing you sitting there playing the guitar took me back to the good old days. I loved singing and being in the band. Where have all those years gone? I would love to go back there, even if it was for a day, so no please carry on. I want to sing along with you.' Tilly joined in, she could not believe she was remembering the words from most of the songs that Pete was playing; It felt like a big shift had lifted from her heart. A few bottles of wine came out, Tilly was in her element, so was Pete, they got through most of the covers of songs they used to play and sing to. She asked Pete, if she could have a go playing his guitar, it was years ago since she last played the guitar, or piano for that matter. Pete handed over the guitar to Tilly, she got herself ready, plucking at the strings, trying to familiarise herself again with the notes and chords of the guitar, which is something thankfully, you never forget. She started singing you make me feel like a natural woman, which was one of her favourite songs, it was a song that frequently came into her head, that she regularly used to sing. The hairs on the back of her neck stood on end, she felt all goose bumpy, and feeling very emotional again, as if the words would not come out of her mouth. she regained her composure, then continued to sing the song, Pete had come nearer to put his hand on her shoulder, for moral support, as she was singing, Pete joined in, in certain parts of the song. 'Pete, this is just brilliant, I am so pleased you carry your guitar in the car,' smiling as she spoke. I thoroughly enjoyed this evening. I never thought I would sing and play guitar again, but I have.' 'There you go, you see, you have not lost your voice at all, I said that to you the other day, I have enjoyed this evening too.' 'Hey Tilly, have a guess at the time ?' 'Erm, I would say about 10.30 to 11pm.' 'It happens to be midnight.' 'Really' said Tilly. That time has gone too quickly.' 'Pete, I have booked a table for tomorrow for 2pm? Isla will meet us here at about 1ish, is that ok?' 'Yes, that's fine,' said Pete, 'I will get here at around 1pm,' Pete continued, 'I have not been to The Swan in years.' He walked over to Tilly, they gave each other a hug and a kiss. Tilly watched him walk to his car. Tilly closed and locked the door, and went and sat in the lounge.

I can't believe it, she thought. This has been absolutely wonderful, why did I get myself into such a state of anxiety and panic, it's gone so quickly, and still another lovely day to look forward to. Tilly got herself a drink of water, she did not want a heavy head tomorrow morning when she woke up. After a good night's sleep, Tilly woke up to the warmth of the sun pouring through the windows, then the clouds would cover the sun, making her bedroom feel a little dark, but the sun soon appeared again. Tilly looked out of the window gathering the energy of the sun ready for the day ahead. She had a big stretch, swung her legs over and started humming some of the songs she sang from the night before. Tilly heard her mum in the kitchen busing herself, putting things away, folding the tea towels. 'Mum, is that the kettle I can hear boiling? Please could I have a coffee, if you are making a drink?' 'Yes pet, of course I can do that for you.' While she was waiting she sent a text to Isla, to make sure she could still make it for lunch. Isla must have had her phone in her hand, a message came back straight away. Absolutely yes, can't wait to see you and Pete a bit later. Tilly enjoyed her cup of coffee, and watched a bit of morning telly with her mum, with some toast and marmalade. 'Hey pet, you seemed to have a good night last night, I was dancing in my bed and singing.' 'Mum, sorry did we wake you up?' 'I had such a lovely evening with Pete.' 'No not at all,' replied Edith. 'I really enjoyed myself listening to you both, this sort of thing does not happen much anymore. It took me back to my dancing days with your father. I do miss going out, I used to be out all the time, but age and my health problems have scuppered that now.' 'I am loving you living here, I know it's not forever.' 'Yes I know mum, I totally understand you, I love living here too. Well at least you had a dance whilst in bed.'

There was a knock at the door, it was Isla. 'Sorry If I am a bit early, I was ready early so thought I may as well leave in case I headed into heavy traffic.' 'No need to apologise, mum can't wait to see you after all these years.' Edith was feeling like a queen, all these visitors, wanting to see her. Isla went over and gave Edith a big hug. 'So lovely to see you, Edith, you look well.' 'Well, the same can be said of you, goodness pet, you have not changed a bit.' 'Well, I'm not sure about that, but thank you Edith.' Tilly came down the stairs all ready for lunch with two of her best friends. 'You look lovely Tilly,' 'so do you, Isla,' Tilly replied. 'Pete should be here soon.' 'Have you had a lovely time Til's?' enquired Isla. 'Yes, absolutely. It has been lovely to see Pete after all these years.' Without another word said, there was a knock at the door. Isla opened it as she was nearest to the door. 'That must be Pete,' said Tilly, 'can't think I am expecting anyone else at this time' she said laughing. Isla opened the door.

" It absolutely is.'" 'Hello ladies,' standing at the front door with a big smile on his face. Isla smiled, not really knowing how to greet Pete, she had only met him a few times, before she knew it, Pete had given her a hug. 'Hello Isla, nice to see you again, I do remember you, you were sometimes with Tilly, when we played in the band, when Bob got to know Tilly.' 'Yes that's right, that's going back some years,' replied Isla, as they moved into the lounge. While Tilly got her coat and bag. Pete went over to Edith to say hello. 'If I did not know any different, I would say you were giving me the eye pet,' Edith said laughing. Pete had a cheeky grin on his face as she spoke. 'You have the same twinkle in your eyes, just like my mum had.' Pete replied. Tilly came back into the room. Pete went over and gave Tilly a hug. 'Ok folks, are we ready? Bye Mum.' They each said goodbye to Edith. 'Have a lovely time together, enjoy, see you all later. They all walked out the front door, Tilly with keys in her hand,

'I will drive us to The Swan.' 'Are you sure?' Pete said 'Yes positive you have driven all the time, it's my turn, you can enjoy a drink. It's so nice for us to all be together.' Pete sat in the front, Isla in the back, already chatting about their lives present and past. They arrived at The Swan. 'Oh this looks lovely Tilly,' said Pete. 'Yes it is lovely here, the food is good too,' said Tilly. 'So let the trio go and enjoy,' Isla said. They were shown to their table. They have done this place up,' Tilly said. It is done out in art deco style, an era that Tilly loved, with big comfy sofas and chairs, art deco lamps, and artificial trees with twinkling lights adorning the leaves and branches. 'This is so pretty,' Isla said. 'Certainly changed since the last time I was here.' Isla continued. The waiter arrived with drinks and food menus, for them to peruse. 'Are you going to have a drink Tilly?' Pete asked. 'Well,' said Tilly, 'I think I will have one cheeky glass if white wine,' smiling at Pete. 'So what do we all fancy from this wonderful menu?' Pete enquired. They each gave their preference in meals to Pete, who then gave the information to the waiter, who had brought their drinks over. 'So, are you having a nice piece of fillet steak Pete?' Asked Tilly. 'Well, I have to confess, as we have been sitting here I have seen a few steaks being served, and they look delicious, and also noticed that the people are thoroughly enjoying them, so that's me sorted with my meal,' laughing as he spoke. 'So Isla, where do you live now?' Pete enquired. 'Oh, I live in a village called Alnwick, I suppose it's about a 20 minute drive, not long really. I have lived there for a few years now, but before that I had been living in Italy, in the Tuscany region. It was very beautiful living out there. 'And she cooks a mean spaghetti Bolognese,' Tilly piped up laughing. Isla and Pete both laughed along with her. 'So what made you come back to good ol Blighty? Pete asked. 'Well,' said Isla, 'my daughters live here, and I have grandchildren, who I missed terribly when I was living out in Italy, and not seeing my grandchildren growing up. The phone calls and speaking to my daughters and grandchildren does not replace seeing family and spending time with them. So we decided, well actually I decided, as my husband did not really want to come back here. I don't have any regrets about coming back. I experienced a wonderful life out there, but felt the need to be back with my family.' Pete wanted to ask more, but felt it was too inappropriate to ask more questions. Yes, I love where I live, Isla continued. 'That's when Tilly and I bumped into each other on the beach in Bamburgh. I was up visiting a family friend, and decided to have a walk on the beach before heading home, and I spotted a familiar face, sitting alone on the bench, and now our paths have crossed, we will always be in each other's lives again. It's been wonderful spending time with my very best friend, and now you are here too, thanks to Tilly contacting you. It's amazing how life works and manoeuvres itself around, so people from your past actually cross your path again.' 'Yes, I agree with that one Isla, never thought I would ever speak to Tilly again, let alone see her and now get to see you too.' Pete replied. 'What's to be will be, ' Tilly added. They all raised their glasses "ching ching" They all said, 'here's to happy memories and making new memories.' 'So Pete, where are you living now?' enquired Isla, 'I live in Cornwall in a town called Padstow.' 'Wow, how did you end up living down there if you don't mind me asking?' 'no not at all, Isla.' When I got divorced, I just felt that I needed a new life and somewhere completely different. My daughter was at Uni in Exeter, I just felt drawn to Cornwall. I spent many happy holidays there with my parents when I was a young boy, and I was able to see my daughter, which was a bonus. I am a Sculptor, and still play guitar, so luckily I can move anywhere as I work for myself. I joined the band in a local pub, and play there most Friday evenings, unless we have a gig to play in other pubs or a function.' 'That sounds like a wonderful way to live, Pete.' replied Isla. The waiter returned with their food, and served them their meals. 'This all looks lovely Tilly, good choice to bring us here,' said Pete. They all enjoyed their lunch, chatting and laughing in between. 'So, Pete are you seeing anyone,' Isla asked. 'No, not me, funny you should ask, I was sharing some of my dating faux pars to Tilly only the other night. When I look back now, they were so funny, but at the time, I was embarrassed, and seemed to meet women, who were very demanding and controlling, a bit like my ex wife. That is one road, I never ever want to travel ever again.' 'Oh that's a shame Pete, you could be missing out, but I do get you on that score.' Do you have any hobbies, Isla?' Pete enquired, Isla was feeling a bit uncomfortable, she wondered if she had interrogated Pete too much about dating again. Isla carried on with the answer to his question. 'Well yes, I am an artist. I used to paint a lot when I lived in Italy, the scenery was magnificent to paint, I could spend hours just sitting up in the hills, near the mountains, or sitting amongst the lemon and orange groves. But since I have been back here in the UK, I have not picked up a paint brush, I feel I have lost my confidence.' You are so good Isla, maybe when we have our meetups, we could perhaps get the paints out and get lost in our painting,' Tilly replied. 'Yes, why not Til's, we can certainly do that.' I am also interested in spiritualism. I love crystals, and like to meditate every day. It really helps me to feel more balanced and less stressed. In fact Tilly and I meditated together at my home, it was so lovely sharing that with Tilly. I also have an interest in tarot cards, and crystals. It has been very helpful, when I have felt overwhelmed.' 'You know Tilly, I have always thought you were that way inclined, you have that type of energy.' Tilly looked at Pete, in a strange way, ' how do you know about energy?' 'I feel the same energy as both of you, but never discuss it with anyone unless they have that certain energy around them. I have dabbled, with the cards, and the pagan side, but I try to meditate every day by the sea, it too helps me to release any pent up stress. So, it looks like we are a trio with the same beliefs in Spirituality.' They all looked at each other in the eyes, they are the windows to the soul. 'Wow, I now understand why we have always got on Pete, that has answered a lot of questions, as to why I turned to you, when Bob was having one of his narcissist arrogant moments.'

'Pete, I have not told you, but Isla and I are going to London in about 4 weeks, we are going to go to some of the old haunts that we went to when we went to live in London, well, that's if they are still there, we fancy a reminiscence of the 60s and 70's.' 'That sounds fun,' Pete said, smiling,' it's good to have girly times away. Yes, we are looking forward to our girly time away, a good excuse to do some retail shopping, see a show, and generally to chill out for a few days.'

Tilly was sitting at the table and could not but notice, there was some chemistry between Isla and Pete, they just seemed to get on with one another. Tilly felt a pang of jealousy, as she knew that Pete had always had a soft spot for her, but this felt different and Isla was really enjoying talking to Pete. I don't know why I am feeling a bit jealous, thought Tilly, but it has triggered something in me. 'WHY' when I turned him down. But, he is a very handsome older man, caring, sensitive and knows how to make a woman feel special. Maybe this was my purpose for me ringing Pete to bring Isla and him together, "mmm" I wonder. 'You alright Tilly.' asked Isla 'you seemed like you were elsewhere just then.' 'Yes, I'm fine. I often find myself doing that, sorry. I am listening to you both, feeling guilty about the thoughts, especially as Isla is a married woman, and Pete lives down the other end of the country. She could see the eye contact Isla was giving Pete, and visa versa. They had now finished their meals and ordered a sharing dessert, as they were all full up from the beautiful food they'd eaten. Leaving the dining table they went to sit on the comfy sofas to have coffee and liqueurs. Pete and Isla sat on the sofa together, Tilly sat opposite on the comfy chair. Tilly had all sorts of thoughts passing through her head, thinking that they looked good together, wondering what Pete was thinking about Isla, it was a minefield in Tilly's head. It was well past 5pm by the time they left. They had laughed, nearly cried, knew all about each other, and found they shared the same spiritual values, and vowed to meet up again. 'How about you both come down for a visit to Cornwall.' said Pete. Islas eyes lit up. 'Yes I think that's a lovely idea to come to visit you, thank you for asking us,' said Isla. They settled the bill, and left. They were all a bit tired on the way home, but had had a great time. They arrived back at Tilly's house. Pete and Isla both wanted to come in to say goodbye to Edith. When they got in, Edith was listening to her favourite music of the big band era, where she loved to dance with her friends, she regularly listened and watched the old 1940's Hollywood musicals. 'Hi Edith,' Isla said, ' I just wanted to come and say goodbye to you,' she went over to give her a big hug.' Have you all had a good time?' Edith enquired.' 'Yes it's been really lovely. The Swan has been revamped into an Art deco style, and looks very elegant.' 'That sounds lovely, Isla. don't forget to come and visit when you and Tilly meet up, You are always welcome.' Thank you Edith,' said Isla. Isla went to say goodbye to Tilly, knowing they were meeting up on Friday as they had their massages booked. 'Bye Isla,' they gave each other a hug. 'See you Friday' Tilly said. Isla then went to say goodbye to Pete, who gave her a bigger hug this time and a kiss on each cheek. 'Would you like to keep in touch?' Isla asked Pete. 'Yes, that would be nice, to keep in contact.' They quickly exchanged numbers and Isla left to start her journey home. Tilly watched on, she knew that Isla liked him, she was never one to give her number out, let alone ask to keep in contact, or where she lived when they were young. Pete came over to Tilly and sat and spoke to Edith, having a last cuppa with them. Edith had cooked supper for herself, and was feeling cosy in her armchair. Pete followed Tilly into the kitchen.

'You ok, Tilly,' asked Pete.'Yes of course, I thought it was lovely that you and Isla got on so well.' 'Yes', said Pete 'she is a lovely lady, just like you Tilly, it's been so nice to see you and Isla and to be with good female company.' 'Likewise Pete, you are a very special man.' Tilly went over and planted a big kiss on his forehead, they gave each other the biggest hug. 'Oh I needed that Pete.' said Tilly 'And so did I. We are so lucky to have this friendship, thank you for contacting me Tilly. I am going to the b&b soon, as I have a long drive back tomorrow and need some sleep, as you kept me up late for the last few nights.' They both started laughing again. 'Yes that's fine Pete, I totally understand,' replied Tilly. 'I will come and say goodbye before I go. I have so loved coming up here Tilly,' Said Pete. 'So have I Pete, I have enjoyed it immensely.' They drank their tea in the kitchen, Pete said his goodbyes and left to go back to the b&b. Tilly went into the lounge, kicked her shoes off, and just relaxed into the sofa. Her thoughts were very muddled indeed, funny how you know that you are best of friends, nothing else, but have thoughts of jealousy. HELP: I am doing what I always do, that is over analysing and thinking too much. I have got them paired up already, even though Isla is with her husband, and Pete is not looking for a relationship. Tilly put her thoughts to the back of her mind, and started to watch the film Edith had on, it was another one of her hollywood 1940s musicals with Ginger Rogers and Fred Astaire, she was totally engrossed with the dancing and singing along to the song

Edith loved reflecting over the past. She felt that life now was more of a challenge, then making new memories in her life, she continued reflecting on the lovely time she had in the last few days. Edith looked across to her daughter merrily singing away. 'You know Tilly,' Edith exclaimed, you should start singing again, and playing guitar. You have a lovely voice, I heard it the other night, and when you and Pete were singing together, you had a lovely harmony between you.' 'Thanks Mum, maybe one day who knows?'

CHAPTER 9

The next day Tilly was looking out over the fields when she saw Pete pull up, her tummy felt like butterflies, the same feelings she had when he was arriving. She called her mum to let her know that Pete had come to say goodbye, she went and opened the front door to let him in. 'Hi Pete, all ready for the journey. 'Yes,'as promised I have come to say goodbye.' He had a beautiful box in hand, that he had saved it until now to give to Tilly. He came in and gave her a big warm hug, he left the box out in the hallway. 'So glad you came round and said goodbye, I have had such a wonderful time in the last few days, Pete.' 'No, thank you Tilly, it's been brilliant. I have enjoyed our time together, we must do it again.' Pete disappeared into the hallway to get the box that he had brought round for Tilly, he came back into the lounge holding the beautiful box. 'This is for you Tilly, I wanted to give this to you years ago, but our paths never crossed again, once the band split up, so I kept it at my studio, never thinking that I would see you again.' 'Oh Pete, what a beautiful box, thank you, I'm so excited as to what is in it. Goodness Pete, this is heavy, it's not a bomb is it,' she said laughing, 'No, exclaimed Pete, just open it you will be very surprised.' Tilly sat down on the sofa, and gently opened the box, she pulled back the tissue paper, it was a piece of sculpture that Pete had made of Tilly, she struggled a bit to pull it out of the box, but when she saw it was of her, she was overcome with emotion. 'Pete, I don't know what to say, it is beautiful, so this is the sculpture you made of me that has been sitting on the shelf for years,' replied Tilly. She got up, and went over to Pete, and gave him a big cuddle and a kiss on the forehead. 'Thank you so much, I shall treasure this forever.' 'I'm just pleased I have been able to give this to you, it has been on the shelf collecting dust for years. It's my pleasure, I loved sculpting you. You were and still are a very pretty woman.' Edith walked through the door to be greeted with the sculpture of her daughter sitting proudly on the coffee table. ' Mum, look what Pete has done, he had made this sculpture of me years ago, look it's beautiful.' 'WOW Pete, you certainly have a talent, it's so lovely.' 'Thank you Edith, I'm glad that you like it.' replied Pete. ' Have you come to say goodbye to us?' enquired Edith 'Yes I sure have, thank you for your hospitality, you have a very warm cosy home, and thank you feeding me, it's just been great, and for letting me watch your 1940' films, you so remind me of my mum, it been a pleasure,' as Pete put his arms around Edith, she threw her arms in wild abandonment around Petes waist, as he was to tall, for her to reach his neck, Pete bent down and gave her a kiss on her forehead. 'You are one special lady, I know where Tilly gets her wonderful energy from.' Tilly was standing in the corner, laughing. 'Sorry Pete, think mum got carried away, I think you may have pulled,' they both laughed, as Edith said 'why not, I don't get to cuddle many men nowadays so I made the most of it.' with the glint in her eye, that Pete so recognised in his own mum.

'I thoroughly enjoyed your cuddle Edith, yes we all need cuddles' 'Your very welcome Pet, don't leave it too long next time, you're welcome to stay here anytime, there's plenty of room.' Edith said her goodbyes and went and sat down in her cosy chair, wrapping the soft fleece blanket around her. Tilly followed Pete to the front door, they gave each other another hug, 'Bye Tilly,' 'Bye Pete, speak soon, text me when you get home, so I know you are home safely.' 'Yes of course, bye.' Tilly watched him go to the car, she shed a few tears as she saw him drive off, bibbing his car horn, as he disappeared round the corner. She felt an emptiness now that he had gone. She stood and stared for a few moments, then went to get herself ready for her counselling session. 'You ok Tilly,' asked her mum, 'Yes I'm fine, I have had such a good time with Pete.' She looked down at the sculpture of herself in her younger days. 'Mum I can't believe Pete did this for me, what a lovely thing to do.' 'I know pet, it is such a beautiful piece of creative art, he must think a lot of you in fact, he does think a lot of you, you can see it in his eyes, shame you don't feel the same. Are you going to keep in touch with each other?' 'Oh yes, of course, we are in each other's lives forever now as friends. He has invited Isla and myself down to stay in Cornwall with him, which we have both agreed to go and stay. Yes he is a lovely man, very caring.'

'That would be nice, a visit to cornwall.' Edith replied. 'Pet, have you got your counselling session today?' 'Yes Mum, I only have one more session, after this one. I am feeling so much better and am getting to understand who I am now. I still have a way to go, but it's a work in progress towards a more fulfilling happy life. When I come home do you fancy a meditation, and a look at the cards?' 'Oh yes, that would be good.' 'Ok Mum, I need to get ready now.' Tilly went up the stairs to get dressed, just taking 10 minutes, to ground herself and reflect on her weekend, it had made Tilly feel more confident, in herself knowing she can spend time with a man without constantly feeling anxious and panicky, she had got so used to Bob's put downs and gaslighting. When he could see her getting stronger again, he just knew how to pull the rug from beneath her, as she spiralled back down to anxiety and depression, a place she knew only too well. Pete had shown her what it was like to be treated properly and respected. She could feel another shift in herself, and recognising that she was not on the bottom rung of the ladder, but just over half way up. She felt good that she had a friend for life, who knew her well. She gathered herself together, went downstairs. Tilly said goodbye to her mum, and opened the front door. The weather had turned quite blustery again and rain clouds were brewing overhead, she picked up her umbrella, and started walking to Aromasense for her weekly therapy session, holding the scarf which was covering her nose, ears and most of her head. She reached the therapy centre, and was greeted by Sophie. 'Hello Tilly.' Tilly took a seat, and for the first time, did not feel fidgety, or anxious as she was waiting, she casually, looked at the pictures on the wall, which she had not really studied before, because of the anxiety she was feeling. 'Hello Tilly, are you ready for your session,' Lucy enquired. 'Yes of course, thank you Lucy.' Tilly followed Lucy to the therapy room, Tilly went over to the cosy chair, in the corner of the room, by the window that overlooked the little high street. 'So Tilly' asked Lucy, how are you?' 'You look very different Tilly, your body language is much more relaxed and open, and your shoulders are not up by your ears, in fact you look really well.' Actually Lucy, I feel the best I have felt in years, I seem to have shifted a lot of my past feelings and emotions from my thoughts. I have noticed that when I get anxious and panic sets in, I start talking to the anxiety and panic, and sit with it, until the feelings of anxiety have passed through me, gradually dissipating. I have learnt this technique from meditating, and have learnt to listen to my body, and what it is trying to tell me. I feel a lot calmer, learning this has certainly helped the process. So I am now getting to know myself, and trying to understand how I got into this place of such unrest. I'm not saying all the anxiety has gone, but I seem to look at things so differently.' 'Oh Tilly, that's fantastic to hear you speak like this. When did you first start to find these things out about yourself?' 'I suppose, a few weeks ago now, I had a male friend whom I had known for years. I found his number and contacted him, he actually came up this weekend, and went home today. Before he came up, I kept getting these feelings of great anxiety, and my head just felt spacey, and feeling nauseous, but I just kept trying to talk to myself, and asking why I should feel like this. I thought I was going to pass out when he knocked at the door, just through feeling anxious and panic stricken, but over the last few days, I have relaxed with him and had a lovely time. I realise I put a lot of pressure on myself, which creates anxiety. I did want to ask a question, if that is ok Lucy' 'Tilly, of course, how can I help ' 'Well, since my last session with you I have noticed that my head does not feel like it's constantly busy, how has that happened?' 'Last time Tilly, we spoke a lot about your marriage and how you felt. You said you had not spoken to anyone about what had happened, so it was constantly going on in your head, the feelings, the hurt, betrayal, the pain and suffering that you have held in for many years. Now that you have spoken about your marriage, the mind does not need to question your thoughts so much, unless you are retrieving data from the past. Tilly, journalling is a wonderful tool to help clear any feelings or thoughts that come up, again assists in clearing negative thoughts.' 'Thank you Lucy, that is such a help, actually I am going to get myself a notebook and start journalling. I used to do a lot of writing, so I will thoroughly enjoy this.' 'That's ok Tilly, that's wonderful. You have come on in leaps and bounds. You certainly have been doing a lot of work on yourself, this is when we start to heal from our past traumas. The anxiety comes up because you are going out of your comfort zone on all levels.

Although you have known him for years, never suffering abuse from him, it's actually the fear of not being good enough, not confident enough to be yourself, waiting for a panic attack or anxiety to happen, then not being able to cope, not wanting to show your vulnerability to him. You want him to see you as a strong confident woman that he knew years ago, not who you are at this present time. Tilly you are that strong woman, but abuse takes away every element of yourself on all levels, until you really don't know who you are anymore. That's why it can sometimes take years to recover. These feelings, unfortunately, are the abuse you suffered from your ex husband, it leaves its scars, especially mental and emotional abuse. You get so used to keep being knocked down all the time, you lose who you are, you become codependent, which means being taken outside of your comfort zone, will bring up these feelings of not feeling safe. Tilly I have to ask, you have only ever spoken about mental and emotional abuse, but did your ex husband physically abuse as well?

'Er yes, he did' Tilly replied in a quiet voice, 'Tilly sorry to ask but it plays a big part in how you have felt up to now. Why did you not say Tilly?' 'I felt so ashamed of myself that I let this happen to me, he could be very violent, he used to kick and punch me quite a lot, even my children witnessed it a few times, which is something I never ever wanted them to see, I saw myself as a mother who had failed her children. He once tried to strangle and rape me, but it was only once that happened, it was very scary, I became more breathless the tighter he squeezed his hand around my neck. I just became so scared and frightened of him, everything in life seemed to have fear attached to it, nothing was normal to me anymore, even walking to the shops up the road, it always felt very unsafe for me and my children to go out, then even going out was out of my comfort zone became such a issue for me, trying to control everything inside of me, so that I could feel normal, but it never worked Lucy. I did not know what normal was anymore, but nobody knew, again I felt so ashamed of myself.' Tilly sat with her head in her hands just sobbing. 'Tilly, do you think what your ex husband did to you was ok, because he only did it once?' 'No not all, it still haunts me even today.' replied Tilly. 'I know Tilly, it's very upsetting but it is so important for you to bring issues like this to the surface. You don't want to be still carrying this around for years to come. Any manipulation from a narcissist will leave you feeling lost, and broken, like you have been disempowered. Let's hope today, as it has come to the surface, after being so deeply buried within you, that it will be healed in time. I hope this has been helpful today Tilly.'' Yes it has thank you, it helps me understand myself a lot more, although I am feeling stronger, I know I have more healing to do.'replied Tilly.

'So going back to the original anxiety you were feeling the last few days. When your male friend came up this weekend, your body and mind clicked into overdrive, creating the feelings from the past. It's the male aspect, as you have been emotionally hurt, so your body went into protective mode. If this had been a female friend, there would not have been any anxiety or panic. but you are now learning to retrain these emotions and thought patterns from your past, by not making them important anymore. The more you practise knowing that these feelings and emotions do not serve you any purpose now. Your body and mind will naturally reset itself. When you are in these situations, you will know that when these feelings come up, that your body does not need to go to the fight or flight mode that would normally happen, creating the adrenaline rush, to protect you from fear. This has come from the abuse you have suffered over the years from your ex narcissist husband over a long period of time. The sympathetic nervous system overrides creating the adrenaline rushing through your body, the anxiety is protecting you from fear. You are not in fear anymore, unless you are caught in a situation where the fight or flight is necessary for your survival. Your body and mind needs to catch up, which is exactly what you are doing now with the practice of meditation and body scanning. I hope you feel proud of yourself, you have achieved so much in the last few weeks. I think this gentleman coming up this weekend is what was needed for you to separate these feelings. I always believe everything happens for a reason, nothing is coincidental. Do you feel that this weekend has shown you how you used to be before the abuse set in and destroyed your self confidence Tilly?' 'OMG yes, completely, he has shown me what it is like to be treated properly, and he was very respectful of me. Thank you Lucy, you always explain things so well, I have a mind that needs to understand the whys and wherefore, then when I understand I can process the information.' 'That's good,' said Lucy, ' you seem as if you are coping now, and having an understanding of what happened in your marriage, is how you became full of fear and anxiety.' 'That is the main objective, the narcissist just wants to bring you down, so it boosts them up. Basically they are very unhappy souls, who actually hate and despise themselves. As long as they are getting the attention whether it's positive or negative, they really don't care. They are mainly drawn to empaths and sensitives, that goes for both men and women. They look for the vulnerability, so they are easy pickings, to groom, and mould them into what their wants and needs are. It's a very scary place, especially when you become codependent, by that time you are a lamb to the slaughter, it takes an awful lot of strength and courage to leave these disturbing relationships, there are several types of narcissists, and 9 different levels, so the higher the level, the harder is to leave, as these are the sociopaths and psychopaths, but any narcissist relationship, is always tinged with control on some level. They do not love nor care, they don't have the capacity for any feelings whatsoever, they only think of themselves, The grandiose type, care about status, money and are very ruthless, so they will seek someone who has good finances behind them, then they love bomb, and before you know it, they are telling you how to spend your money or pleading poverty. Don't forget you also had a controlling father, so you have never really known who you are, so Bob's behaviour to you, was familiar, so why would you think otherwise, so don't punish yourself for thinking about how you got this mentally messed up, it purely is how you are as a person, that Bob, knew he could manipulate you, you were at both your dad and Bob's mercy, but you are now getting your strength back, and totally empowering yourself, it will take time Tilly, to find the true you, as you take off the comfort blanket, you are now making your own life choices, and what you want from your future.'

'Oh Lucy, thank you, I do find all this interesting. I have always enjoyed learning how the mind works, and the psychology of a person's mind, actually tells you a lot about them. I have to say Pete, that's my friend's name. We played in a band together years ago, I was a singer, playing guitar and piano, Pete played the guitar. Well one of the evenings when he was spending the evening at my mums house, he went out to the car and brought in his guitar, he started playing and singing, then I was singing, then he let me play his guitar, I found it so emotional, we were singing and playing songs from when we were in the band. I have not sung or played guitar for quite a few years. It felt like I was home again. I now want to sing again, but need a few singing lessons, and playing the guitar has opened up a whole new life, the life I loved before I met Bob.' 'Tilly that sounds wonderful.' said Lucy 'How lovely to have such a talent, you opened your soul the minute you started singing, you allowed a positive emotion in and it felt good. It would be lovely if you felt you needed some singing lessons, to help you feel more confident,' replied Lucy.' 'Yes, I feel that too, it was definitely a spiritual shift, for which I will be eternally grateful to Pete, for having his guitar in the boot of his car' Tilly said smiling, she continued 'Yes, I think I will look for someone who gives singing lessons.' 'Follow your heart and your soul, and listen to your intuition, it is guiding you down a new path to your future. 'I hope this has helped you today Tilly, I am just wondering, would you like to come next week, or do you feel you have dealt with enough to go it alone?' enquired Lucy 'Actually, I was thinking before I came here today, not sure if I need anymore sessions, but if I get to a place where I need more help, can I come back to see you?' 'Yes of course, I feel we know when we can guide ourselves, there are always bumps in the road that crop up, so I am here for you should you need some sessions in the future. How does that sound to you Tilly?' 'Yes that's perfect, thank you.' 'Well Tilly, I wish you all the best. You have come so far in just a few short weeks, that tells me you are now ready to embark on your new journey in life,' added Lucy. 'Thank you for everything. Tilly got up and shook Lucy's hand, walking out of the door, remembering the first time she walked in, the emotional pain, depression, anxiety, and fear of the future, that now, seems such a long while ago. She stood upright, walking tall down the hallway, smiling and humming her favourite song, knowing that finally she was heading down the right pathway. She paid her fee, and said goodbye to Sophie and told her she would see her on Friday.

Tilly walked out of the door, and felt drawn to the little cafe, round the corner, feeling that she needed to just be by herself, indulge in a latte coffee and something sweet to eat. The cafe, as normal, always had that cosy warm glow as you walked through the door, she found herself a table and sat down, the waitress came over with a menu. 'Hello Tilly, how are you?' Asked the waitress, placing the menu on the table.' 'Yes I am fine, thank you?' replied Tilly, and how are you?' Can't complain at all, everything is good, and working here is like a tonic everyday, meeting such lovely people, what's not to like, I'm very blessed.' the waitress replied smiling. 'Oh that's good, yes, I love coming here, it's such a comforting feeling walking through that door.' 'What do you fancy today then Tilly?' asked the waitress. 'Well' Tilly replied,' I would like a large latte, and a piece of that black forest gateau.' 'Sounds like you need some comfort food, pet?' the waitress replied laughing. 'Yes, I suppose I do feel like I need a sugar fix.' 'The waitress left the table to put Tillys order through. Tilly sat thinking how proud she was that she had got through the counselling sessions. Yes, I am going to celebrate with a big fattening dessert. A broad smile came across her face. I do feel so much more together and looking forward to Isla's and mine weekend away, and I have the tools to help me now should I feel a bit shaky. Tilly thought in her head, then paused, but strangely enough I am missing Pete already, and he only left this morning. He is great company, but could just be me leaping into these feelings, as I have not experienced this since I was a teenager. 'There we go Tilly, large latte, and black forest gateaux,' as the waitress placed the gateaux on the table. 'Thank you, 'said Tilly,.' 'Enjoy,' said the waitress.

Before she tucked into her comfort food, she texted Isla, to see if she was around, so they could get the times sorted out for travelling down to London for the weekend and to sort out a time for their massages on Friday. Tilly was sitting enjoying her cake, looking out of the tiny windows in the cafe, the clouds seemed very dark. It was raining quite hard, the brisk wind blowing the rain down the street, gently tapping on the windows of the cafe as it was passing through. Mums with their children, being picked up from school, huddled together under their umbrellas, hearing the children chatting to their mums about their school day, some getting very wet, playing in the puddles as they were running down the street shouting out to their friends on the way home. It took Tilly back to those days, how she misses Sarah and Stanley being little again. She loved those days, she thought they would last forever. She was pondering how fast her life seemed to have disappeared and now a nanny to five grandchildren, she felt very blessed, but knew she had to make the rest of her life count, to be happy, and as Lucy said to her, you have the choices now in which direction you want your life to go. That felt a bit scary for Tilly, she had never made choices before, having been controlled by her father and Bob. Fortunately Tilly is a strong woman, who is finding herself again, feeling empowered is the best feeling in the world, her intuition was telling her to go with the flow, no need to hurry to make decisions, just let life unfold, and gradually she would see a whole new world open up before her." Oh," what was that; it was as if her soul was talking to her, like a gentle whisper in her ear. I wonder if that is what Lucy meant by listening to your intuition, well if that is the case, it has just happened, but I have been meditating, and working with my soul's journey. I guess when you start opening up to your spiritual journey, you start to change, I have felt more peaceful, and not trying to engineer the situations that I think I want in life, but I am going with my inner voice, and just left life unfold, on the journey that is meant for me in this lifetime. Tilly finished her luscious gateau and coffee, paid her bill, and meandered home.

The rain has stopped now, it has turned quite icy cold now. It was getting dark as she left, just taking in the scenery, the trees gently swaying in the breeze, and catching a glimpse of the full moon shining in between the frost glistening on the branches, where there were only a few leaves left on them, as the days were growing shorter. Tilly loved the moon; she felt a great affinity with it, she also knew by her emotions that the full and new moons affected her. Tilly stood at the gate, just peering in her mums house, she could feel as if something out of the blue was going to happen, it was very fleeting and she did not know if it was good or bad, she put the key in the door, and felt the warmth enveloping her, coming in from the cold night air. She now sees this home as a cosy home, she never used to as a child, but sees things differently now she understands her past, and has let go of the bad memories. 'Hey Mum ,' Tilly said as she opened the door. Tilly could hear her mum crying, she rushed straight into the lounge, and went over and put her arms around her. 'Mum, whatever is wrong? I have not seen you like this in years.' 'Edith could not speak, through her tears, as she calmed down a little, Edith started to talk. 'It's Morag,' 'Oh, what has happened to Morag?' said Tilly. 'I have just come off the phone to Jack, Morag's son, who has told me, that Morag, has been diagnosed with a lung disease, she has been having trouble with breathing for quite a while now, when we have spoken she has been very breathless when speaking, this has been going on for a few years now, but Morag, being the strong Scottish woman would not go to the doctors, but Jack has said that she had a bad breathing attack and she collapsed, and she has been in hospital. She is out now but has to have oxygen now, and Morag, while she still can, wants to come and visit me and Jack has asked if he can bring her down next week. I'm so upset Tilly, she is my best friend, we have been friends since infants school.' ' Mum, I am so sorry to hear that. I remember when I was little and Morag and her husband used to visit for a few days with Jack and his sister. It's so long ago, I cannot remember her name. Then Morag would come down with Jack and his sister, without her husband, so I guess he must have passed away young.' Tilly added, as she was drying her mum's tears. 'Tilly, it's so sad, but then I guess, we are getting old, we cannot last forever.' 'Yes Mum, I know, that's why we have to make sure, we have some happiness in life, before we get too old to do the things we wish to do. Mum, when are they coming down? I want to be around to support you, I know this will be hard for you. 'Gosh I have not seen Jack for years, wonder what he's up to these days.' I know, you always seemed to get along so well when you were kids.' 'They are coming down early afternoon next Tuesday' Edith continued. 'I think the last time I saw Jack, I must have been around sixteen. I know it was before I went to London with Isla?' 'How about I put the kettle on Mum, I think you could do with a strong cup of tea with some sugar,' added Tilly. 'Yes, that would be welcomed. Please could I have some of my biscuits?' 'I feel a bit peckish.' 'Yes of course, coming right up.' Tilly checked her phone to see that Isla had replied to the text that Tilly had sent earlier regarding a time to meet on Friday. Pete, had also text to let her know that he had arrived home safely, and he was missing Tilly and really enjoyed his time up in Bamburgh. Tilly took the cups of tea and biscuits into the lounge. Edith had calmed down now, she was shocked that Morag was declining in health, and it brought her own mortality into question. She was thoroughly enjoying Tilly living with her, having Isla and Pete visiting her and having her grandchildren and great grandchildren coming to stay with her; it had brought her home to life, and to Edith as well. Tilly was sitting replying to Pete, that she was happy he had arrived home safely, and that she missed him too. He also mentioned again Tilly and Isla, going down to stay with him. Tilly said she would speak to Isla on Friday to sort something out when they met up for their monthly massage. 'That sounds good,' replied Pete. 'Yes, I enjoy having massages, so relaxing and the aroma of the oils is just divine.' replied Tilly. 'Yes I have had a few over the years,' Pete replied, 'such a pleasant way to unwind.'

'Pete, I hope you don't mind, but I am going to have to end this text. Maybe we can catch up next week, mum has had some upsetting news today, when I look at her, I can see she is sad.' 'Yes of course, no problem, I was going to ask how your mum was. Give her a hug from me.' 'She will love that it has come from you.' finishing with a smile emoji, Pete replied with a laughing emoji. 'Speak next week, take care. xx' Tilly text back smile emoji and xx. 'Mum, are you ok? You look so sad, do you want to talk, or just be on your own, I can go upstairs if you need some time alone?' 'No pet, you stay there, I like having company, you know that, but it has brought up my own mortality pet, that's all, and Morag, is my oldest and dearest friend. It feels like this might be the very last time I see her. We have not really been able to see each other regularly, because we both have health problems now. Morag can't breathe properly, and I can't walk a long way, so not a good mix of being able to meet up.' 'I know mum, it's sad, I am looking forward to seeing Jack and Morag next week, well in the nicest possible way, I know this visit is tinged with sadness Mum. You don't know, until you see her, how bad she is. I can always drive you to see Morag, we can make sure you take your pain killers, plus put some extra in your bag, you should be able to do the hours drive,' 'Tilly, that would be wonderful, if you could do that for me, I would hate to think that was the last time I saw my friend, thank you pet.' Edith said 'Your welcome Mum, you have supported me so much over the years, it's my turn to support you. Just relax, drink your tea, put a good movie on, or watch one of your quizzes. I will go and start dinner.' It's ok pet, I'm fine now.' Tilly went into the kitchen and started the evening meal. Tilly decided to ring Isla, to see if she was around.

'Hello Tilly, how are you?' said Isla, 'Yes I'm fine Isla, just ringing to have a catch up, whilst I'm cooking the meal. Have you got time?' 'Yes of course.' 'Was just ringing to sort out the times for Friday and when we go away for our weekend to London.' 'I know I'm so excited,' exclaimed Isla. 'I can't wait. Tilly continued. 'I was thinking of maybe driving to you and leaving my car at yours, if that is ok and we can get a bus or a cab to the Alnmouth station, to get the train to Victoria. I was thinking of getting to you for 10ish. There is a train to London at 11.15am, said Tilly.' 'Yes that sounds good to me, and of course, you can park your car at mine.' 'Shall we meet at the cafe, for some lunch then go to the therapy centre Tilly?' "Yep, that seems like a good plan to me. Isla we do love meeting at our cafe, we always seem to be the last ones to leave when it's closing time.' laughed Tilly.

'What has been going on with you Isla, how are things with Brian?' 'Well, I did have a conversation about our marriage and lack of intimacy, Brian did not really respond, which tells me everything I suppose, all he said was that he liked the marriage as it was, separate rooms, he says he still loves me, but not in that way, I have often wondered if there is someone else he sees. Just lately, he has stayed out overnight a few times. He did say that I put our daughters and grandchildren before him, when coming back to the UK, when I knew that he did not want to come back here to live. It seems he is still sulking and punishing me for making that decision. He's not like Bob was with you, but it is a form of control, and he is actually deciding whether I can have intimacy with him or not. I did say to him that it's his family too, and his grandchildren, but he has always done what he wanted to do, he has always had his own business, and continued for a short while when we lived in Italy. I do feel sad, I know I cannot live life like his for the rest of my life,' Isla replied in a sad voice. 'Oh Isla, I am so sorry to hear that. Yes we are both in our early sixties, we have to make the best of our lives and be as happy as we can, not have control in our lives in any shape or form.' 'How about you Tilly?' What is going on with you?' 'Well, mum had some sad news today. Jack rang earlier today to say his mum was becoming more unwell, and wants to visit with his mum next week, on Tuesday, as she wants to see mum before, she becomes so unwell, that she cannot contact or see her.' 'Oh that's sad Tilly.' 'Yes it is, it's her very best friend from her school days, but it has brought up her own mortality. There are all sorts of things going on in her head. I did have a chat with her, and said I would take her to see Morag, the thing is, I think she feels it may be the last time that she sees her, it was sad seeing her like this. Guess you never really know what's round the corner in life, good or bad. Anyway Isla, I am going to have to go, I want to keep mum company so is 1pm on Friday at the cafe ok with you Isla? We can continue our conversation then.' Tilly continued. 'Yes that's perfect, I will see you then Bye Tilly, lots of love,' 'Bye Isla, lots of love.' Tilly went downstairs, to see her mum staring into space, 'you ok Mum? you don't seem to be on this planet.' ' Yes pet, just going over my hay days with Morag, when we were wee girls and the fun we had, it just seems to have gone in a flash.' 'Yes I know what you mean mum, just had a similar conversation with Isla' replied Tilly. 'How is Isla?' Yes, she is fine, just a few problems but what would life be, if we did not have a few problems come up. 'I actually think it helps you to make the right decisions in life, and realise you are stronger than you think you are. Right Mum, I'm going to have a bath and chill out for a while. I have enjoyed the last few days with Pete but after the late nights, I'm not getting any younger. Are you going to be ok on your own for a little while?' ' Yes pet, of course. I know what you mean, dancing in my bed, listening to you both singing and playing guitar, was more than enough excitement for me. I woke up an hour later than normal,' laughing as she spoke. "Enjoy," have a relaxing bubble bath.' As Tilly lay in the bath, her mind started wandering to Jack coming down next week. I wonder what he looks like now, he is a few years older than me. I remember having such a crush on him, but we were only young. I still have the letters that he sent me. I found them in the same box, as I found Pete's number. I remember him picking me up in his car, and taking me to the Ice cream parlour, I was fourteen I think at the time. Mmm yes, I remember that first kiss, only once, but it was very memorable, it felt very nice, considering it was my first kiss. We did always get on with each other, there was an attraction between us, I know that now I am older and wiser. I wonder if that's what Isla meant, when she read my cards that you will get a message from someone, that leads to a new man. Mind you, Jack is not a new man, I know him, But....... .I suppose he could be. I have not seen him for years, what about Pete, he has not changed, still the loving caring gentleman as he ever was, it's so powerful how the universe works, had not seen Pete in quite a few years, thoroughly enjoyed the time we spent together, he goes back home, and on the same day mum tells me that Jack is coming down with his mum. Tilly sank back into the bath full of relaxing bubbles, just letting her thoughts go with whatever she wanted to think about. Tilly woke up freezing. I must have fallen asleep, this water is bloody cold, my fingers have gone all wrinkled at the fingertips where they have been in the water so long. She got out and wrapped her dressing gown around her, which thank goodness, had been warming over the radiator. As she sat on the bed, brushing her wet hair, she took a moment to look in the mirror, as she spoke to herself " well I wonder which direction my life will take me, I wonder what my future holds for me."

CHAPTER 10

Tilly was walking towards the cafe to meet Isla, as she turned the corner Isla was there to greet her. 'Hi Til's, it's turned so chilly, shall we get inside where it is warm?' 'Good idea,' Tilly replied, wrapping her scarf around her head to keep the northerly biting winds from giving her a headache. 'Oh that's better,' Tilly continued, as she opened the door, and stepped inside the warm welcoming cafe. 'Look!! there is a table in the corner, let's grab that,' said Tilly. They were in luck, as the cafe was very busy, they ordered large coffee lattes, with homemade soup, and crusty bread. They started chatting. 'Sooo,' asked Isla, how was your time with Pete?' 'He is such a lovely man, so easy to get along with. I have to say Isla, it was lovely seeing him again, it felt like it was only yesterday when we last saw each other. Yes we had a lot of fun together. Pete fortunately always carries his guitar in the boot of his car, so one evening he brought it in and we sang all the old songs from when we were in the band. I asked Pete if I could play his guitar. It was such a lovely feeling having the guitar sitting on my lap with one arm wrapped around the guitar, my other hand plucking the strings, it was a very surreal moment. I really enjoyed playing and singing again. I am actually going to have some singing lessons, to get my voice back to where it was, well nearly,' Tilly smiled. 'He has definitely opened up a side to me that has laid dormant for many years. It has given me back some confidence. I was so anxious before he arrived, Isla, anxiety, panic attacks, all negative emotions, when really I should have been so excited about seeing Pete again, but it turned out ok in the end.'

'Oh that's brilliant' said Isla, 'I'm so glad you had a good time. "Wow," replied Isla, " That must have been a great moment playing the guitar, especially as it has triggered you to want to play and sing again.' Tilly continued 'Unfortunately, my mum had some bad news about her best friend Morag. Jack's mum is very unwell, but she wanted to see mum before anything happens to her, so Jack is bringing his mum down, so I will be seeing him again. I have not seen him for so many years so it will be good to see him.' 'Oh that's sad,' Isla replied. 'The universe is certainly bringing your past to the present Tilly.' continued Isla 'Til's, something has definitely shifted around you. Now your life is starting to move forward.' 'Yes I believe that too.' 'So how are you Isla?' Tilly enquired. 'Have you managed to speak to Brian again?' 'Well no, it's not good really, I think I said on the phone, I am really trying to fix this marriage, but I have to say sleeping in separate bedrooms does not help. I think I said to you when we last spoke that he seems to be happy with this arrangement, in all fairness Tilly, if you have to fix a relationship then it's too broken to fix anyway.' 'Oh Isla, I'm so sorry, so I guess you really need to look at your life, it's not fair on you, especially if you would like intimacy in your relationship. Brian has no right to make the decision of whether you have intimacy or not, it's like a form of control really.' Tilly paused not really knowing whether to ask this question to Isla, but she needed to know what she thought of Pete.

'I have to say Isla, you seemed to like Pete when we went out to lunch on Tuesday?' 'Yes, I did,' replied Isla. 'It was so refreshing to talk to a man who has the same spiritual outlook, a very creative and caring man.' 'Hey,' Isla continued. 'I just thought, do you remember when I gave you a short reading, that I said a man would come into your life through a message, I wonder if that is Jack....?' 'Oh yes, how very interesting.' exclaimed Tilly, 'mmm, I wonder, anyway I need to find myself first. I did actually feel pangs of lust for Pete myself,' replied Tilly. 'I have to be so careful Isla, when you have experienced physical and emotional abuse, it's very easy to fall prey to a man who shows you some affection and emotionally supports you, even if you are friends, it's probably worse as you know them. I just don't want that to spoil our friendship.' Tilly saw Isla's face drop with disappointment. Tilly had a feeling that maybe Isla liked Pete more than she was letting on, she could see her eyes light up when they were all having lunch together on Tuesday. 'I have to say I did have feelings of desire which if I am honest, has never happened before, being married to Bob, and Pete playing in the band, I just never saw him that way. I was shocked that I even had feelings.' 'So,' Isla piped up, 'do you think you and Pete could be an item then Tilly?' 'No not sure, to be honest Isla, Pete has always made it clear that he likes me, he has said a few things that have indicated that. I really do care about him, but as I said earlier, I have never seen him in that way before. That's why I said I have to be careful, I don't want to be hurt again, I would not ever hurt Pete either, so for me I see him as a wonderful supportive friend like he always was when we were in the band. He used to support me, when Bob was being a complete arsehole, and using his control over me.' Tilly continued

'Do you like Pete?' 'Well, if I'm honest I do,' replied Isla. 'I found him interesting, and we just seemed to click, that's why I asked him for his number. I have never done that in my life. As you well know, from when we were teenagers, he has also opened up a feeling I have never experienced.' 'Looks like Pete, has done us both the power of good. If only he knew his power,' said Tilly as they both laughed together. "We are obviously feeling very similar in our lives and not happy.' replied Isla. 'I'm not really unhappy' Tilly continued 'but I would like to meet someone and share a reasonably normal life, whatever normal is, after the marriage I had, I actually don't have a clue, but I would like to find out. And for you Isla, you are unhappy?' 'I see this beautiful soul, my best friend who's husband has totally disregarded you, as he could not have things his own way, then has decided to punish you by taking away the love, passion, friendship, the very things that you need and desire. Isla, I'm not at all surprised that you like Pete, I totally get it, but my darling friend, we both need to find ourselves as women, without a man by our side, we have to be happy in our own skin, be happy with ourselves, empowered, a man has to enhance our life, not make us feel that we are not complete unless they are by our side.' 'Tilly, you are so right, and we have our weekend coming up next week, I'm so looking forward to going away. Tilly, do you still fancy going to Cornwall to see Pete?' 'Yes of course,' replied Tilly. 'I have not been to Cornwall for years, maybe we could do a week, as it is quite a long way, maybe see it as a little holiday. We can book somewhere to stay near Pete. Yes let's get something booked up in the New Year, how does that sound?' 'Perfect,' replied Isla.

'It's so lovely, our paths have crossed again, so nice to have someone, especially my best friend from the past, to go away with, do things with, have a chat with. 'You have opened up my life Tilly.' 'Likewise Isla, you have done exactly the same for me, my moving back to be with mum is lovely, but I dont have anyone up here to do social things with. So let's just say the universe is working for us both, but in different ways and different paths.' 'Tilly, I think we need to pay for the bill, our appointment is in 10 minutes and I cannot run like I used to,' Isla said laughing. 'Me neither,' said Tilly. They both very hurriedly walked to the therapy centre, Sophie as usual, was waiting with her lovely smile to greet them. 'Hello ladies, how are we today,' Sophie enquired. 'Yes we are fine,' they both replied together. 'That's good. Take a seat Charlotte and Holly won't be long.' Within a few minutes they appeared, ready to take them to their respective therapy rooms, for their pamper time. 'See you downstairs Isla when our treatments are finished.' 'Ok.' replied Isla. Charlotte asked Tilly how she was doing, Tilly replied that she had finished her counselling sessions at the centre, and felt more in control of her life, and ready to move forward in a new direction. Charlotte was pleased to hear how far Tilly had come on in the last month. Charlotte blended the appropriate oils. Tilly was laying on the couch ready to be thoroughly pampered. 'So what wonderful oils are you using today?' Tilly asked. 'I have used rosewood, patchouli and lavender. Charlotte could see that Tilly's body was much more relaxed than the month before, so blending these oils together would help keep Tilly's body stress and tension free. Tilly was just enjoying the stresses and tension leaving her body. When the massage treatment was finished Tilly felt so good, wondering why she had not found this sooner in her life. Tilly bumped into Isla as they came out of the therapy rooms. They went downstairs, paid for their treatments, each made another appointment for their next aromatherapy massage. They both said goodbye to Sophie, and walked out into the blustery winds that were howling around the streets. 'Isla, I just love my massage every month. I feel, so relaxed, like all the stress just melts away.' 'Yes, that's how I feel too.' replied Isla I think I'm going to go home, and relax for an hour, and have a nice meditation.' 'Now that sounds like a plan, Isla. I think I may do the same, replied Tilly. 'I have had a busy weekend, late nights, and do feel rather tired. In fact I feel very sleepy.' They said their goodbyes. 'Isla I will ring you to let you know about Jack.' Tilly shouted out, as Isla was disappearing around the corner to her car. 'Ok,' Isla shouted back. 'You will be fine, you know everything happens for a reason, the Universe knows what it is doing. I do hope all goes well with your mum and Morag.' 'Thank you Isla.' Tilly put her gloves on, a hat she had in her bag, and a scarf that was wrapped up around her face to stop the bitter wind that was biting at her face as she walked home. One thing I forgot about was the cold winters up north, she thought, as she hurried through the streets, to get home.

Tuesday had arrived, Tilly was busy sorting out her clothes for the weekend in London with Isla, while waiting for Jack and Morag to arrive around lunch time, and feeling excited to be visiting some of the old haunts that she and Isla had frequented back in the late sixties, not knowing whether they were still standing or been knocked down. Who knows, she thought to herself, we are going for a girly weekend, there is plenty to see and do in London. Tillys mum was also on her mind, since her mum found out about her friend Morag, her mum had been very quiet, and a bit subdued. Tilly knew there was a lot more going on in Edith's head, that's why she wanted to be here with her mum for moral support. 'Mum, shall I start lunch and get it ready so when Morag and Jack arrive we can sit down and eat?' 'Yes, that would be a good pet.' 'I thought I would make a steak pie, with mashed potatoes and peas, something easy, as I'm not sure what Morag can eat. I am going to make apple crumble and custard for pudding.' 'Oh that sounds like good old comfort food to me Tilly.' She went out to the kitchen to make the pie, then the crumble, laying the table ready for lunch. Tilly wanted Edith and Morag to spend as much time together catching up. After she had prepared lunch, she went into the lounge to see her mum sitting and staring out of the window, deep in thought with her hankie in her hands, gently dabbing away the tears, that were flowing down her cheeks, no TV on, no 1940's musical no game shows, where Edith would have joined in she just sat in silence. Tilly went over to her mum and sat next to her gently putting her arms around her.

'Mum, I am so concerned about you, you are definitely not yourself, It's worrying me. I do understand how you feel, she is your best friend, but you are assuming that Morag is going to die next week, she could live another 2 years or more. Until you see her you don't know. You are projecting too far into the future, which is making you feel sad and depressed. We have to live for the moment mum, and take each day as it comes. I used to always be projecting, until I started seeing my counsellor.' 'Yes but,' Edith interjected, 'I lost another friend a few years ago, with a similar condition.' 'Please mum, we are all different in how our illnesses occur, and what the outcome is to be, which is why we only know our birthday and not our last day, we would have a world of people going mental with stress trying to compact everything to their lives, and not living a joyous, happy peaceful life. We know there are bumps in the road, it's called life, we deal with them as they come up. I do get you mum, you are very sensitive like me, but life is a journey, the only thing we know for certain it that we all pass away sometime, whether it young or old, we are all having a spiritual journey of the soul in a human body, the two unfortunately, don't always go hand in hand. Please mum look forward to seeing Morag, and enjoy your time together today, old memories, the good fun times, I am sure there were plenty of those to be had, this is not the last meeting at all.' Tilly said with a big smile on her face, which lifted Edith's spirits up, and a beautiful smile appeared. 'Thank you Tilly, that has helped me you are right, I have been doing exactly that, looking at my own mortality, brooding over my life. Yes, I will enjoy today spending time with my dear friend, and try to live in the moment from now on, and let the future take care of itself. I should know these things by now at my age.' As Tilly gave her mum a kiss on the forehead. Tilly heard the gate unlock, she peeped through the curtains and saw Jack holding his mum's arm and wheeling a trolley with her, with an oxygen tank and a tube attached to her nose. Tilly reeled, at what she saw, she never expected Morag to be at that level that she needed Oxygen 24/7. She was worried about her mum, after having spoken to her only a few minutes ago. 'Mum, they are here, Jack is just bringing his mum up the garden path, I am going to open the door ready for them to come in.' Tilly greeted them both, and welcomed them in, she gave Morag a hug, and helped Jack get his mum into the lounge.

'Look Mum,' said Tilly as Morag turned into the lounge, she saw her best friend Edith, looking quite frail, with a blanket over her legs to keep her warm. Edith looked at Morag, and felt frightened of seeing the trolley with this oxygen tank and tubes attached to Morag. She sat down, and the trolley was placed beside her, they wanted to hug each other, but the best they could do was to hold hands, both feeling very teary, wiping away their tears, they looked at each other for a few seconds, which seemed like minutes, trying to find each others connection from the last time they saw each other which was about eight years ago. Both could get along walking, back then, but this time neither were really able to walk long distances, and both needed some assistance, especially Morag. 'Hello Morag, how lovely to see you, it's been a long time. I'm sorry to hear of your health problems.' 'It's ok Edith, it is what it is, but it's just lovely to see you.' 'Shall I make us some tea? Asked Tilly. 'I can get lunch sorted as well. 'Jack, would you like a cup of tea?' It was the first time since Jack had stepped through the door with Morag that they got to speak to each other, as Tilly spoke, their eyes just naturally met, just like they used to. 'Oh a cup of tea, would be good.' replied Jack. He followed Tilly into the kitchen, Tilly felt a little awkward as to how she should have greeted Jack, Jack seemed to feel equally awkward as well, so they just stood together as Tilly was putting the pie in the oven and sorting out the vegetables, and making the tea.

'It hasn't changed a lot around here has it?' 'Actually, Jack continued, 'I did not know you were here, your mum never said, are you just visiting?' asked Jack. 'No, I am living with my mum, at the moment. I got divorced last year, and had to sell the matrimonial home. I felt I needed some peace, so asked mum, if

I could come back here, until I sort my life out, luckily for me, she jumped at the chance of having some company.' 'Sorry to hear that Tilly,' Jack replied, stirring his cup of tea. 'Lucky for me, you are here today, smiling at Tilly.' I totally understand. My marriage broke down a few years ago, I have been divorced for about 5 years now, then I was in another relationship, and that ended about eight months ago.' 'Oh really!!!' Tilly was quite taken aback that Jack was divorced as well. Well I'm sorry to hear that Jack, it's not good getting divorced, especially when there are children involved, at any age.' Tilly was chatting as she was taking the tea into the lounge, Morag looked up at Tilly. 'Goodness, Tilly, you have not changed much at all, you look very well my dear.' 'Thank you Morag, it must be the genetics' looking at her mum smiling. 'Morag, I am cooking lunch, are you hungry?' ' Yes I am feeling quite peckish. That would be lovely Tilly, thank you, us Scottish lassies, like our food, it keeps the cold out,' she said with a broad smile. Tilly piped up 'just like mum then,' looking at Edith. They all looked at each other and laughed. 'Morag, would you like just a small portion on your plate, or a good plateful?' Tilly said laughing. 'No, just a small portion, I cannot eat like I used to unfortunately.' Morag replied.

'It won't be long, just a few minutes for the pie to cook.' Tilly returned to the kitchen, to get the lunch dished up ready to serve. Jack was still in the kitchen standing at the back door, looking onto the garden watching the last of leaves falling off the trees. 'You ok Jack?' Asked Tilly, 'you look like you're miles away.' Jack turned round surprised, as his head was back in an era that was long ago, but the memories still fresh in his mind. 'Yes, I'm fine, I was remembering all the fun we used to have in the garden, you, your brother and sister, and Janette and me, playing ball, hide and seek, us older ones cheating then the younger ones going and telling on us, those were the days, no responsibilities, carefree, just looking forward to a life that you think you have planned in your head, but then you look back it does not resemble any of the plans that were there in the beginning, maybe just a little but not a lot.' 'Yes they were the good old days Jack. Yes, I have many a time, looking back to when I was in my late teens, the plans I had made, just thinking it just unfolds, and you have your dream life, but my life is nowhere where I thought it would be. But I am learning about myself now, and understanding a lot more of what life is really about.' Tilly was thinking in her head, oh yes Jeanette, I have been trying to remember her name for a few days now, good job Jack has said her name, I don't have to feel embarrassed in trying to guess. 'I have to say Tilly, you look really well, considering you have just come out of your marriage.' 'Thank you Jack, I have been doing a lot of work on myself, inner work, which has helped me tremendously.' 'So what have you been up to?' 'The last time we spoke, you had a job driving a truck.' 'Blimey Tilly, you have a good memory, that was back in the middle sixties, you have a good memory.' 'Yes, I remember when you learnt to drive, you brought a car when you started your truck driving job, you used to come down, pick me up, and drove us to the ice cream parlour, we listened to the music on the jukebox, whilst eating those delicious ice cream sundaes.' ' Yes Tilly, I remember, every time I came down we would go out for a drive somewhere but remember that was the place we seemed to head to.' Every so often their eyes would connect and they held a gaze between them and a few seconds of silence, it's like they were scanning each other's body language. 'Tilly, do you have children?' 'Yes I have a son and a daughter, Stanley and Sarah, and I have five grandchildren who are my world. Moving up here has meant that I don't get to see them as regularly as I would like, but I am driving down to spend some time with Sarah and the girls next Wednesday.' How about you Jack?' 'Do you have any children?' 'Yes, I have four children, three sons and one daughter. My daughter is married and has two children. She lives in Ireland, and my eldest son is married with no children. They both decided to work hard, and have the life they wanted. They are avid travellers, and seem very happy. My youngest son lives in Australia and in the media arena, let's just say he has a varied life with regards to women,' Jack said smiling. 'My other son lives in Shropshire, he is married and has one daughter, he owns a farm, it is so beautiful down that way, when I need to get some peace in my head, I will go and stay with him, he has plenty of room on the farm, so I go and help him with his chores it's so therapeutic.' 'Wow, Jack, four kids, all living very different lives. I have to say my brother lives in Australia, and is in the media as well.'

'So where are you living now?' Tilly continued, 'I have moved around a bit, I can get quite restless sometimes, always seem to have been searching for something new, guess I chase the stars, and see what comes up. I am more settled now than I have been for a few years. I run my own haulage company, and also have a photography business, and living in Scotland, in Edinburgh have been there now for about ten years.' 'You have had a varied life, my life seems very boring to yours, I lived in Sevenoaks Kent for over 35 years, well since I got married.' Tilly was chatting as she was getting the dinner dished up, 'Jack. I don't want to put too much food on your mum's plate, could you tell me how much to put on?' 'Yes, of course.' 'Jack, would you like to get your mum settled at the table, and I can get mum there too.' When they walked into the room, Edith and Morag were still holding hands and merrily chatting away, about the old times, just like Tilly and Jack were doing. They were all seated having their lunch together, when Tilly noticed again, that Jack kept looking at her, but everytime their eyes met, Tilly could feel a glow in her body, just like she used to when they were younger, it was not an uncomfortable feeling at all, but a deep knowing of someone from her past, a strong connection coming back into her life. Tilly cleared the table, Jack helped her to wash up and put the dishes away. 'Hey Tilly, do you fancy going for a quick drink, and leave our mums to have some time on their own?' 'Yes that is a good idea, let's just check with them to make sure they are ok being on their own.' Mum' 'Yes pet.' ' Will you both be ok, if Jack and I go to the pub for a quick drink.' "Of course,' replied Edith, 'go and have a nice time with Jack.' ' Thanks Mum, we will only be there an hour or so.' 'No problem, pet, me and Morag are just fine sitting here.' 'Ok, see you both later,' both Tilly and Jack said at the same time.

'Shall we walk or drive Tilly?,' asked Jack. 'Oh, let's walk, it's not far, get some fresh air in our lungs.' 'We certainly will.' replied Jack laughing, as he pulled the collar of the coat up over his ears. They got to the castle hotel, which had a lounge bar, they found a table by the open fire, the logs were crackling in between the flames, occasionally burning embers would spit out on the rug. Tilly just sat staring into the fire, she was mesmerised by the flickering flames that seemed to be jumping about. She was thinking to herself that she had been with Pete only a few days ago, now Jack. 'Here you go Tilly, one gin and tonic, ice and a slice,' as Jack placed the drinks on the beer mats on the table. 'Well this is nice Tilly, being beside the fire this very cosy. I never thought you would be living at your mums, and then out having a cheeky drink. So where were we, before lunch took place' Jack enquired. 'Well, I think we were giving each other our life stories, 'Tilly smiled. 'Oh yes, we got to the part of you living in Sevenoaks, since you were married, by the way, where is Sevenoaks?' 'Oh it's in Kent. Bob, my ex husband, lived in Greenhithe, Kent, but he wanted to live further out, so that's where we went.' 'How did you start your life up here in Bamburgh and end up down in Kent' 'Well, when I went to London with Isla. We were there for about six months. Isla and I had found a pub which had live music, and there was a band we used to go and watch. Bob was the lead singer, and he started coming over to Isla and I in between the sets, and we got talking and I told him that I played the guitar, piano and sang. He invited me up on the stage to sing with them occasionally when we went to the pub. Bob and I seemed to get on really well, we fell in love the rest is history. What about you Jack?' 'Well, certainly not as glamorous as you, I had a few girlfriends, some long term, but I struggled to commit properly, always looking for the next one, then June came along, she seemed different to the other woman I had dated, I was in my thirties when we got married, which was old back then, but I followed my career and loved photography, I then became a fashion photographer, taking pictures of models, portrait, and weddings came later. I asked June to marry me, she said yes, so we tied the knot, she moved into my house, then four kids later, we seem to drift apart really. But you know Tilly, I have never forgotten you. I guess somewhere deep inside, I have been trying to find another Tilly, but she never appeared. I can't stop looking at you.'

'Mmm, yes, I did notice that at the dinner table earlier' Tilly smiled but blushing at the same time. 'I have to admit, I had a massive crush on you. You were my first sort of boyfriend, the first boy I kissed. I know I was not the first girl you kissed, but somehow you always seem to remember the first boy that kissed you. I remember feeling so grown up, when I was out with you. I have often wondered about you, and where you were.' replied Tilly. 'Yes I have to admit' said Jack 'that I have often wondered the same thing, isn't it strange how things happen that are totally unexpected. 'Hey Tilly, how about we meet up again? Would you like to? I'm staying with mum at the moment, as she is poorly. I still work, well, I'm semi-retired now. My haulage company is still going, but I have stepped back a bit. I have a good manager who oversees it for me, and I just go in a couple times a week, it does not take me long to get here.' 'Yes Jack, I would love to meet up, actually,' Tilly continued. 'I promised mum I would take her to see Morag. She has been sad about her best friend. Yes, that would be lovely.' 'Great' said Jack, 'let's exchange numbers so we can keep in contact. Maybe we could arrange something next week if you are free?' 'Oh I cannot do it next week, I am away in London for the weekend with Isla, not sure if you would remember her? Friday to Monday, and then I'm driving down to my daughters to see my granddaughters on Wednesday until Sunday, so the following week would be good.' 'Oh yes, you said earlier that you were seeing your granddaughters, and off to London, what is sending you off down that neck of the woods?' "We are going to revisit our old haunts, the pubs and venues we frequented, a bit of retail therapy, maybe a show, but not sure if the pub is still standing that we used to go to regularly, or a block of flats. We both just fancied a weekend away, have some fun.' 'Now that sounds like a good weekend away. 'Once we get to know each other better Tilly, maybe we could have a weekend away.' Tilly really did not know what to say, she felt flattered that he offered this, and started thinking in her head, this must be the universe's way of putting us together. Isla was right, a new man in my life through a message, bloody hell, my dreams are coming true. 'Yes that would be nice, but we would have to get to know each other a lot more," said Tilly. 'Of course, I would not expect you to go next week, but maybe the following week.' Tillys jaw just dropped in shock of what Jack just said. 'Tilly don't look so shocked, I would never expect that, only teasing.' Tillys face went instantly into a relaxed mode again.

'Jack I think we ought to get back to our mums to make sure they are ok, they have probably worn each other out, and are snoring, ' said Tilly laughing.' 'Yes I think you are right Tilly.' They walked back, Jack got hold of Tilly's hand and they held hands as they walked back with the icy gusts of wind blowing directly in their faces, and Tilly cowering into Jack's shoulder to protect herself from the cold. They reached Tilly's home. She put the key in the door, and they heard a gentle snoring coming from the lounge. They both walked into the lounge to see that they were both asleep. Tilly went over to her mum and gently shook her mum's shoulder. Edith jumped out of her skin, clutching her chest with fright. Morag started to come round from her slumbers. 'You ok Mum?' Jack asked. 'Think it's time to get you home, have you enjoyed your visit today?' 'Yes, I have enjoyed seeing Edith, it's just what the doctor ordered, we are going to try to meet up again, if you and Tilly could help?' 'Yes Mum, Tilly and I have already said we will make sure you see more of each other.' 'Thank you son, I really appreciate you driving me to see my friend.' 'Mum, it's no problem, you are my mum, I love you, you have supported me so much over the years.' 'Tilly was standing at the side, listening to Jack, and thinking what a caring lovely man he is, very similar to Pete, they both loved their mums, except that Pete had lost his mum a few years ago. Jack got his mum up, and got her coat on, and sorted out the trolley, and gave her some medication. Morag and Edith blew each other a kiss, they were already looking forward to meeting up again. Tilly helped Jack to the front gate. watching Jack help his mum back in the car, he then came back to the gate and put his hands on Tillys shoulders and gave her a peck on the cheek. 'we will speak soon, how nice it was to meet up.' They looked into each other's eyes, 'Yes, it was Jack.' Tilly had her arms folded to keep warm on her way back indoors, she wondered what could come of this meeting, it's still there, that feeling of attraction and chemistry, oh it's so exciting Tilly thought, new chapters in my life everywhere I turn. Tilly felt the warmth of the house, as she walked through into the lounge, stepping inside from the freezing weather.

'Mum, how are you feeling now you have seen Morag?' 'Oh Pet, it was so lovely to see her, I have to say when I saw the oxygen on the trolley, it did scare me a bit but we took it gently, talking about life, and when we were wee girls, we managed a few laughs, but unfortunately Morag, cold not manage laughing for too long, bless her, I hated seeing her like that, but is was wonderful, and so pleased that was not our last time of seeing each other.' 'Well, first of all I'm so pleased that you and Morag had an enjoyable afternoon, you look quite perky Mum,' looking at her mum with a broad smile, seeing her mum smiling back was a good sign. 'What was it like seeing Jack?' Edith enquired. 'Yes I have to say it was good to see him, I used to have a crush on him when we were young, he is going to come down in a few weeks' time.' 'Hey pet, I thought you liked Jack, you were like his shadow, wherever he was you were sure to follow.' She said laughing, 'Well just take things slow pet, you are just finding yourself.' 'I will mum, don't worry, I have got things I want to see and do, do you fancy anything to eat mum?' 'No, not really, that meal at lunch time filled me up, if I want something later I will make a sandwich.' Tilly settled down on the sofa, and watched another Midsomer Murder, she loved doing a bit of detective work, Edith also enjoyed being a sleuth as well. 'Mum, I'm going to have a bath and get an early night, I feel really tired now.' 'Yes, I'm tired too, and have not slept much worrying about Morag.'

It was 11.30am and there was a knock at the door.

CHAPTER 11

'Hello, These are for Tilly Fellowes,' said the lady holding a bouquet of beautiful flowers. 'Oh, that's me,' exclaimed Tilly. 'They are gorgeous and smell divine thank you.' Tilly took the flowers from the lady, walked into the lounge and placed them on the dining room table, looking for the little card that normally accompanies flowers that have been delivered. Tilly found it, amongst the Lilies and Eucalyptus foliage, she opened it up it said,

"So lovely to see you yesterday, looking forward to meeting up with you soon, have a great weekend, "by the way I still have all the letters that you wrote to me.' 'Love Jack xxx"

Tilly just stood looking at the flowers, amongst the lilies, were red roses, lisianthus and gerberas, tied up with pink ribbon. She placed them on the table, but took the card upstairs, Edith walked in, wondering where the beautiful smell of flowers was coming from. Tilly came back into the room, 'Oh pet, those flowers are beautiful, who sent you those?' "Oh they are from Jack, he said it was lovely to see us both, and to thank us for lunch," she said, being slightly economical with the truth, as the card said more in a cheeky way! 'That's nice of Jack to send them,' 'Yes it was mum.' Tilly went back upstairs to find her small case so she could start packing for her weekend away. She wanted to send Jack a text to thank him for the flowers. She sat on her bed, looking at the clothes she had got out, and realised that she had too many, so she got her phone and texted Jack instead, within minutes she had a reply, he wanted to let her know, what a surprise it was to find her living at her mums house. Tilly replied back, saying that she also had kept all the letters that he had sent her too. He replied with an emoji smile, saying he would ring her next week. Tilly then set about sorting out the clothes for the weekend, every so often a feeling of being unsettled kept coming and going, in her tummy, but she pushed it to the back of her mind, and continued to sort out packing. She decided on what she wanted to take with her, and got it all packed, and put the suitcase beside her wardrobe. All that was needed was the last minute bits and bobs, and her rescue remedy.

Tilly felt the need for some space, she laid on her bed, holding the crystals that she felt drawn to, listening to a meditation, which helped her greatly. Although the last few weeks were fun, it has been a bit of a whirlwind, and she needed to bring the energies back into her body, soothing her emotions, spirit and soul. She could feel herself relaxing, and the anxiety she was feeling was slowly dissipating, not really understanding why she was feeling like this. The meditation was about releasing stress and anxiety, by learning to breathe more slowly, feeling safe and secure enough to know that she would be ok. After the meditation, Tilly sent a text to Isla, to make sure everything was still ok for Friday, and how she was feeling excited, Isla swiftly replied that she was also feeling excited too, and would see Tilly around 10am on Friday.

The day arrived Tilly was up early, getting her luggage ready to take away with her. Edith was already downstairs having her breakfast, as she heard the suitcase bumping down the stairs, Tilly then put her luggage by the door and went to have breakfast with her mum. 'You ok Tilly?' 'Yes mum, I just feel a bit anxious again, a bit like I felt before Pete arrived. I hope I'm not going to have these feelings every time I do something out of my comfort zone, I never used to be like this.' replied Tilly. 'You've lost your confidence Tilly, that's all. It takes time to heal Tilly, you've only been divorced a year. You had more years being controlled, then making your own decisions, you became codependent on Bob, not because you are a weak woman, but manipulation, and gaslighting are very insidious, they mess with your reality, you begin to doubt yourself, who you are as a person, that man destroyed you, on all levels. Darling Tilly, please don't punish yourself, or get angry with how your body is responding to these new adventures, the abuse alters your mindset, it's like having to learn everything over again but this time you will be more stronger then ever, also Tilly, I have to add that when you get older, it can be harder to come out of your comfort zone, but that does not mean that your life is over. And you are doomed to staying like this forever, just be gentle with yourself, understand the journey you have just come through, remember your counsellor said anxiety is when you are holding it all together, you are seeing it as failure, it's far from that pet, and getting angry with yourself is not the answer. You are trying new things. It takes a lot of courage to move forward on your own, you were with Bob for many years, you managed when Pete came up, and you thoroughly enjoyed yourself, so do exactly the same, and tell Isla how you feel, she will understand. Tilly you would be surprised how many people suffer with anxiety, it's more common than you think, most people have this facade that they keep up of being confident and fearless, but they have learnt to deal with and handle their anxiety. I had it many years ago now, when your pa was alive, I sometimes struggled to go out socially with him, and stayed in a lot. I lost my confidence, but just do it gradually, you wait and see, you will come back from this period of your life. You will come back from London full of stories and tales to tell, what you and Isla have done, come here pet, let's have a cuddle.' 'Thanks mum,' Tilly replied 'whatever would I do without your wisdom? but I am worried about leaving you too.' 'Tilly, I have managed all these years, I have gotten by, you have brought me a mobile now, so if I am in trouble I can ring you, I've got Maureen next door, and Dot who lives a few doors down, just go and enjoy yourself.' 'Ok mum, I'm off now, I have got everything and taken my rescue remedy, and put my crystals in my bra, Tilly replied laughing. Well whatever floats your boat pet, who am I to intervene with how you use your crystals?' They were both laughing, which was a good therapy for Tilly, if you're laughing you're not anxious. Tilly went over to give her mum another cuddle and a kiss! 'See you around 4ish on Monday. I will text you and ring you to make sure you are ok.' 'Pet, I will be fine, dont worry about me.'

Tilly got her case and bag, and went to her car, she got in the driver's seat feeling a bit shaky, as she was putting her seat belt on, and gave herself a talking to, thinking about the conversation that she had just had with her mum, she did some deep breaths, a little voice inside was saying relax, breath, you are fine, This is a new adventure, see hope and happiness not doom and gloom, you will be fine. She put her hand on her tummy, the solar plexus, and started gently rubbing it gently in a clockwise motion, letting go of the anxiety. The journey was good, not much traffic, she finally got to Isla's, pulled up outside, parked her car, got her case and bag and headed up to Isla's house, before she could knock on the door, the door opened and there was Isla. 'You must be psychic Isla,' Tilly said smiling, you seem to know when I've arrived.' 'I must be,' Isla smiled back, as she made her way back to the kitchen, Tilly walked through the door, put her case down and followed Isla into the Kitchen. She sat down at the table feeling that dreaded feeling again. "Bloody hell" Tilly thought in her head, I don't need to keep feeling this bloody shitty. Isla turned round, looking at Tilly, 'are you ok Til's?' Isla asked, 'you look a bit pale.' 'Yes I'm ok Isla' 'Tilly come on, tell me what's wrong, I can see it on your face, you look worried.' Tilly started getting a bit tearful, Isla went over and put her arms around her. 'Bloody hell Tilly, what's wrong, what's happened?' 'It's just me, nothing is wrong, or anyone else, just me and my silly thoughts that's all.' 'Hey, come on,' Isla said, 'spill the beans.' I just feel so stupid Isla.' I'm sixty one, and getting bloody anxious every time I go out of my comfort zone, even when Pete came up, I was a nervous wreck, so anxious I even had a panic attack. I don't want to live like this. I've had counselling and everything. I spoke to my mum before I came here, as she could tell that there was something not right with me, she sat and explained the reasons why, its to do with my past, not to punish myself, it's the abuse, manipulation and gaslighting that has messed with my mental state, loss of confidence, codependency, everything she said made sense, but here I am still feeling like crap.'

'I have to be honest Tilly, your mum is spot on, what she has said is exactly what I would have said to you. You cannot expect to be in a thirty five year marriage with a narcissist, and think within a year, you would be going on a round the world trip, you are healing, sometimes it can take years to recover and heal, it's a gradual process. Your mum is right, stop putting pressure on yourself, to be this perfect woman. Tilly no human is perfect, no marriage or relationship is perfect, so why are you striving to meet this perfection. So start loving yourself for who you are. Allow these feeling to come to the surface, look at them instead of pushing them back down, this is all part of the healing process, you were always a confident little girl, and teenager, find that part of you, access it gradually, until you can feel yourself becoming you again, and not what Bob turned you into you, believing you were not a good person, and putting his perceptions of you onto you, so that now you firmly believe that his perceptions are true, they are not, never have been. The more you try different things, the more your confidence will come back. People don't realise that after any close contact with a narcissist, whether in a relationship, work, family or friend, it is very debilitating .This is about finding you my darling friend. I will help you and support you like your mum. I do understand Tilly, when Brian and I came back to England, everything had changed so much over the last fifteen years, and I have suffered anxiety on and off for most of my life. Knowing Brian did not want to come back did not make it easy either. I had no friends, did not go out, but Brian found all these clubs, and just left me. I have never been abused, by Brian, or lived anything like you have, but I still suffer from anxiety. I just have a better control of my anxiety knowing and having a better understanding helps, anxiety is about protection of you, you have been living on the flight or fight syndrome for years now, that's the message your body is going to give to your brain, that you are in danger or fear is lurking around the corner, the brain does not know why, it's just learnt to react when the adrenaline rushes in, so it's about retraining the brain to change the neuro pathways to accept a new connection of feeling safe and not in danger. In future, don't tell it off when you get anxious, start putting in a new way of connecting with your thought patterns.' 'Isla, thank you, between you and my mum, you both have helped me greatly.' 'Remember' said Isla, 'when we are away anytime you feel uneasy just grab my arm, or let me know, Its ok Tilly, to feel like this, if we did not feel anything, we would not be living.' 'Now what do you want to do, bus or I can drive and leave my car at the station? I don't mind, I have left my car at the station before.' 'Can we drive, then I can calm myself down a bit.' 'Yes sure, ok lets go, otherwise we will miss the train.' As they drove to the station, Tilly was feeling a lot lighter. Isla looked at Tilly and saw she had some colour in her face. I don't want you to feel under pressure if at any time you want to come back home, it's fine, I want you to have a happy life, not one that's full of anxiety.' 'Yes I am feeling a lot better now, I think sometimes it's apprehension, when Pete came up, as soon as I opened the door it disappeared.' replied Tilly. 'Yes it may well be apprehension, you were living on a knife edge not knowing what frame of mind Bob was going to be in when he came through the door, so you were always apprehensive, then once he came through the door, you knew whether he had a bad day and was going to be abusive to you and throw his weight around. Now look at him coming home, when he was in a happy mood, he had a good day and was civil to you, again the apprehension would go, so your apprehension had nothing to do about whether you were in a restaurant being happy, or Bob coming in a bad mood, it was your brain receiving messages of high alert, whatever the scenario, as I said earlier the brain cannot differentiate as to the cause of the adrenaline being pumped around the body, but your body got into that mode whatever the situation. Yes you're right, you should not have to feel these feelings today, you are going away for the weekend to have a good time and enjoy, I'm your friend you can trust me, you know I'm not going to abuse you, but your brain has its own filter. It's not your fault or your brain's fault, it's now about getting in touch with your body as well as your mind. The two work together, not against each other.'

'I am so sorry Isla, I did not want to start our weekend away like this, I do feel very inadequate sometimes.' 'Er,Tilly, now no more of being sorry, I understand, so from now on the rest of the train journey, lets enjoy the scenery, let's do normal chit chat, going down memory lane, cause that's what this weekend is all about.' 'Absolutely Isla.' Tilly turned to look out of the window, knowing and understanding a bit more why she felt like she did sometimes. To heal from narcissistic abuse takes time to heal. So it was time to work on herself to rid herself of the damage that Bob put on her, making her feel she was not worth anything. They arrived at Victoria Station, to the hustle and bustle of

London, people darting everywhere. 'Tilly it's fortunate, we are not that far away from the hotel.' 'Look Tilly, there's a cab. Shall we grab it?' 'Yes lets,' replied Tilly. 'I think we both need a cuppa or something stronger, when we get to the hotel.' 'Yes, a drink is definitely a must.' replied Isla. They put the key in the door of their hotel room and had the most wonderful view of Hyde park, they were central to everything they needed to visit. The black cabs, weaving in and out of the traffic, the red buses, the array of top class hotels, scattered around the vista. They took a bottle of wine from the refrigerated drinks cabinet, and sat by the big window overlooking the park. They were on the 4th floor, so they could see quite a lot. Cheers, they both "ching" "chinged" with their glasses, here's to a wonderful weekend. Tilly heard her phone ring, she grabbed her bag, and looked at the number on the phone. 'Hello Pete, nice to hear from you, said Tilly.' 'I just wanted to ring to make sure you and Isla had arrived safely and to have a wicked time revisiting the old haunts of the band days.' 'We sure will. Are you ok?' enquired Tilly. 'Yes, good thanks, I played with the band last Friday evening. I was thinking of you, when I was playing my guitar.' Oh that's lovely Pete.' 'Hi Pete,' Isla called out 'Hi Isla, you ok?' 'Yes I am fine thank you.' 'Ok Tilly, it was only a quick call, I will let you get on with your weekend, have a good time, I will catch up next week, and say goodbye to Isla for me.' 'Yes ok Pete, have a good weekend whatever you have planned, bye Pete,' 'bye Tilly.' 'Aww that's nice of Pete to call, said Isla, he is such a lovely man, one of the best men I have met in a long time. 'Yes he is. 'But guess who I saw this week, Isla? Jack came down with his mum.' Isla gasped, putting her hand over her mouth. "Well," Isla probed, how did you get on?' 'Well he came down so our mums could meet up, but we left for an hour, so they could be together without us around and we went to the pub and had a drink. Yes it was nice to see him, and for my mum to see Morag, there was definitely a lot of eye contact. The chemistry and attraction was still there from all those years ago, and yesterday I got a beautiful bouquet of flowers delivered from him. It was a lovely surprise.' 'So where's he at, after all these years?' asked Isla. 'Well, he is divorced, has been divorced a few years now by all counts, he has four children.' "four!!!" exclaimed Isla. Yes three sons and a daughter, two of his sons seem quite settled, but one of the sons seems to be a bit of a loose cannon, I think he said he had a couple of grandchildren, but seems he has led the life he wants to, don't really know to much more, as we were only there for an hour, but we are each taking in turns driving our mums to see other every couple of weeks. He is coming down the week after next to take me out for lunch.' 'Oh this is exciting,' said Isla. 'See those cards, I said there would be a new man. Well technically he is not a new man, but bloody hell, it might as well be, you have not seen him for years. Well watch this space. First no men on the horizon then two within two weeks.' 'I know Isla, been trying to work out how the universe manoeuvres all this around.' 'It's called synchronicity,' replied Isla.

'When we are needing to work through issues or it's time for something positive to happen on any level in life, the universe sets the scene. Tilly, are you going to start overthinking in your Scorpio way? I believe everything happens for a reason, maybe there are lessons to be learnt for you, or they are testing you out somehow, clearly about relationships, so just go with it.' as Tilly sat sipping her wine, feeling calm and peaceful. She looked up at Isla. 'Would you like to have Pete as your friend?' 'Well yes, I would, we have a lot in common, just nice to have a friend if nothing else, to be honest Til's I am married, I am nowhere near finding a resolution to ending my marriage, I guess deep down I still love Brian, but I need to work through those emotions because, he does not love or need me anymore does he? or he would try to resolve the intimacy side of the relationship. Anyway Pete does not strike me as someone who would get involved with someone who was still married, it would not sit with him at all. I am looking forward to seeing him when we go to Cornwall,' 'Well I was thinking of inviting him up for the New Year,' replied Tilly. 'That would be nice to have a New Year celebration.' 'Tilly, what's on the agenda for the weekend, do you fancy seeing a show?' 'Oh yes, that sounds good, 'Tilly replied, 'let's have a look to see if we can book something for tomorrow evening. 'Shall we eat in the restaurant tonight and just chill out, what do you fancy doing Isla?' 'Yes that's perfect Tilly, let's do that, how are you feeling now?' 'Yes I'm feeling ok now.'replied

Tilly. Isla continued, 'maybe we can go shopping tomorrow, go to carnaby street, and just have a wander around, then on Sunday, we can go to the pub, where we used to go and old haunts in North London. I have just found a show at the Garrick Theatre called Bad Girls. It's a musical. How does that sound to you Tilly?' Do you fancy going to see that show, maybe we can get the tickets when we get there.' 'Yes, I have heard good reviews about that musical. We can get dressed up, which is nice,' replied Tilly. They enjoyed a lovely meal, in the restaurant, and decided to have an early night, so they would be refreshed for the hectic day ahead.

    They awoke to beautiful shards of light, streaming through the large windows, where the curtains had not been drawn properly. They ordered a full English breakfast in their room, with coffee, chatting as they enjoyed spending time with each other. 'Well, I Suppose we had better get ready for the day ahead Isla' 'Yes, you're right,' replied Isla, 'so let's get ready and see what the day brings,' as Tilly stood up and did a big stretch waving her arms around, while Isla was looking on. 'So! Carnaby street, here we come.' 'I can't wait to go there, that was really one of our favourite shopping haunts, I wonder if Biba and Mary Quant are still there,' Isla said quizzingly. 'Well I hope so,' said Tilly. They were both ready, and left to go to the tube station, they did not have to wait long before a tube came along to take them to their destination. They started walking along Carnaby street, when Tilly spotted the shop Biba. 'Look Isla, there's a Biba shop over there,' they both rushed to the shop, and went inside, funnily enough it still had the aroma of Opium back in the sixties. They looked around, there was some lovely clothes, but they were mostly up to date modern clothes, not really the sort of the clothes that Tilly or Isla would wear now, however, it did bring back old memories and the days of walking out of that shop loaded with bags of their happy retail therapy days.They carried walking along and Tilly caught sight of a shop which actually had lots of vintage clothes and jewellery, even a few bits of furniture, lamps rugs etc. They were both looking through the window, and something caught Tillys eye immediately, it was a cream Afghan coat, which was on trend back in the sixties and early seventies.

'Oh Isla, I have just seen something I always wanted when I was younger but never had the money to buy one.' 'Oh what have you seen Tilly?' 'Well' continued Tilly, 'do you see that Afghan coat on that mannequin?' Yes, Isla replied. 'Well I am going to go and try it on.' Isla followed Tilly into the shop, and Tilly made a beeline for the coat, it was like an aladdin's cave, full of memorabilia, they were both in their element. She asked the sales assistant if she could try it on, to which the sales assistant came and got the coat for Tilly to try on. She tried on the coat, it fitted perfectly, she was twirling around looking at every angle of herself in the coat. She loved it, and was definitely going to purchase that. 'Well' said Tilly I am going to have that coat, what do you think Isla?' 'Yes it looks good on you Tilly, you are quite tall, and the coat is lovely, long, and in really good condition. Are you sure you are going to wear it?' 'Oh yes I sure will, but minus the platform knee high boots. Maybe we can start a new trend back home with the Boho look.' 'Well then treat yourself.' As Tilly was wandering around, Isla was elsewhere in the shop, when a lovely flouncy maxi dress caught her eye in a lovely Purple colour with frills with a daisy trim around the sleeves and the collar, it had buttons down the front. 'Oh Isla, what a pretty dress.' 'Yes I am just going to try it on.' Isla came out of the dressing room, 'that looks so pretty on you,' said Tilly, 'you only need your platform boots, dangly necklace, earrings then the outfit is complete.' 'I don't think I could balance on platform boots anymore' as Isla started walking up and down pretending she had platform boots on, falling all over the place, they were both in stitches laughing."Mmmm" yes you could be right Isla, best not add platform boots to the outfit.' Isla came out with the dress over her arm, Tilly had the coat in her arms, as they continued looking around the shop finding so many gems and memories from when they were in London in the late sixties. 'Think we have to be careful Tilly, we have no car until we get to the other end and we have to carry what we have.' 'Good thinking Isla, I think I've spent £250 so far, and that's not including the coat,' both laughing as they both loved to spend. They finally got to the till, where the friendly assistant was smiling, I have to say said the assistant smiling, 'I saw you trying to make out you were walking in platform boots, I could not stop laughing, I could not walk properly in platform boots, back in the day, so I would definitely end up in a&e if I ever tried a pair on now.' All three of them were standing by the till laughing, reminiscing about the good old days. 'Wow, this shop is amazing. We are limited to what we can buy as we are travelling light, as we are away for the weekend. Tilly said.

'Yes, it has proved to be very popular,' said the assistant. 'I was not sure when I took this shop on, let alone selling vintage fashion and accessories, with a few bits of furniture and home decor. But the recycling of vintage clothes and how many people love that era, and dress in that era in their everyday lives, furnishing their homes with vintage furniture and decor is astounding. We are online as well. I just started a website a few months ago, you can buy through that media, and I will post it to you. 'Oh that sounds good, please could we have the details' enquired Tilly. 'Yes of course, let me pack up your clothes and bits then I can give you a card. Nice to meet you both.' 'Yes you too, we will definitely be buying on the internet. Bye' they both said together.

They left the shop like the two teenage girls that they once were, pleased with their new purchased items. 'Tilly guess what the time is?' Isla said, 'I would say about 2pm' replied Tilly.' 'No it's 3pm.' replied Isla. 'Oh my, how long have we been in that shop? ' said Tilly. ' Quite a few hours,' added Isla. 'Shall we grab something to eat Tilly? I feel a bit peckish' said Isla, 'Yes me too. Then I suppose we need to get back to the hotel. I think I need a nap before we go out tonight.' 'Yes I can feel one of those coming on too,' replied Isla. They arrived back at the hotel, managed to grab a nap, order a room service meal, and got themselves out by 7.30pm, 'How did we manage that Isla?' I'm not used to rushing like that anymore.' Tilly added. 'Don't know, Tilly, it reminded me of the old days, when we were a bit more sprightly. We were used to rushing around getting ready to go out,' Isla said with a big grin on her face. 'Oh this has just been a brilliant day, Isla, I have not been to see a show in London for years, so I'm looking forward to watching a good musical.' 'Yes it has,' replied Isla, 'let's make sure that we book regular weekends away, so we have something to look forward to.' They got their coats and bags, rushed through the hotel to the taxi waiting for them. They arrived at the theatre, having enough time to have a drink before taking to their seats. Oh it is a nice theatre,' Tilly said, 'I don't think I have ever been to the Garrick before, have you Isla?' 'No I can't recall ever being here, but I do remember some of the streets that the taxi went down. If my memory serves me right Tilly, I think the Marquee club is not far from here, I would love to see what it is there now.' Isla replied. 'Yes, you're right Isla, how about we ask the taxi driver if he would just drive by the marquee club, on the way back to the hotel, at least we get to see where we spent most of our evenings.' 'Yes, let's ask Tilly if we dont ask we won't get.' They were excitedly waiting for the curtain to draw back to see the cast of Bad Girls, then a voice came from out of nowhere. They saw a girl, coming through the stage scenery of prisons, singing I should not be here. Tilly was sitting in the seat wishing she had been able to be in a musical, but her fate never took her down that road. Everybody in the audience was enjoying this musical, the time went very quick and before they knew it, the curtains had drawn, and everyone was heading out to the foyer to go home. As Tilly and Isla made their way out, they saw a whole line of Taxis waiting, they jumped in one that was nearby. Where to, girls? the taxi driver asked. 'Could we ask a favour please? we are visiting, we used to go to the Marquee club that's in Wardour street, and we would like to just pass it, to take us back to those days, then onto our hotel is that ok?' 'Yes girls of course,' the taxi driver said. 'I used to go there myself, had some great nights there and always good bands too. I pass it everyday doing my job,' he laughed. He drove them up to Wardour street, and stopped outside. 'I can see the disappointment on your faces,' the taxi driver said. 'Soho Lofts,' they both said together, "Oh no," Tilly continued. "Where is the excitement and enjoyment of that place, we knew the Marquee club would not be there, shame it's not a restaurant with some music going on. Anyway thank you for taking us past, it's just lovely to see this area. We are down here for the weekend, going over some of our favourite old haunts. 'Not a problem, it was a pleasure, where to now?' he asked. 'Oh, to the Millenium Hotel please,' said Isla. 'Ok.' He started asking them questions about the Marquee club and what they could remember of the bands that they saw, 'Well! said Tilly, 'I remember seeing the Rolling Stones, Rod Stewart, the Kinks, Searchers,' 'and Herman Hermits' Isla added. 'Loads really.' Maybe our paths may have crossed at sometime back then, said the taxi driver. 'Whose to know' said Isla. 'Right girls here we are at your hotel.' 'Thank you so much for taking us past the club, said Isla. 'How much do we owe you?' 'You know what,' said the taxi driver, 'have this ride on me, it's been a pleasure to help you, and brought back some good memories from the past. Ones I had forgotten, so thank you!' 'Are you sure?' Isla said 'Yes it was delightful meeting you both' he said in his cockney voice. They both alighted from the taxi, and together they thanked him again. 'Well how lovely was that, what a wonderful evening we have had. I'm definitely ready for my bed Isla.' said Tilly. 'Me too' replied Isla. "We may have gone back to those teenage years, but my body is saying you are not eighteen anymore, that's for sure.' Tilly replied saying her body was aching too, as their first day came to end. They both slept in until 9am, then struggled to get out of bed, 'guess we need to sort breakfast out Isla? 'Yes good idea,' replied Isla. 'shall we have room service?' Tilly replied. 'Blimey all we have had so far is room service, guess it's there so us lazy oldens can sleep in longer.' Isla said laughing. They both got up, made their way to the table by the window, after ordering their breakfast, deciding where they should go first. 'How about we go to the Sir George Roby pub, it's in the Finsbury Park area,' then have a stroll around the shops, maybe have a walk around the park, said Isla. 'Yes' replied Tilly. 'Or we could head to Camden Town It's not that far from Finsbury Park.' said Tilly 'Yes,' replied Isla, 'actually Tilly, I think that is a better idea, there is much more to see there, so shall we do that first, then go to see the pub last?' Isla replied. Just as they finished deciding there was a knock at the door, their breakfast was being served.

They got themselves ready for the daily delights that would unfold, they got to the tube station and got their tickets and waited for the next tube to arrive to take them to Camden. The journey was not very long, they soon arrived at Camden tube station.

They both stood on the pavement for a few minutes, trying to get their bearings of which direction they should start walking in. Tilly could see if they turned right, they would be heading towards the market. The nearer they got to the market they could see so many unique and unusual artefacts adorning the stalls that were laid out with their wares to sell, lots of vintage memorabilia, bric a brac. They had their eyes on a few bits, but they were too big and bulky to get them back home safely. Tilly stood looking around and caught sight of a stall which had crystals, incense, candles and lots of mystical ornaments. They walked towards the stall, it was laid out so lovely. Tilly was drawn to the crystals and Isla found a lovely Rose Quartz necklace with a lovely ornate chain. Tilly had been drawn to some unusual crystals with beautiful markings on them. They both paid for their items and continued mooching, enjoying the energy of the market. They made their way down to the locks where there were lots of boats of all colours, different sizes painted in lovely bright colours, some had flowers adorning the roof of the houseboat, some had chairs for relaxing in. As they were walking through they could hear music, coming from one of the cafes, they both looked at each other, heading in the direction of the music, considering it was October it was quite warm, the sun was shining brightly, They were drawn to a cafe, which was playing reggae music, as they got nearer, there were people just dancing to the music. it was so quaint and cosy, the tables and chairs were mismatched wooden tables with flowery tablecloths, and a small table decoration. The cafe had a huge range of black and white pictures, all different shapes and sizes, hanging from the walls, a piano sat in the corner. They found a table outside and waited for the waitress to arrive. As reggae music was the theme, the cafe was serving a Caribbean menu. They were overlooking the canal, and saw a few houseboats and just taking in the energy of the place. Everyone seemed to look very relaxed and seemed to just live for the moment. The waitress came to take their order, there was so much going on they did not know which way to look. People watching was one of Tilly's favourite pastimes. She loved the psychology of how people's minds work and their body language. Isla was just sitting tapping her feet to the music, and looking around at all the different types of people that were gathered in this small area. Everyone seemed to enjoy this place, from the locals to the tourists who found themselves in Camden Town, some were jigging around to the music as they passed the cafe, some were just enjoying like Isla, tapping their feet. Tilly and Isla's meals had arrived, they looked delicious. They both ordered Jerk Chicken, it tasted so good. They thoroughly enjoyed their meal, the music, and the vibe of the people around them. They found themselves both jogging to the beat of the music clapping along with everyone else, both smiling and laughing, and feeling so happy. 'There is such good energy here,' said Tilly.

'Well, I suppose we had better get our bums off the chairs, ' said Tilly. They paid their bill, and started messing about dancing and singing as they walked away from the cafe. 'Wow,' said Isla, 'I don't think I have ever danced while walking along the road toward a tube station. 'Me neither' said Tilly. 'This place certainly has a great buzz, just like it used to have all those years ago.' As they were walking further away, the music was fading into the background noise, as they headed to Camden Park tube station on their next journey to seek out the Sir George Roby pub, still linking arms, just enjoying being together. They sat on the tube, looking out as everything was just whizzing past them, all the adverts on the walls. 'I wonder what we are going to find when we get to the pub' said Tilly. Well, that's if it's still there.' Tilly continued. 'Who knows, it could be a block of flats, or houses now' replied Isla. 'I really hope it has not been demolished, Isla, I have so many fond memories.' replied Tilly. They got off at their stop, and walked up the stairs, and came out of the entrance of the tube station. They both stood there in shock, 'OMG' they both said together. 'It's not at all how I remember it.' Tilly said 'So many new buildings, where the shops used to be. I can see a few of the remaining shops.' They were trying to get their bearings. 'Ok, let's go left, 'said Tilly, I have a feeling it's up there.' 'Ok, let's try that direction' replied Isla,' let's see where it leads to,' as Isla followed Tilly up the road. 'Look,' exclaimed Tilly, 'I can see something blue on the right hand side. The pub was painted blue.' Tilly said with delight. 'Yes you're right Tilly, let's cross the road and have a look.'

As they walked nearer, they could see a taller building behind the pub that has been recently built. Tilly stared in disbelief. 'I did not expect it to be the same, but this is just horrible, the place is so run down, there is only a small piece of the roof left.' They both peered through the doors into the lobby area. There was still the same orange wallpaper, but a lot had peeled off, or ripped, some pictures of the groups that played there remained hanging on the walls and debris everywhere. 'This is so sad,' said Isla, 'I know.' replied Tilly 'We have such good memories of this place, all the new and old bands that we saw. I can still see myself on the platform stage, singing alongside Bob and Pete and the rest of the band. I wonder if someone had bought the pub, but did not get planning permission or have the funds to renovate it.' Tilly felt very tearful and sad as she stood outside, thinking back to days in the band and Bob, and having flashbacks of the past good and bad. 'I was so hoping it would still be open, bands still being able to showcase themselves, or just a normal pub that had a nice restaurant.' As she spoke, for the first time Isla realised just how much Tilly could dwell on the past and in such a heavy way, that it seemed to lock her up inside, she could see how this had affected her on a deep level. Isla, was not like that, she was able to pull herself out of the past quite quickly, she was sad, but knows life moves forward like it has to, if it does not, no progress can be made, and the world has to progress whether we want it or not, it is part of evolution, its human nature. Isla looked at the sadness in Tillys eyes, she could see her completely immersed back to the sixties and seventies, her marriage to Bob, it was like one of those old 1920's silent movies where everything was going so fast, you could not keep up with the story! 'Hey Tilly, are you ok?' 'You look so lost,' said Isla, 'Yes I'm ok, sorry Isla, I did not think I would have this reaction, I feel everything in the last forty years has just swallowed me up in my head.' 'Don't be sorry Tilly, we all deal with things differently, I can see your sadness. I did not realise how deep emotions and feelings go with you. I know you are quite a deep person, but now I can see the feelings and emotions you feel, it's like you're moving forward but stuck in the past.' said Isla. 'I know' Tilly said, 'it drives me mad sometimes. I have such conflict within me, I guess it's just who I am. I sometimes have to wrench myself out of the underworld that I seem to disappear into. Yes, the emotions and feelings are very deep, and very real.' 'Shall we make our way back now? it's beginning to get dark.' Said Isla, 'Yes you're right, it is getting dark. Think I need to leave this part of my life behind now, it's about moving forward and not going back, keeping hold of the good stuff.' 'That is a start Tilly but don't change who you are.' As they walked along the road linking their arms, towards the tube station. Tilly realised that sometimes it felt ok going back into the past, and lucky that she could share her feelings with Isla. 'I know' said Isla, 'we all can dwell on the past, we are humans, it's when you cannot move forward, through constantly living in the past, that problems arise Tilly. You have come from control and abuse most of your life, its feels like the happy button has not been pressed a lot, and you go immediately to a place of sadness, misery and reliving in your mind, just think back to an hour or so ago, you were dancing and happy enjoying the music, you were in the present, Camden Town held no sad memories, or potential threats, so you were who you were supposed to be, we come here and you descend back into the past, like you are reliving it all again. I know you have moved forward Tilly, I can see it in you, your confidence has grown, and you are finding you. Don't let the past pull you backwards, that's why they call it the past, because that's where it belongs, it also may be why you get apprehensive when you go out of your comfort zone, your body is alerting your brain, to be aware of potential danger, when in fact there is none, your body has had that so many times, it's time to change your reaction to it now. How about, seeing the old pub, just remembering the happy times we had, before Bob was there singing, a bit like this weekend, we have had fun, and have gone to places, where they hold no bad times. Then as you get stronger, you will be able to look back in the past, and see it for what it is, just part of the journey of life, part of your tapestry has been woven, the threads are now all being sewn together, to finish that chapter of your life, to make way for the new chapter. You, me, all of us cannot change the past, it has brought you to where you are now, giving you the opportunity to close the old book and last chapter, To start a new book, and create the chapters that you wish to write for the rest of your life.' 'Thank you Isla, you're like my mum, you have such wisdom, I do listen and I know what I have to do.'

They put their key in the door and flung open the door. 'Oh, it's nice to be back in the room, I feel so tired again,' said Isla. 'Yes me too,' replied Tilly. 'Think our age has something to do with it, Isla,' as Tilly put the kettle on to make a cuppa. 'Shall we just stay in our room and just chill out,' said Isla, 'Yes lets,' replied Tilly. "We can get our dinner sent to our room, relax and look out over London and all the twinkling lights, the hustle and bustle of the traffic, taxis, people watching from the window going about their lives," replied Isla. 'I think we will have built up a bill for room service,' laughed Tilly. 'Isla, can we do a meditation later, I feel I need to ground myself?' 'Yes of course, I think we could both benefit from that, I am going to have a shower and get into my pj's Tilly.''Yes, once you have had a shower, I will do the same, and just get cosy, get something ordered from the menu, do you fancy a bottle of wine Isla? 'Yes why not,' replied Isla. I have so enjoyed our weekend, but it's gone so quickly' Tilly said, 'Yes it has, but a good time was had for us both.' replied Isla. They sat at the table enjoying their meal, having a lovely glass of wine, looking out over the starry London sky. They finished their evening with a lovely meditation, drifting off to a peaceful sleep.

It was Monday morning and time for Isla and Tilly to make their way back home. They sat one last time having breakfast by the window that overlooked Hyde Park, clinking their glasses of orange juice, 'cheers' said Isla, 'cheers' said Tilly 'here's to more girly weekends away' Tilly added. 'Absolutely agree,' said Isla. They got their bags packed and headed to Victoria Station, to catch their train back to Alnwick, Tilly had her extra large bag, with her Afghan coat and Isla with her dress. They got to the station, the train was already there, and was leaving in 5 minutes. They walked at a fast pace, to find a carriage, they settled themselves down ready for the journey home. Their cases and bags beside them, there was no way Tilly wanted anything to happen to her new prized possession. 'You know Isla I thought we would come home with a lot more bags than this,' 'Yes I thought the same as you Tilly, but maybe we don't need all the clothes and bits and pieces that we used to buy years ago. I am happy with my dress and I know you are really happy with your coat,' Isla replied. 'How do you feel now Tilly?' 'Yes I'm fine, thank you for your understanding,' 'It's not a problem Tilly, it was only on the journey up here, that's what apprehension does, it kicks starts your past memories. You have been absolutely fine, I could see that.' 'Yes Isla, this weekend has really helped me to understand myself more, it's definitely the apprehension which I will work on, when it's a happy occasion, or doing something fun, I need to see it as excitement and not fear.' Tilly said. 'Absolutely' replied Isla. 'The more your life becomes positive and you feel happy, your thoughts will create new neural pathways in your brain that will override the sad and unhappy times you have experienced. Did you know there is a close link between fear and excitement, those butterfly feelings you have in your tummy, come from the same place, when we are fearful we have like a butterfly feeling, maybe feeling a bit nauseous, when we are excited, we can have exactly the same feelings, so it's about changing the mindset. It does take time Tilly, but I know you will do it, not even know that it has changed, that's because your life is changing. There is nothing wrong with going back to Lucy, now you can pinpoint that is the apprehension of being outside of your comfort zone. She will be able to help you recover on that level.' 'You know Isla, I think I may consider that. I can't believe I have done it, gone to London especially how I feel now compared to how I felt Friday morning.' replied Tilly. "We all have anxiety sometimes in our life," Isla said. It's protecting you, letting you know that you are on mental and physical overload, but there is a difference when the anxiety creeps into your everyday life, causing havoc, and making you feel unwell. When you start to understand your spiritual, mental, emotional and physical self, you start to realise that you need some type of balance, if one of these is out of balance by a long way, it affects you on all the levels. That's why meditation, yoga, painting, crafting, being by the sea, being in the woods or with nature, or animals soothes the soul, it also brings all the other elements into balance. If you do feel there is anxiety or apprehension, look at what is causing it, going to the dentist, someone passing away, stress of work, family etc, can create fear and anxiety on the other hand, going on holiday, spending time with friends, going to a wedding, or just going out somewhere nice should bring up the feeling of being excited, about enjoying yourself with people you love, unfortunately even big events can trigger anxiety and fear, it all depends how balanced your mindset is.'

They both sat within their own thoughts looking out at the beautiful scenery that was going past them at great speed. They were only ten minutes away from Alnwick. The train slowed down, as it arrived at their destination. They got their luggage and alighted the train, they walked to Isla's car, and drove back to Isla's home. Tilly put her luggage in the car, and went and said goodbye to Isla. 'I will ring you next week, Isla. I am going down to Sarahs for a few days to see my granddaughters.' 'Have a lovely time Tilly' as they hugged each other. Isla waited at the gate to wave Tilly off, Tilly was wondering what the next few weeks would bring into her life. She knew she wanted a positive happy life, no more dramas in her life, that was all behind her now!

CHAPTER 12

Tilly arrived home to find her mum pottering around in the kitchen, getting the evening meal prepared. 'Hi Mum, how have you been?' 'Yes pet, I'm fine, no problems at all, but I did miss you. Did you have a good time in London?' 'Yes it was great, it went very quickly, but we packed a lot in those few days,' as she went past her mum to put the kettle on, to make a cup of tea, would you like a cup of tea Mum?' 'No thank you pet, I have not long had a cup of tea thank you.' Tilly's phone was ringing, when she looked it was Sarah, 'Hi Sarah, is everything alright your end?' 'Yes mum, I am fine but unfortunately the girls are off school as they both have chicken pox.' 'Oh no, both at the same time!!!, that will be hard work having them both poorly.' 'Yes I know Mum, anyway I was ringing you to say not to come down this week, I don't want you to catch anything.' 'That's ok Sarah, I completely understand. Once the girls are better we can make another arrangement.' 'Did you have a good time away in London?' 'Yes we both had a good time, I have not been home that long.' 'Sorry Mum, I need to go, the girls are scratching like crazy,' 'ok Sarah don't forget to put a good dollop of calamine lotion on them.' 'Will do bye mum, love you.' ' Bye Sarah, give my love to the girls, give them a big kiss from their Nanna, Love you, speak soon.' Tilly was upstairs unpacking and putting her new acquisition on to look in the mirror, I can't believe I have found one. Tilly thought as she looked into the mirror, I think I'll go and show mum my new coat. She was so excited when she tried it on. She proudly walked down the stairs, and walked into the lounge. Edith looked round in shock, her face was a picture. 'What's wrong Mum, don't you like my new coat?' 'Well, I have to say pet, I wondered what the bloody hell was entering through the door, a big furry beast was my first thought, only joking,' said Edith. They were both in hysterics. 'Mum, it's my Afghan coat, I found it in a nearly new shop in Carnaby street. I could have brought a lot home, but I could not carry it all.' 'Hey Mum, don't you remember when I was a teenager, going through my hippy phase, with the bell round my neck, always wanting one of these coats, but never could afford one.' 'Well, err, sort of pet, sorry, I'm still in the moment, when I thought a hairy beast had entered the room.' ' Mum, do you like it?' 'Well yes, it does look good on you, it suits you. It will certainly keep the cold out. That's for sure living up here, just promise me one thing.'asked Edith. 'What's that?' replied Tilly. 'Please don't go and get a bloody cow bell,' Tilly and her mum were still laughing. 'Glad we can still have the laughs we used to have Tilly, laughter is important in life and always will be, the day you stop laughing, you have to dig deep to see at what stop it jumped off at.'

'Have you spoken to Morag, since you met up?' enquired Tilly. 'No I have not, but I am happy that we were able to meet up, that gave me a real tonic.' Just as Edith had mentioned Morag, her phone was ringing, she got her phone and it was Jack, she quickly answered, asking if she could ring him back, as she had just got home. As soon as Jack replied, she felt a tingle go up her spine, at the sound of his voice. 'Oh Mum, I'm in need of another cuppa, do you fancy one now?' 'Oh yes please, could you bring in the shortbread that Morag brought down last week?' It reminded Edith of days when she was a little girl living in Perth, Scotland, living in the same street as Morag. Tilly got round to ringing Jack back.' Hello Jack, how are you? How's your mum doing?' 'Yes, I am good thanks. Yes mum is doing ok. How was your weekend away in London?' 'Yes, it was brilliant, we had a great time, I have not been to London for years, what have you been up to Jack?' ' Well Tilly, mostly thinking about you, and when I can see you.' Jack said in a low voice, hoping that Tilly would be free to meet up very soon. There was a pause as Tilly did not know what to say, it was a good job she was on the phone, as she felt uncomfortable and feeling quite hot. 'Hello Tilly, are you there?' 'Er, yes, I was just taken aback by that comment' 'Sorry Tilly, did not mean to make you feel like that, sometimes I just dont think, the words just come out. Are you around this week?' Jack added. 'Well, yes I am now, as both my granddaughters have chicken pox, so I can't go this week after all.' replied Tilly. 'Sooo, what day is good for you?' enquired Jack. 'Maybe Friday, is that ok for you Jack.' 'Yes that's fine, I can drive down, pop in and say hello to Edith and we go for lunch somewhere nice.' 'Yes, that sounds lovely Jack, what sort of time are you thinking?' 'Well, if I get to you around midday, it gives us a good few hours,' replied Jack. 'Perfect, I look forward to seeing you on Friday.' replied Tilly. 'Yes, me too, can't wait to see your beautiful face,' replied Jack. Tilly came off the phone feeling very flustered, she was not used to a man, giving her so many compliments. She again felt uncomfortable, but thought that maybe as she had never had a man say these nice words, and with all the abuse she had suffered she thought maybe it was her, and needing to get her head around dating again. She rang Isla, and told her what happened, Isla assured her that he was just being nice thats all, and that maybe since you had known each other for many years, he was just being friendly, and not to worry.' 'How about we catch up in the week, Tilly?' 'Hey Isla, that sounds like a plan to me.' Shall we meet up on Wednesday, Isla?' Tilly said, thinking about where they could meet up. Isla do you fancy going to Seahouses? We can go for a walk, and have a pub lunch.' 'Yes that sounds lovely, have not been there for years. Shall I come to you, say about 1ish?' 'Yes that sounds good' she replied. Tilly unpacked the rest of her clothes and went downstairs to check on the dinner that her mum had prepared, which was in the oven. Mmm, that roast chicken smells delicious in the oven, better get all the vegetables on, and potatoes in the oven, can't beat the smell of a good roast dinner, when it's chilly and windy outside, Tilly was thinking to herself. 'Mum dinner will be about 45 mins, are you hungry?' 'Yes very, the smell of that roast is making me feel hungrier by the minute.' replied Edith holding her rumbling tummy.' 'I was just thinking the same thing, to myself as I was coming down the stairs.' Tilly had put the rest of the dinner on, and went and sat in the lounge with her mum.

'I'm so pleased you feel a little happier mum, I don't like to see you so sad. By the way, Jack is coming down on Friday to take me out to lunch.' 'Just remember to take things easy, go slow.' 'Yes mum,' was all Tilly was going to say at this time. The lovely dinner of roast chicken, crispy roast potatoes, and fresh vegetables, yorkshire puddings balanced on the top, and lashings of chicken gravy were ready. Tilly brought Edith's dinner to her, she got her portable tray, and placed the meal on the tray, Edith's eyes lit up, 'ooh the smell of that dinner, You do look after me, Tilly,' her mum said. 'I'm so lucky you are living here. I've got good company, lovely food to eat, laughter and visitors in my house. It's just perfect.' 'Mum, it is a pleasure, thank you for letting me stay with you. I did not know where to go when my house got sold, I felt very lost and alone. How lucky am I that my mum is still here.' 'Then we are both very lucky dont you think?' 'Yes, very lucky, ' Tilly replied. The week seemed to pass very quickly. Tilly and Isla had a lovely lunch at Seahorses on Wednesday. where they had a good catch up, chatting about their weekend away, and thinking where they would like to go next time, a lovely walk along the beach. It was Thursday already, and the nerves were kicking in a little bit. Pete was on her mind, as she said she would ring him. She picked up the phone, to ring Pete, his voicemail came on, so she left him a message.

It was dusk, but soon turned into a clear starry night, she could see that the moon was not quite completely full. Tilly was just sitting on her bed just staring out of the window, with lots of thoughts running through her head. Ooh it looks very cold and frosty out there, Tilly thought. The leaves were mainly on the ground now, with a white frost covering them, with just the brown crispy edges of the leaves showing through. When I moved up to be with mum, those trees were full of leaves, Green and lush, where the sun had given them glorious sunlight, and the tree in its wonder had enough energy to feed the branches to create new life for the tree, now just three months later, the leaves had fallen, to return to the earth, to nourish the soil, so the tree can grow strong, with the new leaves, to feed its wondrous self next spring. Tilly was feeling the need to be cosy and warm, winter is a time of hibernation, where we can allow ourselves to be quiet, contemplate, re-energise our minds, body and spirit in preparation for the Spring, exactly the same as the tree. Tilly, actually quite liked winter, but living up north, it was bitter cold and soon there would be snowfall. She got her candles together, and placed some on her bedside table, and some on her dressing table, lit the candles, and laid back on her bed, and gathered a comfy fluffy throw and wrapped herself up, she put her phone on silent, and just soaked up the silence. She had never felt like doing things like this before, let alone the silence. Tilly never had that space to feel what silence is all about. She was always on her fight or flight adrenaline rush waiting for Bob to return home, to see what type of mood he was in. But she was feeling a peace within herself and a sense of who she was now. She promised herself to give more time to taking care of herself, and not to keep thinking about what the future holds, she was always thinking about the future and not living in the moment. But this feeling of peace, and starting to live in the present would give her the solitude to go deep inside to her soul, to truly get to know who she is. She laid on her comfy bed with pillows plumped up around her, she felt safe and secure, with the throw covering her from top to toe, laying in complete silence and seeing the flames flickering and dancing on the walls and ceiling, trying to see the patterns emerging from the shadows. She did not realise that this was part of her spiritual journey, to release the past and be true to herself. She did not want to move, and had no idea of time. She reached for her phone, and saw a missed call from Pete, it was well past 7pm. She got up, sat on her bed, returning Pete's call.

'Tilly, how are you?' Pete answered, how was your weekend?' ' Pete, we had a great time. We saw a show, went to Carnaby Street, and Camden Lock, and we managed to get to the Sir George Robey pub, I have to say I got upset, its derelict and just been left, the foyer was filled with rubbish but were some pictures still hanging on the wall of the bands that played there, and I could see the stage in the distance and went back in time to seeing us all on the stage playing together with the band back in the day. The whole area has changed, but that's just me, I do get so emotional at times, when it's to do with the past,' said Tilly, 'always seems to take me back, just wishing it would take me forward sometimes' she said making herself cosy with the throw. 'Tilly, I quite understand how you feel. We had good times and we don't like to think it's been spoiled, taking the memories away, but they are in our hearts forever,' Pete said, seeing himself on the stage alongside his band members. 'Yes, you are so right Pete, they can't take those precious memories from us,' replied Tilly. 'How is your Mum? didn't Morag come down to visit her with her son?' 'Yes, Morag, and Jack her son came down. It was good for them both to see one another, they sat and chatted and Jack and I went to the pub, to have a drink, to give them some time on their own to catch up. I have not seen Jack for years, we used to be good friends when we were younger, so it was nice to catch up with him. He is coming down tomorrow actually to see mum and I. We are going out for lunch, 'Tilly replied.' 'Oh that's nice,' said Pete, in a flat voice.' You ok Pete?' said Tilly. 'Have you started work on your new sculpture?' Tilly continued 'Yes of course, I'm ok, replied Pete, it's good for you to go out with other men, it will help you build your confidence. Yes, I have started my new commission. it's getting colder down here by the sea, the storms are brewing. I have had some commissions come in for work so that should keep me busy. I'm playing in the band on Friday. I do really enjoy being part of the band.' 'Oh Pete, that's good, glad you have had more commissions. I do envy you playing in a band, I would love to experience that again. When we were away, Isla and I were talking about coming down to see you in a few months. For a week, we will find a b&b to stay near you. I was also thinking, do you fancy coming up here for New Year? you can stay at mine if you would like to do that?' 'Oh that's nice of you to invite me, not quite sure what I am doing re band engagements, but I will let you know by the end of November, is that ok,' said Pete. 'Yes of course, well look, enjoy your lunch tomorrow with Jack, and we will speak soon. Take care, bye Tilly.' 'Bye Pete, yes speak soon.' Tilly knew instinctively that Pete's voice had changed, when she mentioned Jack's name she did not want to lose Pete, in hindsight she should not have mentioned Jack. She knew that's why Pete did not make a commitment for the New Year, she really had to make sure that she did not talk about Jack, as she was not in any kind of relationship with Jack but the chemistry was there.

Tilly knew she was missing Pete, he is such a lovely person, and she does feel an attraction to him, but the chemistry with Jack was all consuming, and she was not sure what it was about, she kept having little alarm bells going in her head regarding Jack. Being an empathic person, Tilly did not want to upset Pete, and thought maybe sending a text to him could clear the matter up, but thank goodness her intuition stopped her in her tracks, she changed her mind, she knew if she sent the text trying to paper over the conversation, she was getting herself in deeper with Pete, which was not necessary. She had a shower, and got herself ready for bed, her mum had already gone to bed. Tilly laid down and tucked herself up in bed, with so many thoughts in her head. "Oh why am I doing this again?" I promised myself only a few hours ago that I was going to stop thinking thoughts over and over again in my head, regarding the future, and let the universe show me the way when the time is right. 'Her head hit the pillow, she fell asleep straight away, after her busy weekend away with her best friend Isla.

Tilly heard a horn beeping outside, so she guessed it was Jack, letting her know that he had arrived. She opened the door, when he came in, he cupped his hands around her face, and kissed her forehead and then her lips. 'Good to see you again Tilly.' 'Yes you too,' again taken aback by how bold he was with the greeting. 'Edith, where are you? I've come to say hello to you.' 'I am in here Jack, I'm in the lounge.' Jack walked in and greeted Edith with a kiss on her forehead. 'How are you doing?' 'Yes I'm fine, how's Morag,' 'Yes not too bad, Tilly and I will work something out today, so you two can see each other soon.' 'Oh that would be lovely Jack,' Edith said with a broad smile, ' I will look forward to that.' 'Jack, I'm ready when you are.' 'Where shall we go?' Jack enquired. 'There is a lovely pub in Seahouses, called the Old Ship Inn. In fact I went there on Wednesday with Isla if you fancy that,' 'Yes of course, that sounds good.' Tilly and Jack said goodbye to Edith. Jack opened the car door for Tilly, then got in the car, putting his seat belt on, and asked which was the best way to get to the pub. Tilly gave Jack some directions to the pub, it was pretty much a straight road, and about a 10 minute drive, it was the coastal scenic route, which has the most beautiful scenery, which Jack remarked on. 'Well, that did not take long,' said Jack, 'it's really lovely here' Jack continued. 'Yes, my dad was born here, he did not move very far away, from Seahouses to Bamburgh' she said, unclicking the seat belt. 'He was Northumberland born and bred and never felt the need to travel I suppose. I don't think many people travelled back then like they do today. Shall we head off to the pub and grab some lunch?' 'Yes, good idea, 'replied Jack. 'I could sit here all day looking out to sea, it's just so peaceful.' They walked to the pub, got themselves a drink and the menu, and found a table right by the window, looking out over the fields, where the cows and sheep were grazing. Jack had gone to the bar to order their lunch. They sat chatting over their pasts and marriages. 'So do you see much of your grandchildren Jack?' 'Yes, well, with my daughter, I only get to see them when I go to Ireland, it's a beautiful place to live. They live in Killaloe, in County Clare. She does come over, but not very often, her husband owns his own food produce company, and my daughter works alongside him. I try to go over about three or four times a year and stay for a month at a time. I see more of my son who lives in Shropshire. He is a farmer, so I go down there at least once a month. I actually like helping him around the farm. He has cattle, sheep, alpacas, chickens and roosters running around. He has just started alpaca treks, where people can take their children for walks. It seems to have done well in the Summer . He is very good at expanding his business and knowing how to make his ideas work and make money. He is in the process of renovating one of the outbuildings on the land by the main road into a farm shop and cafe. My daughter in law works on the farm too. I will have to take you there,' Jack continued, 'you will love it, and to Ireland my kids would love to meet you. I do have another son, I think I have spoken about him, he's married but they decided that they did not want children. I do see them, but not often, and of course the son in Australia is not married and has no grandchildren.'

'How about you with your grandchildren?' Tilly was yet again, taken aback at Jack's remarks about meeting his family, it's as if he thinks we are already in a relationship, she was not sure about this, but continued to answer the question. 'Yes, when I can, when I lived in Kent it was only a few hours drive away, from here it can be a good five to six hours drive since I have been divorced and have come to live with mum, it has not been that easy, but they all came up in September to stay for the weekend, it was just lovely seeing everyone. I do miss my grandchildren and my kids, but they both have busy lives, and my life is not the same anymore. My son is a transport manager, a commercial mechanic, and drives all the big coaches as well, he does really long hours, they put a lot of pressure on him. My daughter is very creative, and started her own baking business, but works as an accountant for a couple of companies, so she is pretty busy, and that's without looking after the children. I was sad that I could not go down to see her and the kids, but I can sort another time out when the girls are well again, and to see my son as well. They are all coming up here to spend Christmas, my mum is excited, so am I, we shall have a good time.' said Tilly, still feeling pensive. 'Well, let's hope I get to meet them too. I would like to meet your family.' Tilly murmured 'yes maybe.' 'Let's hope we can meet up every week, and sort out that weekend away.' Jack said, winking his right eye. 'Yes, as I said, that will be a few months down the line Jack, I am not ready for anything like that.' Tilly said, feeling a sense of pressure from Jack. 'Yes of course, sorry if I am going too fast.' 'Well you are,' replied Tilly. She was so proud of herself, for saying those words, she would never have spoken her truth in the past. She did feel a bit shaky saying those words, but she was not prepared to be pushed into anything that she felt she had no control over. They sat and ate their lunch, there was a bit of an icy silence between them, she could sense that Jack was a bit off with her, when she spoke to him. Jack broke the silence, 'so what happened in your marriage that made you get divorced?' Tilly was not ready to give Jack all the details, as she did not know Jack's past and was not going to tell all. 'Well, we just drifted apart, once the children grew up they did not need us so much, we realised we had nothing in common, so we decided to divorce, it was a very painful emotional experience, but there has to be something between you for it to work and carry on.' Tilly felt bad about lying, but she was now protecting herself, she was not a victim anymore, so why should she give details of her life. How about you Jack?' 'Well, I have been divorced twice, the first wife, very similar to you, and the second wife. I did cheat on her, I do vaguely remember telling you this when we first met.' Replied Jack. 'So do your children have different mums?' 'Yes, with my first wife, I had my daughter and my two sons, and my youngest son, who lives in Australia, is with my second wife. He is a chip of the old block, he loves a pretty face, I have grown up now and know my weaknesses.' Tilly was sitting there, with a million and one thoughts Jack had told me all his children were with his first wife, that's a lie. Bloody hell, she thought, thank god I did not share my side of my marriage, he really has been a Jack a lad, and Jack by name, he certainly was a gigolo, that was for sure. I guess he's slowed down, not because he wants to, but because he's getting older and has not got the pulling power he once had. Blimey, what I have got involved with here, Tilly thought to herself. Right, ok, I can't make these sorts of judgements, he has been honest with me, just take your time to get to know him, you can't judge a book by its cover. They finished their lunch and had a walk along the beach, although it was chilly the sky was blue. Jack grabbed Tillys hand and she was not sure how to deal with this, so she just held his hand, she could definitely feel the chemistry and attraction. When they got back to Tillys house, Tilly said goodbye to Jack in the car and thanked him for lunch, she had not even finished saying goodbye, when Jack took his seatbelt off, got out of the car, locked it, then followed her indoors and went straight into the lounge and sat with Edith. Tilly went to the kitchen, a little bit unsure of what was going on. I suppose I'm wrong really, thought Tilly, he did come down to see me and brought me lunch. Yes I am definitely putting my defences up, so I need to work on not putting my guard up straight away when I feel uncomfortable. Tilly called out to see if they would like a drink. 'Yes please,' Edith and Jack said together. Tilly made the tea, and brought them in with some cake.

Did you two have a good time today?' Edith enquired. 'Yes it was lovely thank you Edith,' Jack jumped in first to answer, leaving Tilly just sitting there with her mouth still poised to give an answer. Jack ended up staying for dinner and was still there at 9pm, Tilly was beginning to feel on edge, something she never felt with Pete. Edith had gone to bed. Jack moved closer to Tilly on the sofa. She could feel the energy building between them, she had butterflies in her tummy of excitement, all those negative feelings she had, had completely gone. The chemistry and attraction were overriding the red flags. Jack pulled Tilly towards him, and kissed her passionately on the lips, Tilly just melted and kissed him back, he cuddled her and caressed her hair, and gently stroking the outline of her face, stroking her mouth, his hand slowly ventured down her neck to the top of her cleavage, then gently kissing her lips. 'This is nice Tilly,' Jack said. 'I felt like this when we were young but as you were a few years younger than me, it was not right, although I do remember kissing you once, even though I wanted to kiss you every time I saw you.' Tilly again, was not sure how to react or what to say to Jack, he seemed very persuasive, but she just replied that she had enjoyed kissing him again. 'If your mum was not upstairs I would have had your clothes off by now.' Tilly could feel the passion, her body aching to make love to Jack, she was totally under his spell, she had waited years to have this type of passion, she did not even answer him, she knew they would have been naked by now if her mum was not upstairs, but maybe that was a blessing in disguise. Tilly had said that she wanted to take things slowly, but she also did not want to stop kissing him. Tilly pulled away from Jack. 'I think we need to stop now, it does not feel right doing this in my mum's house.' 'I did not expect this to happen tonight Tilly, I'm not saying I did not enjoy the kisses and cuddles. I have just got carried away, that felt so good, we must make a date for a weekend away, so we can be alone, and can make love all night. Right Tilly, I had better get myself together and get back home.' he continued. Jack had left and Tilly was sitting on the sofa, reflecting on what had just happened, her body still quivering with excitement. She felt so confused and mixed up, she had no idea how long she had been sitting there, but a text from Jack arrived to let her know that he had arrived home safely, with an added text of what he would like to do to Tilly sexually, how much he loved her and always has done, he would treat her like a princess, give her anything she wanted to make her happy, there was loads of kisses at the end of the text. Tilly was sitting on the sofa with her jaw dropping, mouth open. WTF is this all about, is it normal to get texts like this when you are older. Part of her was a bit shocked, but the other side of her for the first time in years, felt alive, the pilot light of passion had been switched on inside of her. She felt she could have had sex all night with Jack. There were now many red flags, and Jack knew what he was doing, he knew she wanted him sexually he could feel her body quivering, he had done his work, now he just had to wait for her to take the bait of a weekend away. Tilly wanted Jack now, he had caught her in his net. She did not reply, she really did not know what to type to him, she had never been in this situation in her life. Tilly got herself ready for bed, but could not sleep, she finally fell asleep in the early hours of the morning. When she did wake up it was 10.30am, she had completely overslept, she had not slept in this late for years. Edith was calling up the stairs to her, but got no reply, she even went up to check on her, only to see her sound asleep, so left her until she woke up. The doorbell rang, Edith called down the stairs to ask them to wait a minute as she was coming down the stairs slowly. She opened the door to a person who was hiding behind the biggest hand tied bouquet you ever saw.

'Hello' said the florist, 'these are for Tilly Fellowes,' "WOW," replied Edith, it's beginning to look like a florist shop in here, struggling to try and hold it, it was so heavy, she could not even see the florist's face. 'Thank you.' 'Your welcome' said the florist. Edith placed them on the dining table, in the lounge, there was a card in an envelope, Edith thought it only right not to peek. Tilly finally woke up and came down the stairs. 'Mum' she said, 'did I hear the doorbell ring,' she enquired as she was coming down the stairs. 'Yes pet,' answered Edith, 'you have the biggest bouquet I have ever seen.' Tilly could smell an aroma of fresh flowers as she walked into the lounge, gasping as she put her hands over her mouth. There were two dozen red roses, gypsophila, and eucalyptus leaves wrapped in cellophane, with red hearts, and a beautiful white ribbon tied around the handle of the bouquet. She saw the card attached to the bouquet. While her mum was in the kitchen, she whipped the card out of the cellophane and shoved it down her pyjama top and went back upstairs to read what the card said. Jack had written the most beautiful words in the card, and how lucky he was to have found her again. Tillys phone was on the bedside cabinet, so she rang Jack and thanked him for the flowers. 'So!!!! When are we going away for the weekend,' Jack asked, 'let's get something booked up for a few weeks' time,' he added, hoping to get the right response of a resounding YES. 'Ok Jack,' replied Tilly, 'where

you fancy going then,' 'Tilly, you can choose, how about a nice country mansion, or a 5 star hotel, Friday to Monday, think that would suit us. You choose which area where you would like to stay.' Jack thought to himself how easy it was to get Tilly away for a weekend, I really did not have to work too hard for that to happen, grinning to himself. 'So what about your mum?' Tilly enquired 'Oh she will be fine,' Jack replied, 'I pay for carers to come in and look after her twice a day, as I am working, but I can get them to come in three times a day. Tilly I had better go, as I have phone calls to make about work, ring you later.' 'Yes, that's fine, I'm not going anywhere today,' Tilly replied. Tilly felt like a lazy day with her mum, she cooked them bacon and eggs, crusty bread and extra lashings of butter, and a big cup of hot strong tea. Tilly stayed in her pj's all day. The weather was very dismal outside and she felt cosy and warm by the fire with her mum. 'Oh Tilly, this is lovely, this is the first time since you have lived here that you are actually having a relaxing day, it will do you good.'
'Yes your right mum, the last year or so has had many bumps in the road, coupled with a few white knuckle rides along the way, but a lot of good has come out of this, first of all I am living with you, keeping you company, making sure you are ok. I have my bestest oldest friend Isla in my life again. I have seen Pete, who I never thought I would set eyes on again, and now Jack and Morag. So everything does happen for a reason, when you let go of relationships, careers, needing to feel to need to live somewhere new or living abroad, even though it can seem scary, you just have to surrender and trust, that what is behind the closed door to your future, is better and more fulfilling than you can ever imagine. Going through a mind full of reasons why you can't move forward, has to be changed to having a mindset of thoughts of positivity, knowing things will eventually naturally open up for you, to start your new life, being happy, knowing yourself, your strengths and weaknesses, and the beginning of your wings being unclipped, ready for you to fly high.'

'I know mum, that I am not the same woman anymore. It felt very uncomfortable and so emotional, but releasing myself from the abuse and mental anguish to experience the new and my soul is growing and evolving, not sure in which direction, but it feels good.' Tilly said. Edith looked across at her daughter, with the broadest of smiles. 'Yes pet, I can see your future unfolding, because you are free to be you.' 'Mum, I think I am going to have a duvet day, I need some sleep.' 'Of course, just do what you need to do, I'm fine here.' replied Edith. Tilly snuggled herself under her duvet, no sooner had she got all cosy, Jack was ringing. Tilly did not answer her phone, she knew it would be a good 15-20 minute chat, she just needed some space, so much has happened in the last month. She put her favourite meditation music on, she loved the sound of the waves gently rolling over the shingle, and the noise as the shingle moved as the waves rolled back and forth into the sea. It took Tilly back to a time where the band was asked to do a gig in the Caribbean for a holiday company, they spent a whole three months there, she could still feel the warmth of the sun on her face and body, as she fell asleep. A few hours had passed, and she was woken up with her phone ringing, it was Jack again. 'Hi Jack,' she answered in a sleepy voice. 'Hello lazy bones, been to sleep today have we, some of us have to work you know' Jack said laughing, but underneath he genuinely did not like it that Tilly was relaxing. 'I'm not lazy at all, this is the first day I have been able to have myself for months,' feeling a bit pissed off with him. 'Hey beautiful girl, only joking' Jack could feel Tilly was not happy. 'I hope you dont wake up grumpy all the time, it won't be nice when we are away for our weekend, "Jack replied, again in a laughing voice. 'No, I am not grumpy in the morning,' replied Tilly, I am happy in the mornings.' 'Well, that's good news.' Jack said, 'at least I know now why you did not return my call. I thought that maybe I am your bad books.'

'Have you listened to the voicemail?' Jack enquired. 'No not yet, you are not in my bad books at all, I will listen when we get off the phone, ' she replied. 'You had better listen to it, it will make you feel so horny, you will wish you were with me right now, you will know what kind of sex you will be getting when we are away.' Jack continued 'Have you looked at anything yet?' Tilly could feel this tingling in her body, just listening to Jack's voice. 'Er yes, I will be looking a bit later today, will ring you later if I find something.' 'So what are you up to now? 'Have you received anything else in the post at all?' Jack asked. 'Not that I know of' replied Tilly. 'Well, there are a few more gifts heading your way, I know how to treat you, love you and look after you, you are my everything, I love you Tilly, you are my special girl.' Tilly could not reply, again Jack always seems to shock her with his words. 'Tilly, Tilly, are you still there?' 'Yes I am here,' 'Well,' said Jack, 'what you do say to me.' 'Thank you Jack,' replied Tilly. 'Jack I need to go now, mum is calling up the stairs, will look for somewhere nice for the weekend away, and will let you know.' 'Ok, make sure you do, you know I love you, and love hearing your voice.' Tilly came off the phone, her thinking rather discombobulated, she was feeling a heady excitement about Jack, and the chemistry and attraction was too strong for Tilly to even see what Jack was up to. She went downstairs, sat on the chair looking at her mobile phone looking to see what deals were about and where to go. She pondered over the internet results that were coming up, she went into the kitchen to make some toast and a cup of coffee, and her mum something to eat too. She came back in and sat on the chair perusing all the offers. There was one in the lake district, on Lake Windermere, she was totally engrossed. 'You seemed to have found something interesting over there pet?' Tilly felt slightly anxious, knowing she cannot tell her mum the truth about having a weekend away with Jack. 'Oh yes Mum, Isla and I are thinking of another weekend away, she has left it up to me to find somewhere nice to go.' Oh you two are having fun booking weekends away, hasn't she got a husband, I thought she was married?' 'Yes, she is Mum, but her marriage is not working for her, she thinks her husband may be having an affair so she just wants to take some time away.' Feeling so bad at lying to her mum of all people. The feeling of meeting up with Jack made her giddy, and butterflies in her tummy. She kept being drawn to the hotel in the lake district, she had not been that way for quite a few years. Oh this looks gorgeous, thought Tilly. The Cranleigh Boutique Hotel, the luxurious boutique room, looks rather sexy, it was £250 per night, I need to see if Jack has that sort of money, he seems to have a good lifestyle, if not we can go for a cheaper option, I think I will go and ring Jack now. Jack's phone was ringing. 'Hi gorgeous girl, have you found us something?' 'Oh yes, I have found the most amazing hotel in Lake Windermere, it's called the Cranleigh Hotel. it's beautiful, it's available Friday 7th November to the 10th.' 'That sounds nice Tilly, yes book it' said Jack. 'Don't you want to know how much it is Jack?' 'No, it's fine, just book it and pay the deposit and I will transfer it over to your bank account, later today, send me over your details' Jack replied. 'Ok' said Tilly, 'will you be able to do that now?' 'it's £250 per night?' 'Yes of course nothing is much for my girl' Jack said, 'anyway,' Jack continued 'Tilly I thought you had money from your divorce settlement.' 'Oh yes I do,' Tilly replied, thinking in her head that she had never discussed her divorce settlement with Jack. he came back straight away, 'well then it shouldn't be a problem then.' he said in a gruff voice. 'Oh yes, well I suppose so,' replied Tilly. 'I will book it now.' She rang the hotel and made a booking and paid the £250.00 deposit. When she came off the phone, she had a bit of an anxious feeling in the pit of her stomach, she dismissed it and put it down to nerves, really it was another red flag waving right in front of her, but unfortunately, she was caught up with the passion and excitement of Jack. Even with all the passion and excitement, she was wary as Bob was someone who used to ask Tilly for money, and it felt like something she had experienced in the past, that was flagging up for her. She thought about it, and put the past behind her, knowing that Jack was different to Bob. Tillys phone was ringing again, thinking it may be Jack, but realised it was Isla calling.

'Hey Tilly,' said Isla, 'how are you doing?' 'Yes, not too bad, How are you?' 'Yes I'm good Tils. So what's new?' Isla enquired. 'Nothing really, Jack came down on Friday, we went out to lunch and had a lovely time together. Pete rang me, to see how I was. I have invited him up for New Year! He just needed to check if they were playing any gigs over the New Year. He said he would let me know in the next few weeks.' 'Oh that sounds good Tilly,' 'How is your family?' Isla enquired. 'Yes ok. The girls are feeling a lot better now, thank goodness. So I will sort something out with Sarah to visit another time, not sure it will be before Christmas, as they are all coming here. Anyway Isla, it all works out how it is supposed to be.' How about you?'

Tilly asked, 'Yes I am going to go and stay with my daughters. I'm spending a few days with each of them. I don't really get to spend quality time with them and they are only thirty minutes away, but it's just life, but I'm looking forward to seeing them all.' 'That's nice Isla, always good to see your kids and grandchildren.' 'Hey, guess what Tilly! Isla said 'What,' replied Tilly excitedly. 'I have found a local yoga group, I am thoroughly enjoying it, it's on a tuesday evening, I have been going about a month now,' Isla continued, 'I have made a few friends and one in particular a man, he is in his late fifties, divorced and very spiritual, his name is Dave. "We have only been chatting but this week we exchanged our contact numbers, he has sent a few text messages, just seems like a very gentle soul, we seem to hit it off, when yoga is finished we always seem to stand outside chatting for ages.' 'Oh Isla, how lovely, do you feel guilty at all?' 'Well no, not really, I have not done anything wrong, he's just a male friend thats all, and if he asked me out for a drink, I would bloody well go, Brain has made it quite clear that this marriage is over, it's now just a sham. Life is too short not to.' 'Yes you're quite right Isla, we have to make the most of life and what we have left. There is more behind us, then in front, so just enjoy,' replied Tilly. 'I will,' Isla continued, 'I think he's on the verge of asking me out for a drink, he does not seem to be someone who rushes in and loves bombs, I don't think I would like that, it does not feel natural. Even if he is a good male friend, it's good to have that.' 'I realise how much I treasure Pete's friendship now, but did not when I was younger,' replied Tilly. They both made arrangements to meet up over at Isla's home for a catch up and some spiritual connection, which Tilly felt she needed. They both said goodbye to each other, and are looking forward to meeting up next week. Tilly came off the phone, thinking about what Isla was saying about love bombing and things moving too fast, and she found herself questioning all the things that had gone on in the last few weeks with regards to Jack, and not sharing her weekend away with Jack, Tilly quickly dismissed the thoughts, saying to herself that Isla is different to me, she is more careful, where I have always just gone for something, that's what those thoughts are about.

It was the following morning the doorbell rang, Tilly opened the door to the postman who then greeted her with another big box that needed to be signed for. 'This is for you Tilly,' said Ted the postie. 'Something smells good in there, it's coming through the box, wish more parcels smelt this nice' he said smiling. 'Thank you,' Tilly said. She took the box and went into the lounge, she opened it up to find so many goodies. There was her favourite Vera Wang perfume, beautiful aromatherapy candles, a big box of expensive chocolates, there was some pink tissue paper, right at the bottom of the box, she thought it was part of the wrapping, she could feel that there were more gifts to be opened. She gently pulled out the lovely wrapped items, tied up with red ribbon and on opening, was a bit taken aback there was a pair of black sexy knickers with red lace but not much else. A matching camisole with matching red lace around the top and bottom, and thin lace straps. She was putting the tissue paper together, when she noticed that there was a note at the bottom of the box. It read

"To my beautiful Tilly

I cannot believe you are back in my life

I love you so much, here's to our future together

Cant wait to see you.

Jack xxx

Tilly felt a bit confused again. Her head and heart were not in sync at all, this was way too much for Tilly, she felt like she was being put in a corner, which started the head chat, trying to rationalise everything. Tilly, your just feeling overwhelmed, because you have never known anything like this, her head was saying be careful, but for Tilly, her heart was winning, she had wanted to fall in love, and experience proper love all her life, she and Jack went back years, she felt he was her soulmate then, so for him to come into her life, she felt it was destiny, that their paths had crossed again all these years later. She was so drawn to Jack he was like a drug. Her body was aching to be touched by Jack, to have erotic sensual sex, she looked at the lingerie that Jack had sent her. It was so sexy, she could not wait until Friday, when she would be in Jack's arms. Her fantasies over the years were taking over in her mind. She rang Jack to thank him for all the gifts especially the lingerie and perfume, but he did not pick up, so she sent him a text message, hoping he would see that wherever he was, and ring her straight back, a few hours had passed now, and she kept checking her phone to see if she had a missed call, but nothing, it was not like Jack to not ring back more or less straight away, or just send a text saying when he would ring. She checked her bank account to see if he had transferred the deposit money into her bank account for the hotel, but when she checked the money had still not been transferred over. Tilly felt a pang of anxiety in her tummy, he had still not contacted her. All sorts of feelings were whizzing around in her head. Tilly finally heard from Jack at 7pm that evening. 'Hi Tilly sorry I could not ring, I've been busy with work all day.' 'Jack, thank goodness you are ok, I had all sorts of thoughts running through my mind, thought maybe your mum had been taken ill, or something had happened to you.' 'Tilly, sorry to have worried you, no I'm fine.' 'Jack, sorry to ask. but did you manage to transfer the money over last night?' 'Only I checked my account and it has not been sent, just in case it went to the wrong account.' 'Sorry that slipped my mind, I will try and get it done later this evening.' Jack quickly changed the subject, he also knew the mind games he was playing with Tilly, that they were beginning to work. He knew she liked him, and that they had a past, so he knew how she was a sensitive person, and very empathic, so when she reacted, to him not ringing, he knew she was falling for him, and that he had definitely had her in his net, ready to put bait on the line for Tilly to take at her cost. 'So Tilly, how are we going to meet up next Friday, if your mum does not know that you are going away for the weekend with me?' 'Well, maybe I could just meet you at the end of my road, and we can go from there,' replied Tilly. 'Ok that works fine with me, I cannot wait to see you in the underwear that I sent you, I know what a sexy woman you are, and to feel every inch of your body for three days and nights, well that just blows my mind.' Jack added. Tilly struggled to reply, although the fantasies were racing around in her head, she could not verbalise them. 'Yes, I am looking forward to spending time with you too.' 'Is that all you can say Tilly?' Jack laughed. 'Please do not forget to transfer that money over,' before she could finish her sentence the phone was dead.

Tilly gathered up her laundry, and took it downstairs, her head in a whirl again. She felt so bad that she was lying to her mum, even though Edith understood Tilly had her own life. She knew her mum would have been disappointed that she had only just met up with Jack. She put her laundry in the washing machine, and headed to the lounge. 'So Tilly, are you looking forward to your weekend away with Isla?' 'Where are both going,' she added. Edith had a sixth sense. She knew that something just did not feel right with Tilly, as if she was hiding something from her, but could not come straight out and ask her, she is a grown woman, it was none of her business. 'Well,' said Tilly, 'we are going to the Lake District, the hotel is on Lake Windermere. It's a nice country hotel. Yes, I'm looking forward to it.' 'Oh, it's lovely in the Lake District,' Edith replied, knowing Tilly was hiding something from her, she could tell by Tilly's body language and she kept coughing as though her throat was tense. 'It's so beautiful, I'm sure you and Isla will find lots to do there, a bit different to the London lights, but still a nice and relaxing weekend.' Tilly felt very uncomfortable again lying to her mum, but she is old enough to make her own choices in life, and she was excited to be going with a man for a weekend away. Tilly sorted out her laundry and went back upstairs to put it away. Jack was never far from her thoughts. Just as she got upstairs, Tilly checked her phone to see if Jack had sent the money over, and saw a missed call. It was from Pete. 'Hi Pete, how are you?' 'I'm ok. I have not felt too good this week. I think I had a cold virus, and those horrible coughing fits which makes your bloody head hurt, anyway all good now. So what have you been up to? Anything exciting, have you seen Jack?' 'Er no, Tilly paused ! I am seeing him at the weekend, we are going out for a meal, and to the pictures,' she replied. Again hating herself for lying to one of her best friends. 'Oh that's good, so everything is going alright then with you and Jack?' He replied, trying hard not to show the disappointment in his voice. 'Well, I suppose so, it's early days Pete. Sorry to hear you have not been well, and glad you are feeling a lot better.' Tilly was struggling to talk to Pete, as again she was lying to a man who had always been there for her. She was slowly beginning to see how Pete talks to her as opposed to Jack, but it has not completely registered in her head yet. 'Pete, would you mind if we talk later in the week? I do have a bit of a headache today, and feel a bit sick, not sure why.' 'Yes of course, I hope you're not coming down with the bug I have had,' replied Pete. 'I hope not, take care, speak later in the week.' Replied Tilly. Knowing full well that all the lying and her head going round in circles, and just not feeling right somehow, was the reason she felt like this. Tilly came off the phone. What the bloody hell am I doing, lying to my mum, lying to Isla, well just not telling her is enough, they shared everything, and Pete, who has supported her over the years, when her marriage to Bob, was just full of abuse on all levels. The alarm bells were ringing, but again Tilly dismissed them. She knew something was not quite right, but again put it down to her marriage to Bob, and was always looking for something to go wrong. Bob never acted like Jack, so how could Jack be like Bob? It was Thursday, Tilly was sorting out her clothes for the weekend making sure all her sexy black lingerie had been packed. She was getting so excited but the apprehension was also making itself known to her as well. Jack had still not paid the deposit money into her bank account, she was slightly worried, hoping she would get the money at some stage, but text him anyway. He replied to her text, saying that it would be paid tomorrow, and would text her when he was near to her road.

Tilly had gathered up her suitcase, coat and bag, when she received the text from Jack, she went in and said goodbye to her mum. 'Have a lovely time with Isla, see you when you get back pet.' Tilly closed the door, and walked down the road to meet Jack, as soon as she saw him, her heart skipped a beat and her tummy doing somersaults, he is so handsome and gorgeous, she thought to herself, he gave her big smile as she was walking towards the car, when she got in the car, he gave her a big kiss on the lips.

CHAPTER 13

"Ok, are you ready Tilly? Then let's go." "Yep, let's go, and have a lovely weekend together." As they were driving, Jack had placed his hand on her knee for most of the journey and every so often running his hand up and down her thigh. He certainly knew all the erogenous zones of the body that would cause such high sexual desire. Tilly was yearning for Jack, he could certainly feel by her body language and the way she was moving that is exactly what she wanted, she was losing control and overcome by the sexual arousal in her body. Jack knew what he was doing, he is a master manipulator, that is exactly what he wanted to achieve, the flesh especially near the top of her thigh, is an extra sensitive area to make you feel aroused, and that is what his plan was to tease her, then take it away from her. Tilly was still a vulnerable woman, healing from her narcissist marriage; it can take years to heal from these relationships, but she is a caring empathetic compassionate woman, who had been taken in by Jack. It was easy for Jack to manipulate her, being the overt narcissist he was, he knew she was under his spell.

They arrived at the hotel reception area, it was just beautiful. Jack had carried the luggage to the hotel, they got the keys, and were shown to their room by the porter. No sooner had the door closed behind them, Jack got hold of Tilly, he started to undo the blouse she had on, unclasped her bra with one hand while the other was unzipping her trousers, he pulled her over to the wall, where her body was quivering with sexual ecstasy, her emotions were all over the place, she was undoing Jack's shirt, she could feel his hard penis throbbing against her. She had been waiting for this moment all week. He pulled her over to the bed, where Jack just got on top of Tilly. He pushed his penis very hard inside of her, they both had an orgasm. For Tilly, although she enjoyed the sex, she did not feel any passion from him, in fact she found the sex a bit rough for her. He just got up, had a shower, He called to her asking her to have a shower with him, in a cold voice, as if nothing had just happened between them, it confused

Tilly somewhat, and she started to self doubt herself, thinking she may have done something wrong. She went to the bathroom, got into the shower with Jack, there was no love or affection, he came out with a towel around him, and got himself a drink. She was hoping that they would have snuggled having a cuddle, just lying there, chatting and laughing, and stroking each other, not trying to work out if she had done something wrong. Jack wanted to see just how much Tilly would follow his control, it was all a game to him. She just sat on the bed, waiting for the kettle to boil to make a cup of tea. Jack made a comment about making tea, and wanted her to have a glass of wine with him. She made her cup of tea, and then made sure she had a drink with him. He was sitting in the chair with the TV on watching horse racing, she felt very left out. This was nothing like she had envisaged. "Are we going to eat in the restaurant tonight Jack?' 'Yes, if that's what you want to do?' Jack replied in a normal voice. 'Actually, I'm a bit hungry now, shall I order some food for us?' 'Really Tilly, are you that hungry?' 'Well aren't you hungry Jack?' He totally ignored her, carrying on watching the horse racing on TV. Tilly was getting a bit pissed off already, she may be under his spell, but she could feel that something did not feel right to her. 'Oh all right, ' he said in a grumpy voice, 'if you must order food.'

Lunch had been delivered to the room, and Tilly was sitting on the bed, picking at the food, as she was looking at her phone, Pete was trying to call her, "Oh bloody hell what do I do now!! " 'Who's ringing you Tilly?' 'It's only a friend of mine, I can ring him back another time. It's not important.' 'Ring HIM back,' replied Jack. 'Who is him?' 'Oh it's Pete, we have known each other for years, we met up recently, have not seen him for years.' Tilly could feel that Jack was not happy about her having a male friend. Tilly was beginning to wonder, already if this was wise, but she just thought that Jack needed to relax as his mum has been unwell, he seemed very stressed. Jack went back to bed, after the horse racing had finished, and asked Tilly to come back to bed as well. As this was beginning to feel quite a tense situation, she got back into bed and snuggled up to Jack. He was on his phone and then turned his back on her, as he said he had work to attend to, but she still laid next to him. 'I hope you are going to wear the underwear that I bought you, and the perfume. Have you brought that with you?' Jack said when he finished his phone call. 'Yes, I have brought them with me, it's my favourite perfume.' 'Come and give me a cuddle, you do look lovely today Tilly,' he said. He began to kiss her, caressing her breasts, and gently running his tongue over her nipples, she could feel herself getting aroused again, as was Jack fully aroused. The sex seemed to go on for a long time, with Tilly pleasing Jack most of the time, but the chemistry was like a firework display, Tilly thinking to herself that maybe she had been a bit judgemental with Jack, and this time she enjoyed the sex more. They both fell asleep waking up about 6ish. 'So shall we have dinner down in the restaurant?' Tilly enquired. 'Yes, I said earlier that was ok, I do remember where we are going,' said Jack abruptly. 'Ok,' said Tilly. 'No need to speak like that as you did not really answer before, I wasn't sure that's all.' Jack gave Tilly a look as if to say don't question me. They got dressed, went down to the restaurant.

They both ordered the fillet of steak, with peppercorn sauce, small crispy potatoes and peas, with an ice cream medley for dessert, added with an expensive bottle of wine that he had ordered. Jack and Tilly were chatting over their meal, when Jack brought up the phone call when Pete had rang earlier. 'So, who's this Pete then?' 'He used to play in the band,' replied Tilly. 'He was such a support when I was going through bad times with Bob, he just seemed to understand me.' 'Well, I have to say I'm not happy for you to speak to Pete or whatever his name is in this relationship, l love you so much that the thought of you speaking to another man would really upset me.' replied Jack with a sorry looking face. 'Well if that's what you want, I won't contact him again.' replied Tilly, knowing it would break her heart if she could not communicate with Pete. 'I know how these situations work. That happened to my first wife. I had a female friend, and ended up leaving my wife for her.' Tilly was shocked, she did not say anything, but Jack had told her that with his first wife they had drifted apart, and cheated on his second wife, so he'd been lying to Tilly right from the beginning. They were just finishing their meal, when Jack asked again if she was wearing her sexy black underwear, Tilly replied that she was. He asked for the bill to be put on the account that was in Tillys name. As soon as they went back to the room Jack started taking his clothes off and asked Tilly to do the same. Now the red flags, that she had been in denial of, were not going away so quickly now. Tilly complied with his wishes, and got into bed with just her black panties and cami top. As Jack started to caress Tilly, he put himself on top of Tilly and really pushed his penis hard into her again to the point where it was hurting her. Tilly felt so uncomfortable, he was a lot heavier than her. She felt she could not escape, once he finished with the sex, he got up again showered and put the TV on. Tilly was now wondering what the hell was going on, there was nothing, no emotion, no intimacy, just sex, she felt like she was auditioning for a porn video. All she wanted was some love and affection, she felt very rejected, and got herself ready for bed. She felt absolutely worn out sexually, she had not had sex for quite a few years. Then to have this rough type of sex, which was not particularly what she had in mind spending time with Jack. She pretended to be asleep when Jack came to bed, comparing the time she had spent with Pete, when he came up and how different she felt. Pete treated her with respect and was a gentleman. She gradually drifted off to sleep, not quite sure if she could make it to Monday.

On Saturday, they went out on a boat trip, around Lake Windermere. As they were on the boat, Jack got a phone call from one of the carers, who had rang to say that his mum had become very unwell. The carer felt that he needed to be there with mum, and they would have to leave when the boat trip had finished. Now Tilly did not want anything to happen to Morag, but was so thankful, that this put paid to the rest of the weekend. She was more than happy that she was leaving the hotel and Jack's controlling ways, but was slightly worried about what she would say to her mum. It was not fair to use Isla. They got back to the hotel, packed up their belongings, and went down to pay. Jack told them it was an emergency regarding his mum, fortunately they did understand, but did want to charge money for the hotel room for the Saturday night even though they were not going to be there. Jack got his card out to pay, but was declined, he then searched for another one in his wallet, which was again declined. Jack acted embarrassed, but deep down he did not care, he knew those cards would not go through. He turned to Tilly and apologised asking if she had a card with enough money, Tilly reluctantly used her card, now the bill had reached £625.00. Tilly would have been happy to pay half, but Jack insisted when he discussed the weekend away, that he would pay, and would never think of asking a lady to pay for the weekend, he was a gentleman saying he could afford the weekend away. 'Tilly, I won't be able to drop you off at your home, I will drop you off at the nearest train station to Bamburgh, so I can head up to Scotland.' Jack said with a false look of sadness 'That's ok.' replied Tilly. She was quite relieved, she was not sure what to make of the time they spent together, it certainly was not anything that she thought it would be, in fact it so resonated with some of Bob's behaviour, but somehow different, she really could not put her finger on it. She did not inquire with regards to the money, as Jack's mum was unwell, and not really being the appropriate time to ask. Jack dropped her off at Berwick, where she was able to get a train direct to home.

 As she got hold of her case, she espied a nice little b&b with a sign saying vacancies. She waited for Jack to disappear, as he thought she was going straight home. Once his car was out of view, she went and knocked on the door. A smallish lady answered the door, with grey hair done in a 1940's style, full makeup, a 1940's dress, with an apron tied around her waist, wearing a pair of rubber gloves and a loo brush in her hand. Tilly was smiling to herself, she had never been greeted by a loo brush before. 'Can I help you?' The lady enquired. 'Well, yes I hope so, I see you have vacancies, I don't suppose you have a room for two nights do you?' Tilly was hoping that the answer would be yes. 'Yes my dear, come in, let me get rid of the loo brush, we don't need that while we are getting you booked in.' Tilly saw her wandering down the hallway, to discard the loo brush. 'Right, now were we? as she flustered around the desk trying to find a pen. Tilly waited patiently. 'Oh here we are, the pen, silly me, I am always losing pens,' she smiled. 'Now I have got a lovely cosy room upstairs that overlooks the beautiful views, I think you will like staying in that room.' Yes, that does sound nice, thank you,' said Tilly. 'Not sure if you are interested, but in the winter season I offer evening meals, as it's not so busy.' ' Yes, I would like that please, what time is dinner?' Tilly enquired. 'I do evening meals for 6.30pm in the dining room where you have your breakfast.' She replied. 'Sounds wonderful, I look forward to my evening meal.' replied Tilly looking forward to spending some long awaited time on her own. 'Ok Tilly, is it ok to call you Tilly?' 'Yes of course' she replied, so let's get you settled in your room. Follow me, by the way my name is Jessica, but people call me Jess for short.' 'Good to meet you Jess.' Tilly picked up her case, and other luggage and followed Jess to her room. She opened the door. Tilly was so happy. It was such a cosy room, the little leaded windows were very cute with white anglaise curtains, with peach tie backs, the bed had a lovely floral peach bedspread, a lovely bedside lamps which gave out a soft warm ambiance to the room and in the corner, a selection of books and games. It was so quaint. Tilly put the kettle on, opened her case to put something more comfortable on and just lazed on the bed, as it was a dreary day, she put the bedside lamps on and cosied up under the duvet. She was reflecting on the weekend, well one and a bit days to be exact. She did not think she could feel this bad in such a short space of time. He was like an escaped animal, the way he had sex, was like something back in the stone age days. I know I cannot continue with this, whatever this is.... Knowing the universe has divine timing, she was glad she went this weekend, now knowing that she would not waste anymore time on him. Tilly had to play this, as she was owed money. She had promised her mum that she would take her up to see Morag. How the hell is that going to work!!! Now I know why he picked the most expensive bottle of wine, he knew he was never going to pay for anything. Right, I am done with this bloody reflection. I am going to enjoy these couple of days. This is the first time since I got divorced, leaving my matrimonial home, that I have had some space that has nothing to do with my mum, but nobody knows where I am and I can just relax. Unknowingly to Tilly, her mum, knew something did not feel right with her daughter, she could sense it, she also realised when looking out of her window that Tilly's car was still there, also knowing that Isla would have knocked on the door, and not waited outside. Edith was concerned for Tilly for she does not really know where she is and just hoping that she was truthful about her staying in the Lake District.

    Tilly later looked out of the window, and decided to go for a quick walk, as it was getting dark outside. She only went for a quick stroll to see what was around so she had some idea of where to go tomorrow. It was getting chilly so she headed back to the b&b. When she came through the door, she could smell the homemade beef cobbler cooking. She went upstairs and got herself together for her evening meal. Jess, the landlady, showed Tilly to her table. There was also another couple who were eating as well, on the next table, they politely said hello to each other. Tillys evening meal was brought to her table, it looked so good. She had a glass of wine, then tucked into chocolate brownies with fresh cream for pudding. Tilly could not wait to go upstairs to her cosy room, Tilly opened the door, the lamps were still on, she put the TV on and found a pile of books beside the TV, she found herself a good romantic book to read. Mmm, I think I need to read what a romantic weekend or even life should be like. Tilly thought, I don't think I have ever experienced romance or normal, well I guess one day I might. Fortunately she had put in some PJs and dressing gown, and squashed the sexy nightwear behind the netting in the case. Oh I am so loving being on my own, I don't think I could have done anything like this before as I had lost all my confidence. Now I feel strong enough to be my own person, who does not need to be with a man, who thinks he can treat me like some prostitute. She made herself a coffee, and snuggled down to read her book, things have certainly turned out as they were supposed to be. She thought to herself. As Tilly was reading the book, she came across something similar to what had just happened to her, about this woman called April, who fell for a man who treated her badly, in every way, she did manage to escape him, and was getting to know herself again, as she had had a succession of abusive relationships, but this one was the one who had taught her, what she needed to know about herself, over the last few years. Tilly was hoping that she could get to the end of the book by tomorrow night, if not she thought, I will pay for it, I need to see how this woman ends up in her life, maybe I can get a few tips as I am not going be drawn into these damaging men anymore. Having said that Pete is a gentleman he is lovely.

Tilly woke up bright and early feeling very refreshed, she got dressed, went down to have her breakfast, then decided to go for a walk. She felt she needed to be with nature, so walking around the woods that were nearby, with the frost crunching underneath her trainers, the wind gently blowing through the trees, some were so high, she stood and looked up, it was like the trees were an umbrella sheltering her from the gusts of wind every so often. She came across a little river, where there were a few ducks, their little webbed feet, making tiny waves as they paddled past. Oh my goodness, this is just perfect, she made her way out, to find the cafe that she saw last night when she went for a wander. She did not realise how far she had walked, but she soon saw the little cafe, with the open sign on the door. She opened the door and found a table, it was quite busy. She ordered some cheesy chips and hot chocolate with marshmallows, and just sat people watching. Some people with southern accents, some with Scottish and even a bit of German going on to. Once Tilly had finished. She headed to the train station to see what time the trains were going to Bamburgh, there was a train due at 11.15am on Monday, she would be home by midday. It was certainly getting chilly. Tilly could see the moon as the light was fading. She strolled back to the b&b, and sat and chatted to Jess. At this time of year it was relatively quiet, so it was easy to sit and have a chat. They covered all subjects, and found out that Jess was also quite spiritual, using crystals and smudge sticks to cleanse the energies, when she felt that the occupants of a room left a negative energy in the room. Tilly sat by the fire, while Jess prepared an evening meal, it was only Tilly tonight, so they sat and ate together, which was nice for the both of them, they shared a bottle of wine. 'Thank you, I have loved staying here, I will definitely come back here when I feel I need to recharge my batteries, needing some space,' Tilly replied. 'I'm so pleased that you have enjoyed your stay. It would be lovely to see you again. I thoroughly enjoyed meeting you and the wonderful conversations. It is very refreshing to meet a like minded soul.' Jess replied. 'Yes it certainly is. 'I am going to go up to my room now to get my case packed ready for the morning, and enjoy my evening of peace and quiet. Oh by the way, may I ask, I have found a book that I have started reading. but have not managed to finish it all, can I pay for the book, so you can replace it with another book?' 'Oh don't you worry about that, just take the book, nothing worse than not knowing the ending of a book, if you ever come back just bring it with you.' 'Oh thank you, that is so kind. I will definitely be back,' Tilly continued 'so yes I will bring it with me. Goodnight, I will see you in the morning for breakfast.' "Goodnight, " said Jess. "Sleep well.' 'You too,' replied Tilly. Tilly woke up quite early on Monday morning, feeling quite sad she was leaving. She loved this time on her own, she enjoyed herself there, more than the time she had spent with Jack. She got all her luggage together, had her breakfast, paid for her bill, and headed out to the station. She boarded the train, heading back home, not quite sure what to say to her mum, should she ask questions, which Tilly knew 100% would happen. She was feeling quite sheepish. The train pulled into the station. She was hoping that there was a taxi available, but had to wait about 10 minutes. While she was waiting she was feeling so guilty for lying to her mum, as her mum would know that she was not telling her the truth.

'Hi Mum, have you been ok?' 'Hello Pet,' 'Yes, I have been ok. Did you have a good time? You are back early, thought you would be later than this.' 'Well Yes, Isla had to go to her daughter's to look after her granddaughter this afternoon.' replied Tilly, already knowing that her mum had her suspicions. 'You must have left an exceptionally early pet, the drive is a couple of hours or more.' 'Oh, we went by train,' Tilly said, now knowing 100% that by her mum's tone, that she had an inkling that she knew something. 'Oh really,' said Edith, 'there is not a direct link from Bamburgh to Windermere, it takes hours. You literally have to go up to Scotland and come back down to the Lake District.' Edith replied. Tilly could not hide, her face was burning, she felt hot, and hated lying to her mum. She was thinking how the bloody hell have I got here, lying to my mum, lying to Isla and Pete, all because I got swept along on this weekend of passion, that was more like a damp squib. How has he managed to manipulate me? I would not even know when that took place, it's so subtle and equally scary. 'Tilly, if you want to talk you can pet. I know something did not feel right from the minute you stepped out of the door.' 'Oh, Mum I'm so sorry, I met up with Jack for a weekend away, I did not know how you would take it, I've never done anything like this before.' Tilly knew her mum would never interfere in her life, it was because she was concerned about her. 'Oh Tilly, it's not for me to judge you, are old enough to make your own decisions, and run your life as you see fit.' 'I will say Tilly, I knew you had a crush on Jack years ago, you used to follow him around like a little sheepdog.' 'Morag has had a lot of problems with Jack with regards to money, he is a heavy gambler. She has given him money, bailing him out so many times, she now refuses to help him, he is living with Morag, because he has lost his home.' Tilly stood there shell shocked, the colour drained from her face, she was not ready to tell her mum that she had paid for the weekend and it answered his need to watch racehorsing Friday and Saturday, seeing him get agitated he was obviously losing money that he did not have, and the reason why his cards had been declined. 'Mum,' said Tilly, 'I have something to tell you. When we were away Jack got a call from one of the care nurses, who advised Jack to go home, as Morag had been taken poorly. I don't want to upset you, but I think you would be angry with me, if I hadn't told you.' 'Oh no,' Edith sat there in shock, 'but I only saw her a few weeks ago.' Tilly went over to her mum to comfort her. 'I have not heard from Jack since he dropped me off at Berwick station.' 'So, where have you been Tilly?' 'I stayed in a little b&b in Berwick.' Tilly replied 'I felt I could not come home, as I had lied to you.' Tilly started to cry, 'I'm so sorry mum, I have never lied to you, I have never felt the need to, I feel so stupid.' Tilly was still crying as she realised she was only being used for Jack's pleasure. she felt so stupid to fall for this. 'Look,' said Edith,' we all have to experience different things in life, particularly relationships. How will you know who's right for you, if you dont have different scenarios to explore?' 'I will text him shortly,' replied Tilly.

Tilly got her case unpacked, put her clothes away, then sat on the bed, texting Jack about Morag, he finally rang her on Tuesday morning. 'Hi Tilly, it's Jack, sorry I have not rang, it's been very hectic here, mum is in hospital, she is still in there.' 'Jack, don't worry, I totally understand the situation,' 'still' she paused. 'I suppose you can go and check on your own home, while your mum is in hospital, to make sure it's ok.' 'Yes', replied Jack. 'Funnily enough I was going today to collect the post and make sure everything is ok, it is not far from mums, she lives in Edinburgh too.' Tilly is now beginning to realise how much Jack lies, where he lives, his money situation, but something inside of Tilly still wanted to fix this man from his fate. 'Ok Jack, I will let you get on, I will wait to hear from you, my mum wanted to know how your mum was, that's all. 'By the way, are you going to transfer the money over?' Before she could say goodbye, Jack had ended the call yet again, but the empathic Tilly, again put the weekend down to him worrying about his mum. The reality of it all, was that Jack was not close to his mum anymore, because she refuses to bail him out anymore. If Morag did pass away, he had a sister and Morag has changed her will, to read that when the house is sold, the money Morag has given him, is to be taken of the final settlement to be given to his sister, and any remaining money is then split between the two of them. Which means he will not have enough to buy another home. His business has been bled dry by his gambling, and was only thinking of himself in this matter. Tilly was still in shock, how could this be happening? She thought, we have such a chemistry and attraction, he must be my soulmate, to have this connection with him. She sat quiet for a while working out what this is all about. Tilly had come a long way from her divorce and how broken she felt. She felt a surge of power rise up, as if her intuition wanted her to feel this power surge for her to start looking at this situation on a rational level. Tilly for for first time started to think about all the red flags that had come up, all the alarm bells she had been shown, but decided to push them away into the back of her mind, but now was the time to bring them forward again to look at them for what they really are, before she got so deep into the relationship, she would be swept away in yet another narcissist relationship. Tilly felt confused, for she felt the same type of feeling that she experienced with her ex husband only this was so different, in fact she would say it was worse. She knew where she stood with Bob, he would throw his weight around, with a few punches and kicks, swearing and shouting at her, her whole life with Bob was treading on eggshells, never knowing what type of mood he would be in when he arrived home. But Jack was different, he would be silent, not talk, give nasty undermining comments that were detrimental to her, then an hour or so later, he was the kindest sweetest man. He was not a man of many words, in fact hardly any, he stonewalled her as well, but would send flowers, chocolates and gifts, to make her feel special, love bombing her. When they were away, she felt she was auditioning for a porn movie, he was so cold and distant, no empathy. Tilly was beginning to see what the weekend was all about. It was Jack coercing her with gifts and putting her under pressure to have a weekend away. Tilly had told him that it would be a few months down the line, but here she is five weeks into seeing Jack, and there she was booking the hotel, and now over £600 out of pocket. Tilly, was thinking that there was no way she could never speak to Pete, how the bloody hell did I agree to that proposition.

Right Tilly Fellowes you need to wake up and wake up fast, mum has given me the most valuable pieces of information. He is homeless, lives with his mum, has no money, horse racing is obviously his work, he is just lying constantly, I don't think he even has a business left. I need to put a stop to this now, maybe this was a blessing in disguise going on that weekend. I now have more information which has been revealed to me. Maybe, this is all for a reason, actually it is for a reason. 'Tilly,' called Edith, 'would you like some lunch?' 'Yes please mum, I will be down in a few minutes.' 'Ok pet,' Tilly came downstairs to help her mum bring the lunch to the dining table. 'So pet, how are you now? You seem to look as if you are feeling a bit calmer,' as Edith looked intently into Tillys eyes to see what reaction she would give. 'Yes I am Mum, I do need to talk, I need to get things in perspective, what you have told me about Jack and what I have experienced has helped me put things into place in my head.' 'Mum, I don't think Jack tells the truth at all, he has led me to believe that he had his own home, was financially comfortable, and still worked part time with his own business. He also told me in the beginning that he and his first wife drifted apart, that's why they divorced. He cheated on his second wife, turns out he cheated on them both. I'm not sure I can trust him, his moods change very quickly. I have only known him for a few weeks and I am already beginning to feel I am not in control of my own mind and thoughts, quite weird really.' Tilly looked away from her mum, as she spoke, as she could feel the tears welling up in her eyes, she did not want her mum to see how upset she was. 'Jack said he did not want me talking to Pete anymore, he acted like we were in some long term relationship, I cannot believe that I actually agreed to it. This has certainly brought up deep feelings within her, that she needs to sit with to be able to process. How the hell do these narcissists get into your head so quickly, it's so scary, Mum?' 'Oh Tilly, I'm so sorry, I did not know how far you Jack had moved on, but he's clearly not for you. I cannot tell my daughter what to do, but you are going backwards, not forwards. That's why I said to take it slowly, I knew his past from Morag. It's not my place to start telling you things, as he may have changed from those days. Looks like he has not changed one bit. 'I have to ask Tilly,' Edith added, knowing that Tilly was feeling slightly agitated, but she felt it was best to ask now, so that the saga was over and done with. 'Does he know you have money in the bank from your divorce?' Edith knew by Tilly's facial expression, as she turned round that something was afoot. 'Please Tilly, please don't tell me he knew.' Tilly sat at the table, feeling so hot and flustered, angry and tearful, mustering up the strength to say "Yes". 'Ok, pet, look don't get in a state, I could see earlier that you were feeling upset, I could tell then that something had already happened, is that so?' 'Yes Mum,' Tilly was feeling like she was a little girl again who had thrown her ball over someone's garden and broke a window pane on the garden shed. 'The thing is Mum, I don't actually recall telling him that information, it's not something I would discuss. But I do remember when I booked the hotel, Jack said to me "well you have money from your divorce don't you?" and I replied "well yes." 'Oh mum, how clever is he, he caught me out with a simple question.' Tilly was feeling so stupid. Her thoughts were racing ten to the dozen, how the bloody hell am I here in this situation, tears were streaming down her cheeks, searching for the words to come out of her mouth. 'Yes, I paid the deposit for the hotel, and then the final bill, as his cards all declined.' 'So how much does he owe you Tilly' Its £625.00' Tilly said in between the sobs,' I know I have been a fool, I thought I would have learnt my lesson with Bob, the thing is Mum, they are similar in their traits but act differently, I did ask him if he wanted me to pay my half of the bill, but he was adamant that he was well off and he would want to pay for the weekend. As he had a lot on his mind with his mum I did not want to put pressure on him. 'Tilly, now calm down, it is not your fault,' replied Edith with a sympathetic look. 'He did say he would pay the deposit before we went. I did ask a few times before we went away, but he never transferred it over to me. We ate in the restaurant, drinks, room service that was £475.00, They wanted an extra night that's why they wanted that amount of money. I did let him know how much the room was at night, he said at the very beginning make sure you book something that is expensive and luxurious, so I followed what he said.' 'Right Tilly,' said Edith feeling sorry for Tilly who had clearly been conned, by somebody she thought of as a close childhood friend. 'When you ring him to ask about Morag, ask about the money he owes you.' 'Mum, I'm so sorry I have completely messed this up for you, seeing Morag again.' 'Now Tilly, don't be silly, Edith said, I am thankful that I got to spend that time with her, I never thought I would ever see her again, and she is now in hospital.'

Edith got up and put her arms around Tilly, 'Pet, we can all get carried away with passion, chemistry and attraction, said Edith, but it does not mean it lasts forever, Jack is a charmer and very charismatic, I could see that when I first saw him. You can have all those elements in a relationship, but there has to be more to it, a sense of feeling safe and secure, love and trust that goes much deeper, that's what makes a relationship special. I know you won't want me to say this, but I think maybe he was hoping you may bail him out of any debts he has, or maybe hoping that you would buy a home, so you can live together.' Tilly, sat clasping her hands to her face. 'You know mum,' realising what her mum said, 'I think you could be right, even when his cards declined, he did say to me, well you have enough money to pay.' 'Pet, put this down to a narrow escape, in future, do not give your data to any man unless you are sure he is being genuine, give it at least three to six months, never discuss your financial situation, your past history regarding relationships, or anything else, unless you feel comfortable telling them.' 'Mum, I thought he was my soulmate.' 'Well, maybe he was, but came back in this lifetime to give you a lesson, on finding your self worth, to value you and not going back into the behavioural patterns you had with Bob. Thank goodness you have realised so early on, it shows how much you have grown and evolved. No man has the right to tell you who you can and cannot see, what to wear, how you behave, or anything else for that matter, you are your own person. Tilly, when you speak with him with regards to the money he owes, if he does not pay in the next week, do not prolong this as he may be doing that, so he still has contact with you. You may have to cut your losses on this one, you are better away from him. Please Tilly, don't think it's just about money, it's the principles and morals that I look at,' explained Edith. 'I really need to get myself together before I ring Jack, I am so bloody angry at him, I think I could explode, and that definitely won't help matters. You know Mum like you said it's not about the money really, it's the fact that he lied, knowing full well, he did not have the money and had no intention of paying for it.' Tilly saw a wine bottle on the table, she grabbed that and a glass and filled it to the brim. 'I don't think I have ever seen you drink a glass of wine in two minutes, Tilly.' 'Mum, I am so angry, I don't normally feel this sort of emotion, but I am sick to death of how these narcissists think they can do as they please, and not give a damn or care about the pain they have caused, their feeling of entitlement, I am so done Mum, all the feelings have come to the surface again. I need to see where they come from, what makes me drawn to these types of men.' 'Well, that's good Tilly, it shows how strong you have become, we all have a limit of how much we can tolerate. Your dad may have had a temper and was very controlling. I am certainly not condoning that in any way, but today's abusers are in another league completely.'

After an hour or so had passed, she texted Jack to see if she would get a response from him, she was only going to enquire to see if his mum was feeling any better. He did text back after a few hours saying his mum was getting worse, and that he would ring her later. Tilly felt she could not tell her mum the news as it would send her spiralling down herself. Tilly was on her phone texting Stanley as she had not spoken to him in a while, and Jack's number appeared on her phone ringing her, she went upstairs to take the call. 'Hey Tilly, how are you,' Jack said. 'Yes, I'm fine. Thank you, sorry to hear your mum has got worse. Let's hope that she starts getting well again.' 'Why are you laughing Jack, what is so funny?' Tilly added. 'Just had a flashback to our away day,' Jack said. 'You were trying to look so sexy in your cami top and lacy knickers, but it was not much of a turn on.' Tilly could feel her energy dropping like a stone. Everything she had built herself up to be, strong and confident went in seconds, she had always had hang ups about her body, especially after having her children, which left her with stretch marks and boobs a lot lower than before, but she was proud she had fulfilled herself in carrying her two babies in her womb and watching her tummy growing bigger waiting to meet her beautiful babies, that experience will never leave her. Bob's remarks always made her feel that she was not worthy of being loved and desired as his wife; this had a massive impact on Tilly. Now with Jack saying what he said, she felt so embarrassed. Tilly found her composure 'Oh really' Tilly came back, she was not going to take anymore shit from him. 'So what about your performance, it was nothing like the text you sent me, about how good you are between the sheets, quite frankly I found it rather disappointing actually Jack.' Tilly was so shocked with herself, where did that come from she thought, that's not like me. Jack did not answer, he was not used to a woman putting him down, he then came back as the victim. 'Well, I have been worried about my mum, it may have affected my love making skills.' Tilly was aghast, who the bloody hell does he think he is using his mum's poor health on his sexual performance. We were actually discussing your mum, until you decided to devalue me. Tilly knew she needed contact so her mum knew what was going on with Morag. 'Er, while we are on the subject of the weekend, I would really appreciate the money you owe me, I don't have

£625.00 spare, if you wanted me to pay my half you should have said, I would not have had any problem with that at all.' 'Tilly, I can't believe you have discussed money at a time like this.' replied Jack. 'The same could be said of you, being detrimental about me, laughing rather inappropriately don't you think?' Tilly could feel her anger rising. She ended the call, sitting staring at the wall, how the hell did that just happen? In a few minutes he's made me feel worthless, insecure and my self esteem has nose dived in one sentence. Although Tilly stood her ground this is something she had never experienced in her life, even though Bob made Tilly feel worthless, he had never used that tactic on her. Jack did not ring back. For Tilly that was just as well, her body was shaking with anger, her stomach was hurting, she felt sick and her head was all over the place, she felt hurt, and emotionally bruised, how can a man make you feel like this, this has been such a whirlwind in the last few weeks. Tilly composed herself and went down stairs. 'You ok pet? I heard you raising your voice which is not like you. 'Yes, sorry Mum, I had words with Jack, he is something else. Oh by the way Morag is still in hospital.' She put her coat on, got her phone and went for a walk down to the beach. She had tears running down her cheeks, only this time last week, she was so excited for her weekend away, now she was in bits. She kept going over in her head what she had done wrong, self-doubting herself, how she physically felt about her body, she could not even talk to Isla, as she had not told her about the weekend away. The biting wind from the North sea was blowing the tiny sand granules stinging her face, and sticking to her face as her tears were falling down her cheeks. She covered herself with a big cosy blanket scarf to protect herself. Although it was cold it was exhilarating and definitely cleared away the cobwebs. She stood and looked out to sea for a few minutes, going over in her head that she was worthy, she owned herself and was starting to love who she was and deserved to be loved and cherished, just as she would love and cherish her man. I have to keep thinking this, I have come too far now, to go back. That's not my journey anymore, it's about moving forward all the time. She turned and glanced over her shoulder one more time at the sea, before taking a slow walk back home to her mum, pleased that she had worked this man out before he took a hold on her life.

CHAPTER 14

After spending that time on her own at the b&b, Tilly felt that after Christmas it was the right time to look deeper into her life with regards to where her future was going and what she wanted to do. Fortunately she had enough funds and savings to buy a house and maybe start a small business. After going to London and finding the vintage shop which she loved, it has given her the same idea there is nothing like that up where she lives, so it would be a specialised shop, and the lady who owned the shop was online too. Tilly was looking forward and ready to forge her own life now. Tillys phone was ringing, it was Isla, she felt guilty answering the phone especially as Isla will definitely ask how things are with Jack. She knew she needed to speak with her at some stage. 'Hi Isla, how are you,' Tilly enquired. 'Hi Tils, how are you doing? It seems ages since we last spoke, so what's new, how are you and Jack?' 'Yes I'm fine,' Tilly spoke in a rather quiet voice. 'You ok?' 'Well sort of Isla, 'I have something to tell you, but I don't want you to be angry with me.' 'Tilly, you could never make me angry just tell me, it can't be that bad surely.' 'Well against my better judgement I agreed to go away for the weekend with Jack, a lot sooner than I wanted to, but felt pressured into going and I could not tell mum, as I did not think she would like that, so I said I was going with you... Isla I'm so sorry to bring you into my lies,' Tilly was getting upset as she was still processing what had happened with Jack. 'Oh Tilly, don't get upset, of course I don't mind you saying that to your mum, I would have done the same if that had been me.' 'Really,' Tilly said. Astonished that Isla replied with that answer. 'Yes really' Isla continued 'there's nothing wrong in that, you're just being economical with the truth, not having to tell your mum.' 'But Isla, I am sixty one not sixteen' she replied. 'You are living with your mum if you lived on your own, no problem, it's only because of your situation.

'So what happened?' 'Yes, you are right Isla!!! You will never believe it but Jack has traits of a narcissist; he has lied to me on so many levels of his life, well we were only there one day. One of the carers looking after his mum, rang and told him his mum was unwell, and he had to go home, thank goodness she rang because I don't know if I could have lasted until Monday. He was so selfish and made me feel very insecure, when I see you I will fill you in. I did see the red flags again, but I was in complete denial, I just kept thinking it was me, due to my past experience with Bob, but no… it was not me at all, I'm so pleased it was five weeks and not five years, I have not got that time to waste on men, who think they are entitled to do what the bloody hell they want to do. It has made me feel a bit wobbly, but I'm stronger now thank goodness.' 'Oh no Tilly, I'm sorry to hear that, I know when I last spoke to you, you said about the attraction and chemistry, and that he may be your soulmate, I thought how brilliant it was. Tilly, did you know on a spiritual level the universe sometimes sends in a soulmate on that level to test you out, they trigger you with their selfish ways, try to control you, so you start to realise that you are worth more than how they make you feel. You then start to question their actions, speaking your truth, not being compliant with any of their bullshit. It's called empowering yourself, once you get to that point you are near the finishing post, because you have seen behind the mask that they put up, once you have seen them for their true colours, they either retreat, or try to continue with the facade, but Tilly it looks pretty much like you have done that, so that is fantastic. I know it can be very painful.' replied Isla, hoping that she could help her best friend understand how some soulmates cross your path. 'Really, can that happen, Isla?' 'Yes of course.' 'They have come in with the attraction and chemistry, so you start feeling connected. This combination is so powerful, it takes over your whole being, otherwise it would not work. The universe wants you to be strong to find who you are, not what somebody wants you to be. Of course soulmates do meet, feeling all those emotions, but their journey is to work together in this lifetime and enjoy their soulmate union.' 'Thanks for that Isla, that actually has helped me understand a bit more

'How are things going with Dave?' 'Well, I have to say that we went for a drink together last week, and he was the perfect gent. I really like him and I think he likes me too. He has said some nice things to me, and I have to him as well, but still being married to Brian, does not make this easy, but for the time being, I see Dave and I as friends, should it go further, then I will need a conversation with Brian about divorcing.' said Isla feeling more content in her life. 'Oh Isla, that's great news, so pleased for you, just take it slowly, my journey with Jack has felt like I have been hit by a steam train. I'm still trying to process my thoughts mainly on what a stupid cow I was to get pulled in so easily.' replied Tilly still reeling with anger with her altercation earlier with Jack. 'Tilly, please don't beat yourself up, you just got carried away, it's easy done, you also knew him from your past so you had an element of trust that you would not have had, had he been a complete stranger coming into your life. Tilly, do you fancy lunch at the cafe? It seems ages since we sat in that cosy corner, watching the world go by and just chatting.' 'Oh Isla, yes,yes,yes. I would love to meet up' 'Well how about this Thursday, is 1ish ok' said Isla. 'I will come and pick you up. It's bloody freezing out there, I can see Edith as well.' 'Perfect' said Tilly, 'I look forward to seeing you, enjoy your yoga class tonight.' 'Yes I will, see you soon bye Tilly' 'Bye Isla.' No sooner had the call ended, Pete was calling her. 'Hi Tilly, how are you? Just thought I would let you know that I can come up for the New Year.' 'Oh Pete, that is lovely news, you can stay here if you want,' 'are you sure Tilly?' 'Yes I'm sure mum said it herself, she loves seeing you.' 'Brilliant, er' Pete hesitated, 'I have to ask Tilly, I hope this is not encroaching on your time with Jack, I don't want to cause any problems for you?' standing crossing his fingers that he was not on the scene anymore. 'Pete, you certainly won't be doing that, I have found out that he is not really a nice person at all. Put it this way he has traits the same as Bob, anyway Pete there was never a relationship, well not from my side, but from his side yes, we just went out a few times that's all.' Pete tried to keep his happy voice at a tone that did not show his excitement. 'Oh no Tils, sorry for you having to experience that again.' 'You know Pete, I think everything happens for a reason, you were right I needed to be able to make comparisons with men, but having Bob then Jack, I definitely know what type of man I would like in my life.' 'Pete was hoping that Tilly would say him….. but on reflection, was pleased she did not, as he did not want to be on the rebound from Jack, as she was still accepting who he was as a person. I can dream that one day Tilly sees me that way. Tilly has been thinking a lot more about Pete, she was starting to get a comparison on how Pete and Jack are so different. 'Pete, can I run something past you? I have been thinking about my future, and I feel it's time to get my own home again, and thinking of starting up a business up here, but not sure where, what do you think ?' asked Tilly. 'Well, I think it's brilliant news, it shows you are ready to be independent, and create your new life, a business sounds good, do you have any ideas yet Tilly?' 'Oh yes I do. Do you remember when I went to London with Isla, when we came across that lovely vintage shop in Carnaby Street that sold vintage clothing and decor. I really like the idea of recycling vintage items. A lot of people are using vintage memorabilia in their homes, dressing in vintage clothing. I would love to find a place big enough to incorporate other businesses, renting out pitches for other crafters to sell their items, a display area for artists, well everything including sculptors, potters, a place where you can create a community for musicians to play, for people to come and enjoy. there does not seem to be anywhere for this type of thing up here.' 'Wow, Tilly you certainly have come up with a brilliant idea. You seem to have a pretty clear plan, creating a community that helps all creatives to come together. Yes of course I would always help you, it sounds exciting to be involved with something like this.' "Oh Pete, you sound more excited than me,' 'she said laughing, 'I will come to you for help if that's ok, you have had a business for years, but this is definitely something I will think about once I have everything in my head down on paper.' They carried on chatting for at least another hour or so each bringing and sharing their news with each other. 'Pete it's been lovely talking to you today, thank you, I need to go as I'm going to my meditation group tonight.' 'No problem Tilly, your welcome, yes it's been just great chatting to you. Enjoy your evening, take care, lovely lady.' 'I will. You too, bye.'

   Tilly came off the phone to Pete feeling the most positive she had felt in months, looking forward to the meditation group she was attending at the therapy centre, in fact it is Lucy the counsellor whom she saw holding the sessions. As she was getting ready, she saw that Jack was calling her. It had been quite a few days since she had heard from him. 'Hi Jack, how are things with you?' 'Oh, not so good,' Jack replied, 'I have called to let you know that mum passed away last night, her breathing just got worse, she had pneumonia as well.' 'Oh Jack, I'm so sorry to hear that news. I will let my mum know, at least they got to see each other one last time. Will you let me know when the funeral is, as I would like to come and pay my respects and for mum too, as she would not be able to deal with the stress.' 'Yes of course, can we meet up Tilly. I feel I have neglected you lately.' 'To be honest Jack, I have realised that I am not ready for any relationship with anyone, I am still finding who I am. I don't need to get caught up in emotions that I am not ready for, if you want to be friends that's fine with me, 'Tilly replied. Jack was very surprised with Tillys reply. 'Oh right, ok Tilly, I did not expect that, I am rather disappointed actually.' Jack had never had a woman who spoke like that to him before, he was so used to women following his command. 'Actually Jack, I'm surprised you are bringing up this subject, considering your mum has just passed away, I would have thought you would have enough to organise with the funeral arrangements without talking about relationships. Anyway Jack, I'm on my way out, don't forget to let me know when the arrangements have been made.' ' Bye said Jack in a despondent voice, 'bye Tilly replied. 'She felt so proud of herself no way was she putting up with Jack's arrogance any longer or being treated like his possession. She was thinking on her walk to the meditation group, " who the bloody hell does he think he is?' 'Tilly felt quite annoyed that his call was about his poor mum and then it goes right back onto him, selfish bastard. I will tell mum when I get back home, I need to be able to spend time with her. Tilly got to the therapy centre, and was greeted by Lucy, her counsellor, and several other people. It looked so warm and inviting. The candles and incense sticks were giving a lovely ambiance to the room. There were predominantly women, but a couple of men had joined the group. They all sat in a circle. Lucy asked everyone to introduce themselves. Tilly felt a bit nervous, she had not done anything like this before, when it got to her turn, she was actually ok. Lucy looked at her and smiled as if to say well done, you would not have done that six months ago. Tilly was happy that she went to the meditation group, they were lovely people, with good energy, a great way of making new friends. They all discussed their meditation, and what they had experienced. Tilly felt a bit silly saying what had happened in case it was not right, she did start to join in when the meditation was finished and surprised herself with the information she was getting through. 'It's time for us to end the meditation group tonight. I cannot believe how quickly the time has gone, has anybody got any questions they would like to ask about the meeting tonight?' The room stayed silent, but with smiles on all the faces. 'Well, I take it from your smiles, you were all happy with the meditation tonight?' Tilly spoke up and said how lovely it was to have a group to go to with like minded people, then everyone joined and agreed with Tilly, they were all looking forward to the following week. Tilly was not looking forward to going back home, as she had to have an awkward conversation with her mum. When she got in, her mum was still up.

'Mum, I need to speak to you, I have had some sad news,' Tilly went across to hold her hand. They are hands that had made such beautiful clothes, now looking quite frail. 'Jack rang me earlier to say that Morag had passed away last night in hospital.' Edith turned to Tilly, her eyes welling up with tears. 'I know this sounds a bit weird,' said Edith, 'but I had a dream last night about Morag, I felt maybe something had happened, it was as if she was saying goodbye to me, but I was not sure if she had passed, or was on her way to the spirit world.' She gently sobbed into her handkerchief. 'Oh Mum, I'm so sorry for your loss, and that you never got to see her again. I know you have known her since you were a little girl, and was your best friend.' Tilly sat and cradled her, until she felt more peaceful. 'I will go and make us a nice strong cup of tea.'

Edith turned off the TV, and just went back over the good memories of her childhood friendship and the memories of both their husbands being friends, the four of them, going dancing, and enjoying going out for days, before the children came along, then more memories were made together with their families. Tilly brought in the cups of tea, it was just what Edith needed. 'Mum,' said Tilly, would you like me to stay with you tonight?' 'No Pet, it's ok, I just want to be on my own, but thank you.' 'Well if you are sure, if you do need me, shout out for me.' 'Thank you pet,' Edith drank her tea and went to bed. Tilly sent a message to Isla to cancel their lunch date as she did not want to leave her mum, she knew her mum would be grieving. Tilly let her brother and sister know, as they both knew Morag, after the families spent time together for holidays, Christmas and birthdays. Jack contacted Tilly to let her know the funeral arrangements, she informed her mum of the date asking if she wanted to go. Edith replied 'I don't think I can go Tilly, I am not feeling too well at the moment and the drive there and back would be very tiring for me. I don't feel strong enough.' 'That's ok, Mum , I will go and pay our respects to Morag, I will sort out a wreath and you can write your tribute to your dear friend.' Tilly had seen her mum decline over the last couple of days since hearing the news. Tilly was concerned that her mum was thinking bad thoughts of her dying, like she was a few months back. Tilly felt the need to ring Pete, she just needed a friendly voice to talk to. 'Hi Tilly, for what I owe the pleasure of your call?' 'Hi Pete, 'Tilly you sound sad, are you ok?' 'Yes mum's best friend Morag has passed away. I'm just so worried about mum, she goes into these dark places when things happen like this, especially as she is getting older.' 'Oh sorry to hear that Tilly, but unfortunately that is part of life, we eventually all have to leave the earth to return home again.' 'Tilly can I ask, would it be ok to come and visit you again, I thoroughly enjoyed my stay with you?' I hope you don't mind me asking, when you have rang to tell me the sad news.' 'No, of course not. Actually, I think this may be the tonic that mum needs right now Pete.' replied Tilly, thinking to herself it would be lovely to see him too. 'Maybe I could get the train up, it's a lot quicker than driving.' 'Yes of course,' replied Tilly. 'It would be lovely to see you, when were you looking at coming up as I have Morag's funeral to attend this Tuesday? What about Sunday the 23rd and go back on Wednesday?' 'Yes that sounds good, I can come and pick you up from the station, it will save you hanging around for cabs and buses. Will warn you Pete, it's bloody cold up here in the Winter.' 'That's ok Tilly, it can be bloody cold down here as well, I will bring my thermals with me, 'laughed Pete. 'Oh how very fetching' Tilly replied laughing. 'Would you like me to book a room for you?' 'Yes, if that's ok,' replied Pete. Tilly was secretly happy that she was seeing Pete again, they had such a fun time on his last visit. 'How about we catch up next week, let me know what time your train gets into Bamburgh? Take care Pete.' 'You To Tilly, look forward to seeing you soon.

'Tilly was standing in her bedroom looking out of the window. Well that was a nice surprise Tilly thought, and he is coming up for New Year as well. First she must go to the funeral which she is not really looking forward to. Tilly knew she had to talk to Jack about ending the friendship and the money he still owed her, but before the funeral was not really the right time. Tilly rang Isla, to let her know that Pete was coming up again. Tilly also wanted to know how she got with Dave the other evening. 'Hi Tils, how are you?' 'I was just thinking about you, we both seem to be busy at the moment. How's your mum?' she enquired. 'Yes, not too bad, I just did not want to leave her, she seems to have gone downhill since I told her the news, how are you?' 'How did your evening go with Dave?' 'Aww sorry to hear about your mum Tilly, so sad, especially as you get older your friends gradually disappear. Right, yes Dave……. Well, we have been out a few times this week, and we had a kiss the last time we went out, when he dropped me off up the road. It felt very strange kissing another man, but it was lovely to kiss someone again, to experience those feelings. We see each other quite regularly now, we are really enjoying each other's company, we like doing the same things. I think Brian may have his suspicions, but in all fairness he is seeing someone, so what can he really say. Dave has asked the question about my marriage and if I would ever get divorced. I could not really answer, but in the last few weeks, I have found myself thinking about the future. I really don't want to waste anymore of my life trying to fix a marriage that can't be fixed. I want to be happy and enjoy my life without wondering if Brian is coming home that night and what he is up to.' 'You Know, Isla, you are so right, that short episode with

Jack has really jolted me into what type of relationship I would like. I have always gone for charming and charismatic men, just like Bob, I have probably met a few more before I met Bob, but never recognised it. I would like someone who is kind and caring, and we both have similar interests and an understanding of each other,' replied Tilly. 'Well, correct me if I am wrong, but Pete completely fits the bill in every way. 'Is he coming up to support you with your mum,' said Isla. 'Yes, I think so, but he did not want to say that. I have been thinking about him lately but although he likes me, I don't know whether he would want a relationship with me. We have been friends for a long time and I would not like to mess that up if something happened between us and we split up.' Tilly replied. 'Well see how it goes when he comes up. You never know he may been the one all those years ago, but you needed to experience and do that journey with Bob, because there was something you needed to go through to help you grow and evolve spiritually, now he has come back into your life, he is not in any relationship he is a lovely man and nice looking to.' replied Isla. 'Mmm, yes' replied Tilly, 'perhaps I will see it from a different angle, I get so fixed sometimes as to what I think I need, but maybe the universe has a different path and plan.'

'Soooo, what happened when you were away with Jack? Isla continued, Tilly went a bit quiet. 'Are you there Tilly, are you ok?' 'Yes, I am here, I just don't know how to put it into words that's all.' 'Ok,' replied Isla. 'Well, before we went away, he was sending me flowers, my favourite perfume, chocolates, then in another parcel that he had sent me was a pair of sexy black lace knickers and a matching camisole. He was always very sexual on the phone, and would send me sex texts, which I did find very sexy and a turn on, he certainly knew what to do, and knew what to say. On the journey there he kept moving his hand on my thigh. He knew exactly what he was doing, I felt like I wanted him to stop the car and rip his clothes off. When we got to the hotel, we literally had sex as soon as the door was closed. There was no love or affection. Once we had sex he got up and went and had a shower, then put the TV on and sat watching horse racing, he was glued to it, we had sex three times that day. I felt like a prostitute, just there for his pleasure. It was horrible, I know this sounds terrible, but I was glad he got that phone call about his mum being taken unwell. I don't think I could have stayed until the Monday, I felt dirty and used, I have never ever felt like that with Bob, and that is saying something, especially as our marriage was awful, this was just a dirty weekend to him, for me I had expectations, of feeling loved, wanted, cuddles, kissing and holding each other in bed chatting ….. But there is more.' 'Bloody hell Tilly….. More!!!!!'

'Yes more,' Tilly continued, 'he told me to find a hotel, an expensive one, as money was no object, and wanted a top class hotel. He asked me to pay the deposit then he would transfer over the money, but he didn't, and everytime I asked he made some lame excuse, even in the beginning I said I would pay my half, but he refused saying he would pay. Then when we checked out, he knew his cards would decline, he tried them all, to show that he was trying to pay the bill. Then asked me to use my card to pay. It was then £625.00 out of my bank account for literally one day. Because his mum had passed away, it's not really the right time to ask. I did tell my mum, who then told me that Morag had told mum years ago that he was a gambler. That Jacks mum, had bailed him out, he lives with his mum as he had his home repossessed and not even sure if he actually has a business, but has blatantly told me that he does have a business, but semi retired, has money and his own home, all of which are lies, I just feel so stupid Isla, how the hell did I get into this mess. So Isla, that is the story. The only best bit of the weekend, was when he dropped me off at a railway station as he did not have the time to take me home, I found a lovely b&b and stayed there for two days, which helped me to reflect on my life, realising that I am now ready to find my own home. I want to start a small business selling vintage clothing and home decor, like the one in London that we found.' 'Oh my god Tilly, what a journey you have had, but you see from all the bad feelings you have about yourself, you have reflected now on how you want your life to be, which is fantastic. So now you have a direction in which to go in, you should be proud of yourself. I always say everything happens for a reason, but you must get your money back, what a horrible bastard he turned out to be.' replied Isla, shocked that her best friend had to go through this. 'Yes, the exact same words I used, he is a complete and utter bastard, I am only going to the funeral for my mum, to pay her and my respects to his lovely mum, nothing else. I never ever want to see him again after that. Although I think he still thinks we are together in a relationship. He must be very deluded. If he thinks I am giving him my money to bail him out he can think again. I'm truly done with him.' replied Tilly, who was really still seething from his behaviour over the weekend. 'Oh Tilly,' it sure feels like he would want you to bail him out, just shows how arrogant he is. And to treat you like that when it comes to intimacy, knowing your past, he does not give a shit does he?' 'I'm afraid not. Pete did say to me that I needed some comparisons with men in relationships, so I can know what my needs and desires are. To be honest he is quite right, but not this sort of comparison.' 'Have you told Pete about Jack?' enquired Isla 'No way,' said Tilly. 'I said we were meeting up a few times but that was it, I think I would be ashamed of myself to even say anything.' 'I know' replied Isla. 'I understand, that's not an easy thing to declare that to anybody, least of all to Pete.' 'Yes I completely agree with you Isla. I just dont think it's the right time, after all Pete and I are not in any type of relationship. I am just going to enjoy him coming up for a few days, at least this time round I won't be anxious and nervous.' 'Tils have to go, I'm meeting Dave soon and I need to get ready.' 'enjoy your evening Isla, let's try and meet up in a few weeks.' 'Yes, we can still have a chat on the phone,' replied Isla. 'Yes that would be good, I think we are going through similar situations at the moment, ' replied Tilly.

 The day had come for Tilly to go to the funeral of Morag, she set off quite early, as it was nearly an hour's drive and it was at 11am. She was not looking forward to seeing Jack, but she was doing this for her mum, who was very upset when Tilly left the house, as Edith was feeling very guilty that she was not saying goodbye to her dearest friend, but she knew she could not have coped with the funeral as she was feeling very frail. Her health issues had gotten worse over the last few months, her emotions and own fears had played on her mind a lot in the last few weeks.

She knew Tilly was not going to stay for the wake afterwards, and that comforted her not being on her own for too long. Tilly arrived at the crematorium making her way to the chapel, she saw the funeral cortege as they turned the corner to make their way along the cemetery road, Tilly could feel her eyes welling up, the last funeral she went to was when her own father had passed away. For Tilly it evoked all those emotions when she saw her fathers coffin in the back of the hearse, although their relationship was not the best, she always loved her father. As the hearse drew nearer, she could see all the beautiful tributes adorning the car, bright beautiful colours of red roses, yellow gerberas, purples and pinks some just had letters like Mum, Nanny, It looked like Jack's daughter had come over from Ireland. His middle son and their children. She caught a glimpse of Jack, he looked sad, sitting in the back of the car, like a lost soul, Tilly could see his vulnerability, she had never seen that side of him before, he always comes across as confident and a go-getter in life. Everything is good in the hood he used to say. The tributes were laid outside the crematorium as the coffin was gently taken off the hearse. She saw Jack look at her, but he put his head down, he did not acknowledge her as he passed her as he was walking to the front seats, watching his mum's coffin being placed on the plinth, with the curtains either side waiting to be drawn when the funeral service had finished. Tilly felt very emotional as she knew one day she would be doing what Jack is doing today. Once the funeral service had finished, she walked outside and looked at all the floral tributes, she did see one from Jack's youngest son, who lived in Australia. Jack walked over to Tilly, he put his arms around her, holding her tight crying on her shoulder. Tilly could not push him away in his hour of need, and responded back, comforting him through his grief. 'Are you coming back to the house?' Jack enquired. 'Well I wasn't, I did not want to intrude on your private time with your family.' 'Don't be silly, I want you there, I need you there.' Tilly did not know what to do, she just wanted to go back home to her mum. Jack was in such a state, she felt obliged to support him especially on such a sad day. 'Please, Tilly, please, 'Jack begged her to stay. 'Ok, but only for an hour or so, I told my mum I would be back after the funeral service.' 'You can meet my family. My son and daughter, my other son is travelling in Asia at the moment so could not get to the funeral, and the youngest, could not get back from Australia. You can see my sister. She would love to see you after all these years, you are practically one of the family.' Tilly started feeling a bit anxious. She felt trapped, she really did not want to meet his family, as there will never be a relationship between her and their father, but could not see a way out. She followed the funeral cortege to Morag's house, parked up and went in. Jeanette, Jack's sister came straight up to her and greeted her with a hug and kiss on her cheek. 'So good to see you Tilly, after all these years, you look well,' she said. 'Thank you, you do too, so sorry about your mum passing away, we all have such wonderful memories.' Replied Tilly. "Yes, we sure do, to be treasured forever.' she replied. They had a lovely conversation, chatting about the past right up to present day, about their families and the joys of having grandchildren. 'Tilly, it has been so lovely to see you, thank you for coming to mum's funeral. Hope you don't mind, but I need to speak to other members of the family and friends that have come to the funeral to pay their respects to mum. Tilly did not mind at all, although it was lovely to see Jeanette, she felt relieved that she needed to go and chat to other people. She did not feel comfortable at all, she looked around and everybody was engrossed in their conversations, so she quietly slipped away and got in her car and drove home. Tilly was feeling tearful as she was driving home, bringing up memories of her childhood and knowing that this had hit her mum hard emotionally, and seeing her mum getting more frail, she was just hoping that her mum could get through this and her health may pick up a bit. She was so looking forward to seeing Pete again so soon after his last visit.

Tilly arrived home to find her mum asleep in her chair. She went over and bent down slowly to make sure she was breathing, especially after all the thoughts that had been racing around in her head. "Phew" she thought, she could hear her mum breathing, she felt very emotional, she sat for a few moments doing the silent crying when you feel you are going to explode, with such forceful emotions, but silent cry from the inside. Tilly was certainly ready to release herself from the past, and how it had made her feel. I can't do this anymore, she said to herself, I'm in my sixties and just starting to find myself, but my life has always been pleasing everyone else. I have totally forgotten about me, not my children or my grandchildren or Pete, but the bloody men I have encountered, seem to quite easily manipulate me. I have just stood there watching myself doing this, it's as if I'm addicted to the narcissist, but can't escape. Well I am so done, no more, I need to release myself from this negative addiction, trusting myself to find me, and not from a man, especially a narcissist. She felt quite exhausted after the silent crying. Realising she was slowly waking up to the fact this was none of her fault, the only thing she ever did wrong was to love too much, to give of herself, for absolutely nothing in return, no love, no intimacy, no connection, no communication just constant self doubt, struggling to find what normal was for her. She saw the strength in Isla, even the people in the meditation group, but Tilly never felt worthy enough to feel anything else, but the wrath of the narcissist, who despised himself so much inside and took it out on her. She even knew with Pete, although he has always treated her properly, she pushed him away when she was younger because she did not feel she deserved to have a man treat her with respect, she had no comparisons, her own father did not think she was worthy of love, she grew up with that assumption that if her own father cannot love her, then there must be something wrong with her. So she would attract the same type of man, because this is familiar to her, which is the biggest destroyer of love and happiness. A man who is so emotionally unavailable, can never love, because of their own trauma. Instead of working on themselves, they become entitled, the victim. You can try and fix them, which leaves you depleted, no energy, self doubt, a shadow of your former self, where they have drained you. Tilly heard her phone ringing. It was Jack, the ringing of the phone had disturbed her mum, so Tilly went up to the bedroom to take the call. 'So where are you?' Jack Bellowed down the phone. 'Err!!!! Excuse me Jack, who the hell are you talking to?' 'Well you stupid cow, leaving and not even saying goodbye' Jack replied still bellowing down the phone. 'As I said, who do you think you are?' 'Actually Jack I'm so bloody done with you, and your controlling ways. I'm sorry you lost your mum, but unfortunately as normal you only think about yourself, no emotions whatsoever, I don't need your shit in my life, I want the money you owe me. Then we are done. Just leave me alone.' Tilly was seething, she had never felt such anger, let alone let it out. 'Well,' Jack said I was going to dump you, you are too emotional and sensitive, you are not anything like you used to be when you were younger, I was really hoping I had found the one, but unfortunately not,' replied Jack, still shouting down the phone. 'Well, just as well, I have finished this whatever you want to call it. And yes you're right Jack, I'm not the same as when I was younger, thank god, that's because I was with a selfish bastard for 35 years, I have not got another 35 years to waste on you. You are so shallow, you think you can still pull women and use them to your advantage. Well, I have news for you, those days are gone.' Tilly ended the call abruptly, feeling as if there was some space back in her head. Thank god, Tilly thought, I am relieved that it's finished. I did not realise how much head space he was taking up. I am certainly not carrying on just for money, if he pays me what he owes me, all well and good, if not I will just have to put that down to my naivety. She went back downstairs, to check on her mum.

'You ok Mum?' You were sound asleep when I came in.' 'Yes pet, just feel a bit drained that's all, I have had a lot of pain in my body for the last few days.' 'Maybe Mum, it's where you have felt so emotional with Morag passing away, could be something to do with that.' 'Are you ok Tilly? I heard a loud voice coming from upstairs, Jack upset you again,' enquired Edith with raised eyebrows, have you been crying she continued.' 'Er… yes, sorry Mum, did not mean to wake you up. That man makes me feel so angry, in fact I have finished the so-called relationship, friendship, whatever you want to bloody call it,' Tilly said with her head bowed down. 'Tilly, he was supposed to come back into your life, for you to release the thoughts that you have carried over the years, that he was your soulmate, you secretly wishing you was with him and not with Bob, but it turns out they were both the same type of men, both controlling in different ways, let it go now,' 'Tilly, sorry to ask, could you make me a cup of tea please' 'Yes of course, replied Tilly I am in need of a drink myself, but mine is a large glass and a bottle of wine, to steady my anger.' On a lighter note, I also have a little surprise for you.' 'Oh I'm intrigued,' Edith replied. Tilly was back in the lounge giving Edith her cup of tea and some biscuits, with a bottle of chilled wine, and a very large glass. 'Well,' said Edith, enjoying dunking her biscuits in her cup of tea, whilst she was waiting for the surprise. 'Well your favourite man is coming up to see you. Pete is coming up this Sunday for a few days. I am picking him up from Bamburgh train station, he said he cannot wait to come and say hello to you and give you one of his big hugs.' Replied Tilly. 'I will look forward to seeing him where he is staying?' He's staying at the b&b?' 'Yes he is. I am really looking forward to seeing him, and at least this time I won't feel so nervous, I enjoyed our time together last time he was up.' 'Oh, I thought he was coming up in the New Year?' Edith enquired 'Yes he is still coming up in the New Year. He said his work is quiet at the moment, and wanted to come and visit us.' ' I really think there's more to it than that pet, he really does care about you, he has done for many years, but probably too scared to say how he felt for being rejected, he is very sensitive Tilly,' replied Edith. 'Yes I know, it's weird but things are so unravelling in my head and my life now, it feels like all these feelings and emotions are coming to the surface, but they are helping me to understand how although I love, I've loved men whose hearts are closed, but then I realised that my heart is closed as well, but not in the same way, my heart does not know how to love someone who has an open heart full of love, that is what I need to work on now, Tilly had tears streaming down her face.' 'Oh my darling Tilly, I'm so sorry, I know that comes from your childhood, and how your father made you feel, because you are so sensitive, you needed to feel that love from your Dad.' 'Mum, no need to say sorry, this is my life journey. I now know that I have had to meet these men, they have given me the lessons I needed to learn to grow and evolve in this lifetime. It has had to be painful, it had to be with these types of men, who I have loved passionately and had a connection with, for me to feel these deep emotions that are coming to the surface, so they can be released from the past. Below are all the layers that are covering my whole being, my true authentic self, not living with the perception of how Bob saw me, gradually taking me over, so I did not know who I was anymore, I was completely disempowered. Jack, although it was short, I have spent years fantasising about him, only to find out he is like Bob, has completely shattered me emotionally. With Bob, he groomed me to be what he wanted me to be, and I lost my self worth, had self doubt and did not think I was good enough or that anybody would want me. Those layers are being peeled back gradually, to reveal who I truly am. It's painful and tough. It is now time to find me, to be whole again, on every level, especially my heart and soul. So, it has always meant to be this way, so I could learn, on my spiritual pathway.' ' Tilly, You have come such a long way I know you will find the love and the happiness you are so seeking. You do know who you are, you need to trust and believe, continuing to love yourself.'

Tilly went over and gave her mum a big hug and a kiss. 'Tilly, I have to ask, when I was asleep earlier, I felt as if someone was laying on my chest, not sure if it was a dream or not,' Edith said with a broad grin. Tilly answered even though she felt embarrassed to say. 'It was me, you were not dreaming when I came in, you were so still, I wanted to make sure you were still breathing, so I put my head on your chest to make sure, Silly I know,' Tilly said with a quiet voice. 'I thought it was, I could feel you,' they both laughed together. 'Well it's nice to know I am still breathing,' Edith said looking up with a tear in her eye. Tilly sent a brief message to Pete, to make sure that everything is still ok for Sunday. Pete replied back that he had bought his train ticket for Sunday. The train would be arriving at Bamburgh around 10.30am, and that he was looking forward to spending some time with her. Tilly replied that she would be at the station to meet him, and spending time with him too. Tilly was sitting on her bed. The night sky was crystal clear, with that crisp cold air, you could feel it, just looking at the sky. All the stars were twinkling, and just peeking over one of the roof tops, was a crescent moon getting ready to reach another powerful full moon in a few weeks time. When Tilly was a little girl when she saw a crescent moon, she always felt a fairy was sitting right on the edge of the crescent, she was still looking for her tonight as she looked over the rooftops. She was thinking of all the things she had achieved in the last six months, and joining her meditation group was something she enjoyed immensely. Looking back she would never have thought that she'd be joining a group, but she has gained so much confidence along the way on her spiritual journey, as she could see herself unfolding and releasing things from the past, that does not serve her any purpose on this new road, living at her mum's cosy home, made her feel safe and secure, was something that Tilly had needed all her life, but now she was beginning to feel safe and secure within herself, which is one of the most important things anyone needs to feel and achieve, as abuse on any level, affects how you feel. Fear, and anxiety take over the role of ever feeling safe. Tilly was thankful, for all the support she has had, and wondering how her life would unfold. Feeling excited and not fearful.

CHAPTER 15

Tilly had received a text from Pete, to say what time he was arriving. Tilly was so excited, she could not wait to see him. Tilly replied to Pete's text to let him know she would be waiting for him on the platform. She only had to wait for a short while, when she saw Pete's train pulling into the station. As soon as they saw each other, they gave each other the biggest hug ever. Pete gave Tilly a kiss on her cheek. 'Oh it's so good to see you Pete.' "Yes me too, It's lovely to see your smiling face,' said Pete. They both walked back to the car, with Tilly linking Pete's arm. Pete, do you want to check into the b&b first? 'Yes, why not. Shall we have some lunch as well, I am feeling quite hungry.' 'Sounds good to me,' replied Tilly. They drove back to the b&b chatting like they always did, about family, work and what they'd been up to. Tilly could see Pete out of the corner of her eye just looking at her, then glancing back to look forward on the road ahead. 'I just love it up here. I know Cornwall can have that rugged coastal look which I love, but up here the scenery is stunning. The coastal views are beautiful.' 'Tilly, do you think we could find the time to visit Holy Island? I would love to visit there and take some pictures.' 'Yes, I don't see why not, it is such a beautiful place.' "We can do that tomorrow if you would like to?' 'Great,' said Pete. 'I will look forward to that tomorrow, glad I put my camera in the case now.' They arrived at the b&b and Pete booked in. Tilly went up with Pete to put his luggage in the room. 'This is cosy, never been up here to the rooms before, only the pub area.' 'Yes it is pretty snug,' replied Pete. 'It's the same room as before.' As Pete was sorting out putting his clothes away, Tilly stood looking out of the window, which overlooks the quaint little church. 'Pete, do you fancy a roast at mine this evening? I will be cooking for mum.' ' Yes please,' replied Pete. I love your roast potatoes and yorkshire puds.' "Ok, done.' 'Mum is so looking forward to seeing you. I think she has a soft spot for you,' said Tilly smiling. 'Aww, I have a soft spot for your mum as well, as I said she reminds me so much of my mum.' They both went down to the pub, ordered some drinks, took a couple of menus, found a table and sat down. Tilly only fancied something light, a jacket potato with prawns and salad, was just right for her. Pete ordered a hefty steak and ale pie chips and peas, which when came up was the biggest pie ever. Pete's face lit up, he certainly loved and enjoyed food, he said he was a frequent visitor to his local pub in the village, where the food was so good, especially the fish menu. The fish being freshly caught and cooked, was second to none. They continued to chat. Pete was so wanting to know if Jack was still on the scene, but knew to ask that question was not appropriate given that it was too soon upon his arrival. There were never any silences between them, they both enjoyed the love of music, playing the same instruments, both having a sensitive side, so they both knew they could share their thoughts and feelings in a healthy way. Pete paid the bill, and they headed back off home.

'Hello Edith,' called out Pete, running up the hallway into the lounge. He went over and gave her a cuddle, 'so sorry to hear about your friend.' 'Pete, how lovely to see you.' I was not expecting to see you until the New Year, could you not keep away from Tilly and me,' she said laughing, putting on a coy face. 'Thank you Pete. Yes, Morag was my very dear friend, we had been friends since we could walk.' 'Wow, that is a long time Edith.' 'Oh the secret is out now, how did you guess… changing the subject so he could cheer Edith up, 'I can't stay away from my special girls, now can I? Especially Tillys roast potatoes and those delicious yorkshire puds.' Pete replied. Edith laughed at Pete's comment. 'So what are we going to watch on the TV today, is it a quiz show, a bit of columbo, or a Razzamataz 1940's musical?' 'Well, how about swingtime, I have not seen that for a while?' 'You know Edith, I may get you up, and we can have a twirl around the lounge, how about that on a Sunday afternoon.' Edith just giggled. 'I wished I could twirl around the lounge, but I don't think the legs would let me, they would get twisted, not knowing which way they need to go,' laughing as she spoke. Tilly could hear all of this in the kitchen, where she was clearing up and getting the roast dinner prepared. She loved the fact that her mum and Pete got on so well. Halfway through one of the slow dance routines, Pete got Edith up, 'come on lets just dance on the spot, when you have had too much let me know.' He gently pulled her up holding her hands and held her waist to keep her steady and just gently swayed from side to side. Edith was in her element, she had not danced with a man for years, in fact not since Wilfred had passed away. She was completely taken back to the 1940's herself, she nestled into Pete, enjoying the feeling of being held while dancing to the music, she could feel a few tears drifting down her pale cheeks, when the song finished, Tilly was watching from the kitchen. She was just thinking what a beautiful man he was, such a kind soul, Tilly loved the fact he had a connection with Edith, which gave him comfort of not having his mum around anymore. Pete, gave her kiss on her cheek, and gently helped her back into her chair. 'Oh pete, thank you so much, I really enjoyed that little dance with you, you know you have a good rhythm! I used to love dancing. Wilfred and I always went dancing on Friday and Saturday nights, dancing to the big band sounds, back in our twenties.' Well, I'm glad that made you happy, I'm sure we can have a few more dances before I return to cornwall.' Tilly made her way into the lounge, holding a tray with tea and cake for them all to enjoy. Tilly and Pete sat on the sofa together watching the film with Edith. After they had their evening meal, Edith decided to take herself off to bed, she enjoyed laying in bed, listening to the old music, as she calls it, leaving Tilly and Pete to spend some time together. 'Tils, thank you so much for the lovely roast dinner you cooked for us. Your roast potatoes and yorkshire puds are just gorgeous.' 'Now I know why you wanted to come up again,' she said laughing, as Pete leaned towards her and gave her a kiss on her cheek. 'Well, I aim to please,' replied Tilly, smiling. 'Let me know when you want me to take you back to the b&b.' 'Why are you trying to get rid of me?' ' Pete, please don't think that, I'm just happy you are here, but I just thought you may be tired, that's all.' 'No, I never took it that way, I'm never tired around you, you know I like being in your company, I always have. If you fancy it, we could have a drink at the pub?' Pete asked. 'Yes Pete, I think a nice glass of white wine, sitting by the cosy fire would be good for the soul, ' replied Tilly. 'Ok then we shall go and have that cosy drink by the fire,' replied Pete. 'I will go and get changed, and let mum know that we are popping out for an hour or so she does not worry.'

Tilly came down the stairs. They both got their coat, and gloves, Tilly checking in her handbag to make sure she had her keys. 'Right are you ready Pete to brace yourself for the cold icy night.' They opened the door to blustery winds that were icy cold. Tilly put her arm through Pete and snuggled up as they went down the road. 'Bloody hell, Til's, I'm freezing my nuts off here' he laughed, 'blimey I thought Cornwall got cold, but this is something else.' 'Well I did say it got cold up here, have you packed your Thermals? you are going to need them on Holy Island, it's very windy,' Tilly smiled as she spoke. Pete answered, 'of course I have.' The b&b was only a short drive away, they parked up and went into the pub. 'Hey Tilly, hey Pete, what are you having to drink?' Tom, the landlord asked. 'I would like a small white wine spritzer,' Tilly said, 'and I will have a pint of your lovely Northumberland ale.' Replied Pete. Tilly found a table with some comfy chairs to sit on, luckily by the fire. Pete followed her over, they sat for a few moments in silence, both realising that something was happening between them, which is putting this friendship onto another level. 'So Pete, how is the band going,' enquired Tilly, trying to make conversation which normally flowed very easy. 'Yes it was good last Friday, more and more people are coming on that evening so the word must be getting out, which is brilliant, we play lots of covers of the 70's 80's music which gets people dancing and enjoying themselves.' 'I think that's brilliant Pete, I know I have said it before, but I do envy you.' 'Well maybe when you come down to stay, you can make a guest appearance, playing guitar and singing if you would like to do that?' Pete replied. 'I would love that, just worried that my voice is not up to standard and playing the guitar too.' 'Tilly, when I came up last time, you sat and played the guitar, it sounded really good, it's just about getting your confidence back that's all.' 'Yes your right Pete, about the confidence, I would so love to sing beside you again. Just as she spoke her phone rang, she checked, it was Jack. Tilly just did not answer the call. 'You ok Tils,' asked Pete, 'you did not answer your phone, you looked slightly worried about answering the phone.' 'Oh it was just Jack.

I can speak with him tomorrow.' 'Oh err ok,' Pete replied in his quiet voice whenever Jack's name was mentioned, his energy just deflated in seconds, that's why he was holding back, but deep down inside, he really had to know what was happening, he loved Tilly he always had. Everytime there has been an opening something has always stopped him from asking. Tilly could feel instantly that Petes energy had changed, she felt bad, she would never want to hurt Pete. She was beginning to see the difference in her feelings, but she was also scared of losing Pete if he did not feel the same as her. 'Pete,' said Tilly, 'he just wants my bank details for the money he owes me.' As soon as she said it, she knew Pete would ask. 'How does he owe you money?' Bloody hell, what have I done, she thought to herself, she always felt so comfortable sharing things with Pete, she just totally forgot. 'Sorry to be nosy, but are you having some problems with Jack?' 'Well, er, no not really, I had paid for something for him, and he was taking his time to repay me,' Tilly said in a loose term, so as not to enlarge the subject. 'Tilly I think I will go to bed now, if that's ok, with you, I do feel rather tired now, must be the journey catching up with me.' Pete said. 'Yes of course, I understand' she replied, she also knew this is how Pete goes when Jack's name is mentioned. She knew she wanted to be truthful with him but would not know where to start. Pete walked Tilly to the car, to make sure she was safe, they gave each other a hug, a kiss on the cheek to which Tilly responded with the same.

Pete laid in bed, with all sorts of thoughts and feelings going on in his head, he tried to find a comfortable position putting the duvet up, flicking it over, as he was getting hot and stressed, puffed up the pillows, then pushed the duvet off himself, this seemed to go on for hours, little did Pete know that Tilly was doing exactly the same thing as him. This situation was going to bring up some uncomfortable conversations. Especially as they have only recently reunited after not seeing each other for quite a few years and not even knowing whether each other was still in the world. Pete finally drifted off to sleep and didn't wake up until 10am. Tilly had got up early but did not want to disturb him by ringing. Tilly had contacted Jack who was not impressed that Tilly had finished this rather short relationship, well that was

Jack's view of it. Tilly saw anything but a relationship with him. she also felt that he had only paid the money to her, as a softener to her changing her mind. Tilly wished him well, and hoped that he would find the right woman who wants to be controlled on every level, made to feel insecure and feeling like she is auditioning for some porn movie… Tilly had now gone past any stage now of pretending to be nice to Jack, actually it was more sarcasm, something Tilly used a lot, it was just her way, without shouting. She does not want to be seen as a victim. She pulled herself together feeling a lot lighter knowing that she did not have to go through any more insecurities with Jack's behaviour. It was 11am, and she was starting to get concerned about Pete, no sooner had she had those thoughts, he rang her. 'Good morning Tilly, you ok? I cannot believe that I did not wake up until 10am, it's so cosy and warm in this room.' Well you must have needed that sleep Pete.' said Tilly. 'Yes, I certainly did,' Pete replied as she continued, ' how are you this morning Pete?' 'It took me a while to get to sleep, things going on in my head that's all, but I'm raring to go,' he said laughing. 'I was the same actually, I could not get to sleep either, better check to see if there is a full moon or new moon looming,' she said laughing. 'So Pete, do you still want to visit Holy Island?' 'Yes, I would still like to go, if you want to.' Pete said. 'Yes of course, I love it there. I will need to check the tides, so we don't get stuck there, bearing in mind that the days are shorter now as well, as soon as I know I will ring you back.' 'Ok hear from you soon, ' replied Pete. Tilly came straight off the phone, found the tidal times, and rang Pete back straight away, sorting out a time for her to pick him up. She hurriedly got herself ready, she found some jeans, a top, her trainers, brushed her hair, put it up in a claw hair clip, then pulled down a small piece of hair either side so it did not look like it was just scraped back. 'Mum,' called Tilly, 'I have made you something to eat for lunch, there is a flask of tea for you with some cake, I'm off to pick up Pete, we are going to Holy Island for a few hours.' 'Ok pet, thank you. I do feel tired. I will probably have a doze this afternoon.' Tilly arrived at the pub with Pete waiting in the car park. He opened the car door, 'Pete, have you got your thermals on as you will need them where we are going?' Tilly laughed as she enquired as to what Pete had on under his jeans. 'Well, actually I have, I took your advice,' Pete said laughing.

   Tilly and Pete set off to Holy Island, it was not that far away. As they were driving, Pete was taking in the scenery. I am so pleased I asked you if we could visit Holy Island,' as he turned to her with a warm smile on his face. 'The weather is going to be kind today as well, so it says on the weather channel,' he continued, as he was playing around with his camera settings, making sure he had the right lens with him. 'I wished I could take good photos,' Tilly said, `I'm absolutely useless, I seem to just take random pictures, but they are either blurred, not straight or I missed something out of the picture.' Turning to Pete, with a broad smile. 'So how about you take some pictures with my camera? I can show you certain angles to hold the camera so you get a better shot.' 'Yes, then maybe I can start taking some good pictures.'replied Tilly. They were so busy chatting, Tilly nearly went past the turning, she quickly swerved so as not to miss it. 'Blimey Tils you did not say we were on a race track, as he was holding on to the door handle as she swerved left so as not to miss the turning, 'are we here already?' 'Yes nearly, only this road to go down, and we will then cross the road to the Island. 'Sorry Pete,' Tilly was laughing. 'I did not mean for you to be hanging on for dear life as I turned into the road.' 'No you're fine,' Pete said as he adjusted himself and the seat belt in a joking voice. As they crossed the road where the tide had gone out, Pete could see the ruin of the monastery. The Island looked a lot bigger than he thought it would. 'Is there anywhere to eat there?' 'Oh yes, people live on the Island, it has a couple of pubs, with a few shops. The main pub is called the ship inn, it is over 700 hundred years old. You will find some amazing pictures to take in there too.' Once they parked the car, they went straight away to the monastery. Pete had his camera ready, 'don't forget, if you see some pictures you would like to take, let me know?' 'Yep, I would definitely like to have a go with a proper camera,' Tilly replied.

   They were busy walking to the old monastery, Pete was totally enthralled with the views, as it was quite windy, the grass was blowing in the wind, the landscape was very rugged. Pete decided to walk near the edge and he saw how much the Island had been eroded away by the fierce north winds, and the waves hitting the side of the rocks. It was so beautiful, although it was windy, you could still see the sun with shards of sunlight peeping through the clouds whizzing past, 'Wow this is very fresh walking on this Island, certainly blows the cobwebs away Tilly.' 'Yes it does get very windy here, as there is no protection from the wind, and the north sea can be very rough especially when you have the north easterly winds blowing in from the sea, the waves can roll in and crash halfway up the side of the Island.' Tilly replied. As they got nearer the monastery, they were searching for the perfect angles to take pictures. 'Pete, when you are ready, could I take some pictures? I have found a few I would like to take.' 'Yes of course, just give me 5 minutes, I'm nearly done.' Pete walked over to Tilly giving his camera to her, he bent in close to Tilly to show her where to press to take a picture and a guideline of where the picture should show up in the viewfinder. Tilly could feel Pete's breath gently on her neck, she felt very tingly inside, she could also feel the same from Pete, but neither of them said anything to each other. But they just seemed like they just wanted to be together. 'Tilly, do you feel peckish at all?' 'Well yes, I was thinking that too, I feel rather hungry myself. It's getting rather cold here now. Shall we head for the pub and get something to eat.' They walked back to the pub, which was on their way to where the car was parked. They ordered hot chocolate and soup of the day for two. While they were waiting. Pete took a quick look around the pub, to see what he wanted to take after they had eaten. Pete managed to get quite a lot of photos and some abstract. As time was getting on and they had to make sure that they would not get stuck on the Island. They finished their visit on Holy Island, and headed back to the car. There was now an icy wind blowing through the Island.

'Thanks Tilly for taking me there today. I thoroughly enjoyed seeing the Island. I would like to visit again sometime, I found it so peaceful.' 'Yes it is a lovely place. I have not been here for quite a few years either.' They chatted all the way back about different things. 'Tilly, are you still thinking about buying your own home and creating your great business idea?' Pete enquired. 'Yes, I have been looking at property, so I can see what I have to do to start my business. Obviously I need some money behind me, as I am not working yet, just trying to work out the best solution.' 'I'm so pleased for you Tilly, it sounds such a brilliant idea. I hope you don't mind me making a suggestion?' 'No of course not, I need all the help I can get' replied Tilly. 'So,' Pete continued 'would it be best to sort out the business first, so you have some money coming in and then buy a property when you are feeling more secure financially, you can stay with your mum, she loves having you live with her. 'What you have just said, Pete, actually is a more sensible way of working. I have been looking at shop units in Berwick, Alnwick and a few smaller villages, but I do need some footfall to pass the shop as it can be expensive. I could buy stock and trade from home, but it defeats the object of what I want to achieve. I really want to create an arty community, as there is nothing up here, also finding places from where to buy my stock. You know Pete, talking to you, I think I will do it that way first, I have so many ideas going on in my head.' 'Just take small steps Tilly, you don't have to rush to complete everything, do your research, make sure it's viable and works for you, do some research on the area, see if the local people would like to have something like this around them. Put down your ideas, the costs that are important. Tilly I hope you don't think I am taking over but I made so many mistakes when I first started my business, we all do, best deal with the mistakes that are money related and work it in a different way.' 'Of course not Pete, I appreciate your support. I have never done anything in my life like this, it feels quite daunting yet exciting.' They arrived back at Tillys. It was getting dark and looking a bit icy on the road. 'Pete, would you like to have dinner with mum and I?' 'Tilly I've been thinking about this, last time I visited you were always cooking the evening meal. How about we eat at the pub where I'm staying? We can always take some drinks up to the room and chill out just the two of us.' That sounds great Pete. I will do something to eat for mum, have a quick change and freshen up.' I will make us all a cup of tea and help you. I live on my own. I'm used to looking after myself so let me help.' 'Thanks Pete, I appreciate that.' They got indoors, Pete put the kettle on Tilly got Edith's tea started then went upstairs to freshen up, and change her clothes, they both really wanted to have this time together. Pete went in to see Edith with a cup of tea. 'Hello Edith, you ok?' 'Yes Pet, all the better for seeing you. I see you have brought me a nice strong cuppa.' 'Tilly and I are going to eat at the pub this evening. Tilly is going to cook you something before we go.' 'She does not have to do that, I can always rustle up something myself, don't be daft you two go and enjoy yourselves.' replied Edith. Tilly came down the stairs and she felt so much better for a freshen up and change of clothes. 'You look nice,' said Pete. 'Thank you, ' she replied. Tilly went and sorted out Edith's evening meal, and made sure she was ok. She sat with Pete and Edith, they were all drinking their tea together. 'Right Pete, are you ready to brave the cold?' 'Yes' replied Pete' Tilly got up and put on her coat, scarf, gloves and everything she could find to combat the icy cold night she was about to step into. Saying their goodbyes to Edith. Pete got his coat and wrapped his scarf around his neck to keep the cold out. They both got into the car, they had to sit for a few minutes, to defrost the windscreen, Pete had got out and cleared the ice that had built up on the windows. 'Bloody hell it's freezing out here' he said.' 'I know' Tilly said 'I can see the vapour of your breath in the cold air, but it's quite warm in here now.' Smiling as she spoke. Pete cleared the windscreen and got into the car with his coat practically over his head. 'My ears' he exclaimed 'I think they have frostbite' they both laughed.

    They got to the b&b, parked the car and went into the lovely warm pub, as it was a Monday, it was quite empty, apart from a few regulars having their pint. They both ordered their meals and drinks, and sat by the cosy fire together, they both knew that the dynamics between them had changed, both their hearts were starting to open. Well! Pete's heart had always been open, Tilly's heart unfortunately not so. Tilly had these experiences, so she could work out who she is, and what she wants in her life. She knows now abuse and trauma can cloud your judgement of people, relationships being the hardest to understand, when you had gathered so many layers over the years, you get lost under the cloak of co-dependency which has now been put there by the abusers, that is how they have disempowered you, leaving you with so much self doubt, you can only relate and perceive yourself as to what had happened to you on a mental level. It gets very confusing, as deep inside you know that you were once a strong confident person, making your own decisions, having a good life, you know you are in there somewhere, but you cannot place where your soul has gone. The healing takes place, but through that healing, you gradually start to find you. Then another relationship ensues, and because of the past emotional pain, fear of doubting yourself, never ever wanting to go down that road again, you lose out and stay exactly where you are, then you may meet someone who really does care about you, but that feeling is alien, you have never before experienced it, but there is also part of you that likes this feeling, thinking this could be good, then you wait for the bubble to burst. Then you could possibly end the relationship so you don't get hurt. It is like being on a rollercoaster of emotions, but then you start to feel like the person you used to be, stronger, able to make decisions again, and not doubting yourself. This can take a few months to years, all depending on the length of time you have been in that previous relationship, and the length of abuse you endured. Working on yourself on all levels is the first part of the journey, it's one of the most important journeys you will ever experience. It can be lonely and confusing, but you can and will come through it. You are then ready to embark on a life of self discovery, knowing yourself well enough to know what your needs and desires are in life. Tilly is coming to this point in her life, by changing her life, looking for a new home, a new direction of self employment, creating a community for musicians, crafters, vintage clothing, that is her passion.

'Tilly, do you fancy taking our drinks upstairs? It would be nice to chat, just the two of us, if you're not comfortable with that, there is no pressure. I would understand,' hoping that Tilly would say yes. 'Yes, let's do that, we are never really on our own.' Tilly replied, smiling from the inside. She got up straight away, got her drink and belongings all ready, waiting for Pete to get up. 'Ok,' Pete replied, then let's make ourselves comfortable and enjoy the rest of the evening.' They went up to the room, there was only one chair, and the bed, Tilly did not know what to do. She sat on the bed while Pete sat next to her. 'Ohh this is nice,' looking at Pete straight into his eyes. 'Thank you Pete,' as she put her arms gently around his neck and gave him a kiss on his cheek. 'What was that for?' 'That's for all the support and help you have given me over the years when we were younger, now you're supporting me in helping me with my new venture.' 'Don't be silly, you know I have always liked you Tilly, you are very special to me, that will never change.' For the first time they were looking intently into each other's eyes, each reading each other's souls, then their lips met, for the first time they kissed each other. Tilly could feel Petes warm lips on hers, he was so gentle when he kissed her, it was like his dream came true, he could have kissed her all night. Tilly would have normally pulled away, but this felt so right. They gently pulled away from each other. "I think we needed to come up for air don't you Tils,' he said smiling. 'I never expected that to happen, but I'm so glad it did.' replied Tilly, 'Yes, some air was needed,' as she leant on Pete's shoulder, gaining her composure, 'I could have kissed you all night and never stopped, it was lovely kissing you, I can feel goose bumps all over my body,' Tilly said. 'So do I. What a beautiful moment we have shared together,' replied Pete, still holding Tilly close to him. Tilly bent forwards again to kiss him, Pete wasted no time in reciprocating the kiss. When they had finished kissing, Pete had asked her if this is something she wanted? He was very much mindful of Jack's presence in the background, but Pete was too much of a gentleman to ask Tilly those sorts of questions, especially after sharing the kisses between them, he did not want to hurt Tilly, but he did not want to be hurt, however much he loved Tilly, he could not handle that. He was thinking how he could ask Tilly about Jack, he was questioning himself, is this the right time to ask such questions, shall I just go with the flow and see what happens? All these thoughts he knew Jack was his rival, but he was also mindful of him as well. Tilly had not yet replied to his earlier question. 'Tilly I'm sorry I don't mean to come on strong, but from the way we kissed it was very passionate. I felt you wanted this too? I have to ask, where does Jack fit into your life?' Tilly felt so uncomfortable, she knew this would come up, but did not want to lie to Pete, but did not feel this was the right time to discuss what happened with Jack. 'Pete, Jack is not around anymore, I went to his mum's funeral, out of respect for my mum and the family connection that's all. Jack was not who I thought he was, he was very controlling, I was starting to self doubt myself, he was constantly lying to me. Thankfully I am so much more aware now, that I took in every bit of information and stored it in my head, so whenever we spoke I would bring up the different things he was talking about, unfortunately the narrative always changed, I never said anything, but always knew he was lying.' 'What about wanting your bank details? Pete enquired, how does he owe you money so soon after knowing you? Tilly sat there, her face transfixed trying not to show any response to that question, but thinking to herself, shit, he remembered what I said, how the hell do I get out of this one. I feel so embarrassed to even tell him, I only shared with Isla, because she is my best friend. Pete saw that Tilly was feeling very uncomfortable, and hiding something from him. He was not going to pressure her into finding out, he knew that Tilly would tell him eventually. 'Oh Pete, I'm so ashamed of myself,' she said looking out of the window, trying to distract herself by looking at the ice forming on the cars in the pub car park, she could not give him eye contact. 'Tilly I'm not some ogre, you know that, but I have always had strong feelings for you. In all the years we have known each other, we have never kissed like that before, I don't want to be hurt that's all, in my heart I know you would never do that to me, but Jack does come across as quite a strong character that could persuade you back to him, I'm too old to play games Tilly.' 'Pete, I promise you, there is nothing going on, I have so much respect for you, I would never hurt you, I do have feelings for you, deeper feelings that I have never had before, and please dont think this has anything to do with me ending with Jack, thinking you are on the rebound, your not.

When I first saw you a few weeks ago, I realised what I had missed all those years ago. I was so caught up in the drama with Bob, that it became my life to make sure I fixed myself for him. I was searching for love from him. Every time he had an affair, I always tried so hard for him to notice me and love me for who I was. In doing that, I completely overlooked my own life. It was like I was in a glass house, I could see out, but could not get out. I had become codependent on him, and felt I could never get my life together unless I was with him, which was completely untrue. 'So' Tilly continued, 'the money he owed me was because he managed to seduce me, with gifts flowers, told me how much he loved me, that I was special to him, sending me texts, that had very sexual overtones to them, I do admit there was a chemistry and attraction, I knew him from when I was very young, and always had a crush on him, when he came down to visit us with his parents. I feel silly saying this, but I followed him around like a little puppy dog, I genuinely thought he was my soulmate. He was the first boy I kissed, so when our paths crossed again, I just thought the universe had put him back in my life, I thought that meant he was to be in my future, but obviously not, they sent him in, so that I could recognise the pattern that I had been carrying for many years, to understand it and break away from it. Anyway, where was I! Oh yes, so he wanted us to have a weekend away together. I told him that would be months down the line, as we had only just met, we were not in any type of relationship and never have been, but to him we were. I was very naive of him, and he wanted me to find a hotel, and asked me to pay for the deposit which was £250. He told me he had a business, was wealthy, and Pete, please know that I am not into money….. He said he would transfer the money, but he did not, I did ask him, he just kept making excuses. From the start I offered to pay half, as I did not feel comfortable, but he was adamant that he would pay… Pete, I am not going to go through every detail, when we have limited time together, but I will say I felt like a prostitute. I had never experienced anything like that in my life. No closeness, no emotions, I felt like a piece of meat.' Tilly started to cry, 'Oh Pete, I am so sorry, that was not me at all, but like a stupid naive woman, I got carried away, then his mum was taken ill, he then had to leave, I didn't wish his mum any harm, but someone was looking after me, I was thinking that I can't do this until the day we were supposed to leave the hotel and go home. It was one of the biggest mistakes of my life. I then ended up paying the final bill, he tried to use his cards, he knew none of them would work and knew I had money in my account. I later found out, his job is gambling, he has no house that had been repossessed, he lived with his mum, the lies just went on and on.' Tilly put her hands to her face, hiding her shame.

'So you see Pete I am not the woman you thought I was, I am not worthy of you. She got up to go, Pete pulled her back gently onto the bed, 'Tilly that would never ever stop the feelings I have for you. In fact I really want to go and punch him in the face, but I don't think that is a good idea.''He put his strong arms around her, cuddling her until she stopped crying. Pete stroked her face and wiped her tears away, he held her until she calmed down. 'Pete I'……. Tilly started to talk. 'Tilly stop right there, you have shared something with me, that is so personal, how about we just put this behind us, it's nothing compared to the feelings we have for each other, so no more talk of Jack, and hopefully you will get your money back.' Pete replied 'Yes, he sent it over a few days ago, I told him that I did not want anymore to do with him, he was rather shocked he is not used to women saying no to him.' Tilly said. 'Well that's a result,' replied Pete. 'I had better go home soon, sorry our time tonight was taken up with this mess.' 'Tilly, it had to come out this way, if this had not been spoken about, it could have put a block between us, Tilly never ever think that you are not worthy. You are beautiful inside and out.' 'Thank you Pete, that means a lot to me,' as Tilly walked over to the window, noticing that more ice had formed on her car, sparkling under the light of the lamps shining in the car park. 'Pete, it's really bad out there,' she said. Pete got up and looked out, 'how about tell your mum, you are staying here tonight, you can have the bed, I can sleep in the chair,' Tilly text her mum, and had a reply almost straight away from her mum as she was still awake, so she did not have to worry. She looked at Pete, 'I don't want you sleeping in that chair, I want you beside me in bed snuggled up and cosy.' Tilly said. They both felt a bit embarrassed; they had never gone down this road before, but as soon as they had undressed they slid into the bed with the covers over them, they just melted into each other's arms, talking, laughing, kissing and just enjoying being together. They both woke up about the same time, looking into each other's eyes. ' Who'd have thought this would have happened? Pete said as he bent over to kiss Tilly on the forehead. Do you fancy some breakfast Til's? before we go back home. 'Yes please Pete, I want to make the most of spending time with you. As Tilly gave the biggest hug ever to him. After they had breakfast, Tilly asked Pete what he wanted to do that day. Pete drew back the curtains, and looked out of the window, 'oh it looks quite chilly out there again today. How about we go for a walk down to the beach a bit later on and spend some time with your mum. Then when we can come back to the pub, if you would like to have a meal here this evening. If you would like to, you could stay over again? Tils there is no pressure you know that.' 'Yes I would like that.' When they got back to Tillys, she had a shower and got dressed. Her mum was still in her dressing gown, which surprised Tilly as she is always someone who got up and got dressed. Tilly knew her mum was not feeling well at the moment. 'Mum, you ok? It was so cold and icy that I did not want to take a chance, driving home, in case I had an accident.' 'It's ok pet, you do what you want to do, hope you both had a lovely meal.' As she was looking into her daughter's eyes which looked so bright, she had not seen Tilly's eyes like that for years, Edith knew that something happened between her and Pete. She was so happy for her daughter. "We are going to spend time with you today, we are going to blow away the cobwebs with a walk on the beach, grab a coffee and then come back and spend the day with you.' 'That would be lovely Tilly. I will look forward to that.' The day seemed to pass too quickly for Tilly, before she knew it, she was looking after Edith preparing her evening meal, getting a change of clothes ready for the b&b, sharing a lovely meal together, then spending the night with Pete. 'Mum, I am going to stay at the b&b again tonight, will you be ok?' Tilly asked 'Yes of course Tilly, go and have a lovely time, thank you for a lovely day.' 'Am I seeing you before you go home tomorrow Pete?' said Edith looking at Pete with her sad puppy dog eyes. 'Yes of course, how can I not come and say goodbye to you? ' he replied. Edith just looked at Pete giving him one of her lovely smiles. 'I will give you a big cuddle before I go, how about that,' as Edith continued to smile at him. 'We can stop by before Tilly takes me to the station. I will see you again in a few weeks. I am coming up for Christmas now, as well as new year, so I will have a nice long stay this time.' 'Oh that's wonderful Pete, I will look forward to that.' 'Mum,' called Tilly, as she was going up and down the stairs, 'I have got your dinner ready. Do you want it now, or just when you fancy it?' 'Thank you, pet, just leave it out in the kitchen so I can warm it up, when I feel hungry.'

'Pete, I've got all my things together, have sorted mum's dinner out, so are you ready?' 'Yes, I just need to get my shoes on, and say goodbye to your mum.' Pete got up and made his way over to Edith, with his shoes in his hand. He put his shoes down, giving Edith a lovely cuddly hug, 'I do enjoy your hugs Pete, they are the best.' She laughed. 'See you tomorrow.' He sat down on the sofa putting his shoes on, while Tilly got his coat, gloves and scarf. 'Mum, we are off now,' as Tilly bent down to give her mum a kiss, 'see you in the morning, just ring me if you need me.' Oh don't fret, I will be fine, I will have my dinner and take myself off to bed, it's nice warm in that bed.' They both said goodbye to Edith. 'Bye you two, have a nice time.' It was not long before they got to the pub, they went up to the room, so Tilly could put her belongings in there, then went down and ordered their meals. They could not wait to be on their own again. They had a quick meal, then went up to the room. They snuggled on the bed, listening to 70's and 80's music. Pete turned to Tilly and as he put his arms around her, he leant across and kissed her lips, Tilly reciprocated, they each started to undress each other, running their hands over each other's bodies, finding the contours to excitement. Tillys body was starting to tingle with arousal, she could feel the difference from Jack, Pete loved Tilly, she could feel that both their bodies were ready to make love, she could feel the sensuality of Pete, He was so gentle, she could feel his hands tenderly caressing her breasts, kissing her neck, teasing her, slowly moving stroking her tummy. Tilly was yearning for Pete, she felt so safe and secure with him, she had finally let go of her vulnerability, enjoying the moment. Tilly had never felt anything like this before, they were like one soul, the desire they both felt for each other was overwhelming, as Pete made love to Tilly for them both to have the most wonderful orgasm. After they made love, they just held each other with their arms wrapped so tightly around each other, both could feel the electrifying energy flowing between them as they gazed into each other's eyes. Tilly was still in ecstasy, never imagining from where she was with Bob, to actually knowing what it's truly like to be with a man who truly cares about you and shows their emotions having no wish to want to control you, breaking you into tiny pieces. 'Tilly, I cannot believe that has happened. It was such a wonderful feeling. I have wanted to experience that with you for so long, but never thought it would happen. I have never experienced anything like that. It was so worth waiting for. Tilly, you are a beautiful woman with a loving soul,' 'and, you are my handsome Prince.' Tilly replied. Pete started laughing. 'I am not so sure about the Prince.' They both started laughing and joking. They were awake most of the night, but they slowly started falling asleep, peacefully in each other's arms. Pete had woken up about 8ish, Tilly was still asleep. Pete got a shower and got his things together. Tilly was awake by now, and put the kettle on for a morning cuppa. 'I had better get some breakfast before I leave, as I will be hungry on the train back down to Cornwall, do you fancy something to eat Tilly?' ' Yes please, just some toast will do.' They both were ready and went down to the pub bar and ordered their breakfast. Pete had the full English and Tilly couple bits of toast and marmalade. They both got their clothes and bits together, going via back to Tillys on route, so Pete could say goodbye to Edith. When they arrived at the station, they had a few minutes together to give each other a kiss and a hug. Tilly did not want him to go, he did not want to go either, but it would only be a few weeks and they would be back together. As the train pulled in, Pete picked up his case, as Tilly was calling out to him to ring her to let her know that he had arrived home safely. 'Yes of course, I will let you know when I have arrived home, take care, speak soon.' She stood on the train station watching Pete's train slowly disappearing. She walked back to her car, turned it around, still in a dream world. I cannot believe this has happened, the connection was deep and sensual, like our souls just joined together. I have missed all those years, I could have had this years ago, she thought to herself. Right, I need to stop this right now!!! As Tilly was going back in the past, it's time to live for today, live in the now. We both needed to experience the lives we've had, so we know what we have is special. I do hope we can get the future we want, we live on opposite sides of the country. She went home to see her mum who seemed a bit perkier than normal, which pleased Tilly, as she has been very concerned about her mum's mental health. 'Hi Mum, you seem a lot perkier today, I noticed that when we came back for you to say your goodbyes.' 'Yes, I am feeling a lot better about myself. Now pet, I am not prying but are you and Pete an item?' 'Yes mum, it's early days, but we have found each other after all these years. I have always liked Pete, but probably buried it deep because I was with Bob, we were both in the band together, Bob would have made things very uncomfortable, plus I have not been ready to love and open my heart until now. At least he is coming up for Christmas now.' She said with a big smile on her face. 'Yes Pete did mention that he was coming up, oh Tilly I am so happy for you, you do make a lovely couple I have to say.'

'Now,' Tilly said to her mum. I need to start on Christmas. It's only 4 weeks away, I have not got any presents, cards or got organised with food, or sorting out the rooms. I need to book the b&b for Pete, we totally forgot when he was checking out, I think I will do that first, just in case the pub is fully booked. I am so excited about having all the family together, it's been a long time.' 'Yes, so am I.' Edith replied 'So what about Jack?' Edith continued. 'I have finished with him, to be honest mum, it was not a relationship, I thought it was going somewhere in the beginning, but I soon realised, when I started seeing the real Jack.' 'Oh mum, by the way, I meant to tell you, that he transferred over the money he owed me, probably a softener thinking I would entertain him again, he was not best pleased when I told him I did not want to see him again. Anyway Mum, thank goodness it was a very quick chapter, and it was not prolonged, where I would be going backwards again. Mum, do you know if Adele is coming for Christmas, have you heard anything?' 'Oh I'm not sure, it would be last minute depending on the weather and the ferry crossing being safe. To be honest, I don't think she will come here, her life is up there now.' Tilly left her mum pottering around in the kitchen, she often just liked to put things away and have a little tidy up, it made her feel useful.

   Before Tilly started on organising Christmas she gave Isla a quick ring. 'Hey Isla, just a quick call to make sure you are ok.' 'Yes' I am good, replied Isla.' ' That's good to hear Isla. I was just ringing to say I don't think I will have time to meet up before Christmas. I have so much to do, with all the family coming to stay. I have to work it like a military precision, to work out where everyone will sleep, and everything else that goes with it.' Replied Tilly 'Oh don't worry,' Isla said 'we can meet up in the New Year, maybe we can have a quick catchup on the phone before Christmas?' 'Yes, that sounds good. How are you and Dave?' Asked Tilly. 'We seem to be getting on so well together. I am going to Lucy Christmas day and Jane is coming over, so we will all be together.' 'What about Brian?' Tilly enquired. 'Oh yes, he will show his face for Christmas day, but he is always out Boxing day, always has been, meets up with his cronies at the working mans club, but I would think a visit to his lady friend is in order as well. I am seeing Dave Boxing day, Isla continued in an excited voice, I am going to him for the day. I am looking forward to it, but we have not really spent a whole day together. I feel a bit nervous,' Isla replied. 'You will be fine Isla, much better than being on your own, then wondering what your husband is up to...Well thank god, I am not at that place anymore' said Tilly. "We are both really done now, " said Isla, "I know my marriage is definitely over, I would not stir things before Christmas, but come the New Year I will be making changes in my life. So how about you and Pete?' 'Yes we have had a lovely few days together, in fact, I stayed at the b&b on Monday and Tuesday. On Monday we just talked and laughed and cuddled and kissed which was so nice. Then on Tuesday we ate at the pub, and spent the night together, this time with a lot more intimacy, it was so nice to feel connected to someone special. Hey Isla, if that situation occurs on Boxing day, just go with it, if that is something you want to do. Brian does not seem to have a conscience so why should you feel guilty. Sorry Isla, please do not think that I am pushing you into something, if you are not ready, I completely get that.' 'No you're not Tilly, but I am beginning to feel that I want more, but yes I will go with the flow.' Isla said with a more confident voice. 'I am going to have to go to Isla, I need to make a start, sorry I hope you don't think I'm being rude to you, but we can catch up in a few weeks.' 'No of course not, I have things to do, but I don't have all my family turning up on my doorstep. Ok Tilly, happy shopping, and getting your home ready for your family. have a lovely Christmas, if we don't get to speak beforehand, enjoy being with your family, and new man.' 'Ok bye Isla , take care.' 'Bye Tilly, you take care too.' Tilly sat on her bed with her journal in her hand, she was thinking about Pete, and the lovely time they had together over those few days. She started writing:

"In the subtle light, those lovely kisses, never to be forgotten."

She doodled all around the paper she sat pondering, how weird life turns out. How she thought that Jack was the one. How their paths crossed again after so many years of no contact, thinking that the universe had placed him back into her life for them to be together, but he was placed in her life, for her to grow and evolve, to know her self worth, that she did deserve to be loved properly, fortunately for Tilly, she learnt very quickly. But she now knew that sexual chemistry and attraction are primal instincts, but for it to work there must be balance to include gentle loving, caring for each other, having each other's backs, when the road ahead gets tough, that is the best connection.

Tilly knows and understands what true love looks like now. Not the type of one sided love, where you can feel intimidated and abused, where you are completely lost and broken. Tilly jolted herself back into the here and now, she was someone who at a whim, can just go into her own head space, completely losing all track of time. The weeks were going so fast, Tilly had done all the present buying for her family. She was looking at all the presents that needed to be wrapped, wondering if she would ever find time to do them. Right now, she thought to herself, I need to concentrate on the Christmas tree. I wonder if mum still has her Christmas tree and decorations in the loft. Think I need to venture up there to have a look to see if there is anything left. She got herself up in the loft where all the Christmas decorations used to be kept when she was a little girl. She was sad to see that there was not much left from when she was a little girl. Tilly was pushing boxes around that her mum had just put there, she knew her mum had put all the things up there, it had an out of sight out of mind feel to it. Something Edith used to say years ago when all her children were quite young. She found some bags of material and the old sewing machine that her mum had used a thousand times to make the clothes for all three of them, and herself. As she pulled a bag out, some tinsel fell out of a bag, she hurriedly pulled it toward her to see what she would find, all that was left was few Christmas decorations that she had saved that Adele, Edward and Tilly had made at school, that she used to put on the tree. I will put them on the tree, better go out tomorrow to get a tree and some decorations. She took the decorations downstairs to show her mum. She was surprised they were still there in good condition. One thing Tilly loved was Christmas. She always loved putting the tree up and decorating it and putting all her candles and christmas ornaments out, this year was not an exception, she was planning in her head what colours she would like.

The kitchen was stocked up with all the Christmas goodies, mince pies, Stollen which was her favourite, every kind of snack, nuts, sweets for the children and the adults, wine, beer, she had thought of everything. Poor old Edith, every time she went into the kitchen to tidy up, more would appear. 'Blimey Tilly, are you feeding your family or the whole of the street,' she said laughing. Mind you, I cannot really say anything, I used to be the same, so you must have got that from me' Edith said laughing. 'Then you would know Mum I would hate to run out of anything.' Tilly replied laughing. She was on her way back from the shops, with another car load of Christmas cheer, A lovely Christmas tree and lots of sparkly baubles, beads and a fairy for the top. 'Oh Mum, I have just got back in time, it has started to snow, I reckon it will be quite thick by the end of the day. Mum, I am going to put the Christmas tree up, is that going to disturb you?' Tilly enquired. 'Oh goodness no pet, I love Christmas, I will enjoy watching you put the tree up, and decorating it. I used to love it when it got dark, we just had the Christmas lights on. It was so cosy.' Edith replied. Tilly came in with so many bags, she sorted them all out. She got the tree out, and knew the perfect place to put it. It was by the side of the fireplace Tilly started decorating the tree. It looked beautiful by the time she had finished the twinkling of the lights, catching the light on the glitter decorations. There were all sorts, bells, ballerinas, little fluffy decorations, angels, cherubs. 'Oh Tilly, that looks beautiful, I have not had a tree up here for many years, unless you were all coming to me. The children will love the tree you've decorated with all the baubles and beads, it looks so homely and cosy.' 'I do hope so Mum, this is a special one this year. Not only is my family coming, but Pete is as well. I feel like my life has done a 360' turn in the last six months, Thankfully all positive. I think I will put some of the presents around the tree, as my room is rather overloaded, I have wrapped some of the presents from you as well, and there's still more to get done. Pete and Tilly have become even more close, they have had regular phone calls. They had many long conversations about their future together, now it seems like everything is falling into place for them both.

The day had finally come, when her family were arriving, Pete was also on his way up, the snow had cleared up, which made the journey a lot easier for them all, as they were all travelling from a fair distance away. The bedrooms were all ready, food ready in the kitchen. Tilly was sitting down having a quick cuppa and a mince pie, when there was a knock at the door, where Sarah, Martin and their brood, bags, presents, toys, and two excited little girls were waiting for their nanna to open the door. Tilly opened the door, to see all their smiling faces, and the girls just leapt forward to give their nanna and great nanny big hugs and kisses. Tilly had not long got Sarah sorted out, when Stanley arrived with his family, Sarah saw them coming up the garden path, so she went and opened the door to greet them. 'Mum,' said Sarah, Stan is here with Frances and the kids.' 'Ok, Sarah, will be there in a minute.' Tilly went to greet Stanley and Frances, and the little ones had all wrapped themselves around Tilly. Edith was in the lounge, sitting with Sarah, playing a game with the girls. The girls saw their cousins, and ran towards them, then brought them to Edith, where she was entertaining all five of them. Tilly just stood back, so excited about seeing all the family together. Sarah and Frances, had unpacked the cases and bags, they had put all their belongings away. Sarah went into the kitchen to make a nice cup of tea which was duly needed. She looked around the kitchen. 'Bloody hell mum, you certainly have not left anything out' she said laughing. 'You can't be too sure, everyone has different likes and tastes.' Tilly replied. 'Well I can honestly say, you have catered for everyone here. Hey Mum what time is Pete arriving, we all cannot wait to meet him.' Sarah enquired. 'I think he should be here around 5ish. He texted me when he left, and that was about 6am this morning. It is a good 8 to 10 hour drive obviously depending on the traffic and the weather. I think he is quite nervous actually,' said Tilly, 'which I can understand, but I know once the ice has been broken, he will be fine.' "Right," said Tilly, "Have you got the drinks Sarah?' Tilly went up to Stanley with his drinks. it was so busy, she did not get a chance to speak with him. They gave each other a hug, and he asked when Pete was arriving, she told him that he would be arriving around 5ish. Tilly's phone was ringing in the corner of the room. It was Pete, saying he was about 30 minutes away. Pete also enquired if Tilly wanted him to come to her home, she knew he would be feeling like this, but Tilly wanted him to meet her family. She told Sarah and Stanley that he would soon be here. 'Ok, I am looking forward to meeting your family. I will check in at the b&b, have a quick wash, change my clothes. Do they know I am coming today?' 'Yes of course, I have told them, they are fine about it, before you ask they cannot wait to meet you.' 'Bloody hell, nothing gets past you, you can read my mind, now that's a bit scary' he replied laughing. 'Too right' she said, 'I can't wait to see you.' I am so looking forward to giving you a cuddle.' He replied. 'Me too,' said Tilly. The only thing is, I will be quite busy with my family being here, but we can still have our time together.' 'Tilly stop worrying, it will work out as it's supposed to, don't put yourself under so much pressure, I can help out.' 'Thank you Pete, see you soon.' 'Was that Pete on the phone Mum?' enquired Sarah, 'Yes it was, Pete will be here in about an hour, he wants to check into the b&b first and freshen up and change his clothes.' 'b&b' exclaimed Sarah, 'what he was doing staying at a b&b?' Sarah asked. 'Well Sarah, I think it's only respectful. That is what Pete wanted to do, and so do I. We are not teenagers, you have not seen me with another man let alone getting up and seeing me in bed with another man.' 'Oh Mum, you are so old fashioned it's not like that today,' Sarah replied. 'Well, it was back in the dark dinosaur years, you could not live together before getting married, you were supposed to be a virgin on your wedding night, and if you bought a home before you got married, you were not allowed to sleep together there. Your grandad would have gone mad should that have happened.' Sarah stood with her mouth open, 'you are kidding me aren't you Mum.' Sarah replying, aghast at her mum's statement. 'No Sarah, that is exactly how it was, and that is how I want it with Pete, until we get settled into the relationship, and know what the future is to be.' 'Sorry Mum, I did not know you felt that strongly about things, you have never ever spoken like that before.' 'That's ok Sarah, let's get the drinks and snacks out on the table. Let's enjoy our Christmas all together.' Tilly walked into the lounge, and saw Edith with all her great grandchildren around her, they were telling her how their schools celebrated Christmas. Edith was singing the old fashioned nursery Christmas rhymes which they all seemed to love. 'You ok Mum?' you have got your hands full, with them all.' 'Yes I'm fine, just enjoying the Christmas excitement, when is Pete coming?' 'He will be here soon. How are you feeling about him meeting the family?' enquired Edith. 'Actually, I feel pretty calm, I know he is right for me, and I know Sarah and Stanley will like him too.' 'Hey pet, could you get me a few mince pies, so I can have them with my cup of tea.' 'Coming right up,

Just as she got to the kitchen to put some mince pies on a plate the doorbell rang. She quickly got to the door with the plate of mince pies in her hand, she opened the door, to a slightly subdued Pete, waiting to meet her family. 'Oh Tilly,' said Pete, 'how did you know I love mince pies?' he said laughing, 'Hands off,' she was laughing. 'They are for my mum.' 'Ok, well let me surprise your mum, and take them to her.' Pete said with a smile. As Tilly got to the lounge Pete was standing beside her. Sarah, Martin,

Stanley and Frances and all the grandchildren stood there looking at Pete with a plate of mince pies. 'Oh, you didn't need to bring your own food Pete, mum has got enough food to feed an army,' everyone just started laughing. 'Pleased to meet you, I'm Stanley, I'm the prodigal son' as they shook hands. 'Pleased to meet you,' I'm Pete. trying to work out very quickly which hand to put the Mince pies in, shaking hands with Stanley. Thank you for breaking the ice like that, I was quite nervous,' Pete replied. Sarah came up, and gave him a hug, so did Frances, Martin shook his hand. 'It's lovely to meet you, mum has told us about you, and now we get to meet you.' Sarah said. Edith sitting quietly, piped up, 'Pete can I have my mince pies, my tea is getting cold.' He's the best, she added, He is kind and gentle. He would never hurt your mum, nor she to him, I love him dearly.' They all raised a glass to Pete and welcomed him into the family. 'Thank you for welcoming me into your family, I feel very humbled to meet such a lovely family and all your children.' Pete felt quite emotional but so relieved it went ok. Stanley, being the joker in the family, said, 'Well if Nanny Edith loves you, mum has strong competition she needs to watch out.' He said laughing. 'So Pete,' he continued, 'what would you like to drink?' 'I think a nice beer would go down well, thank you' Pete said. Following Stanley into the kitchen, Stanley turned around with the beer ready to pour. 'You know, it's really nice to meet you, you seem like a good guy,' he continued. 'I try my best, I want you to know that I would never hurt your mum, I love her too much. We have known each other for years, but now the time is right for us to be together.' 'You know Pete,' said Stanley, 'I already know that.'

Tilly and Pete, had managed to grab 10 mins together in her bedroom. 'It was so wonderful meeting your family today, I feel very privileged.' 'What about your daughter Pete, where is she?' 'Oh she lives in Suffolk. She always goes to her mums for Christmas, she is very controlling and expects Fiona to go there every year, not sure how her partner feels about that. If you like, when you are ready, we could book a weekend to go there, so you can meet her and her partner Paul.' 'Oh, that would be lovely, I will look forward to that, ' said Tilly. Pete left quite late, to go back to the b&b, they gave each other a kiss, Tilly said that he was welcome any time on christmas eve. She did not really want him to go, but this is what Pete wanted, so she had to respect his wishes. The house on Christmas eve was buzzing with excitement, all children were hyped up, with the thoughts of Father Christmas coming to visit them with their presents. Pete had turned up early that morning chatting with Sarah and Frances, the children were already waiting for their dads to take them to the swing park, this gave Edith a little break, and for Sarah and Frances to get prepared for the day ahead. Tilly was getting ready when he arrived. Pete pitched in and helped them get the buffet food ready, so they all could help themselves from the table. It was a far easier way to feed the family, she already had the Turkey to contend with. The more she looked at this Turkey, the more she felt puzzled as to how to get this beast into the oven, but she did not have to worry as Pete seemed a very positive help in the kitchen. He took control of the turkey and got it ready, Tilly had given him the stuffing to sort out. Sarah and Frances looked at Tilly. Sarah said Mum, I think you got a good one here, he's in the kitchen and not watching sport on telly.' They were all laughing, Tilly just smiled at Pete, saying he is a good cook. 'Well, he seems to have handled Turkey in a very professional way,' Frances said. There was so much banter, they all seemed to have the same sense of humour, this was so refreshing to Pete, he loved humour, something that was missing with his ex wife. The children were worn out by the earlier trip to the swing park, plus sweets, and other treats. They were all ready for bed by 7pm, in anticipation of Father Christmas paying a visit to them. Tilly had sorted out the carrots, mince pies and some good scotch whisky in a glass, each one had something to put down by the fireplace, they were so excited giggling and chatting with each other. They all went to Tillys bedroom, as she gathered them around her, she was asking them if they could hear Santas sleigh bells, as he had to go around the world delivering all the presents. The children were listening intently to see if they could hear, you could hear a pin drop!! 'Oh yes I can hear the sleigh bells,' said Lyla. 'Well then it's time to go to bed, as that means Santa's on his way, and will only come here if you are all asleep.' Tilly went and tucked them all in bed, Tilly giving them kisses and cuddles. Their Christmas stockings at the end of the bed waiting to be filled. Within 10 mins they were all fast asleep. Tilly crept down the stairs, so as not to disturb them. Tilly walked into the lounge. 'Well, they are all asleep.' said Tilly. ' I'm not surprised' Sarah said. They were all absolutely tired from the excitement of the day.' 'I just need to sort out with you and Frances, what you want me to put in their stockings. Do you have things to put in as well?' Said Tilly. 'Tilly, you have thought of everything, 'said Frances, 'I just love doing Christmas. So let's sort out presents for them all, so they can be placed around the Christmas tree, and get their stockings filled too.' Pete just sat there in awe of Tilly, and how she made Christmas so lovely for everyone. He had never experienced this type of Christmas before, when he was married, Martin was also looking on too. Within an hour, the stockings were filled, then they tiptoed into their bedrooms. They were filled with goodies, some colouring pens, and little books. Hallie being a bit older, had some bath foam and body lotion, as she loved having baths, and as she said smelling nice. Once this had been done, they were all sitting downstairs, laughing, telling funny stories, playing cards, enjoying a drink. Pete looked at the time, and said to Tilly ' I had better get back to the b&b in case they lock the doors. 1 have made sure that I am not over the limit and did not overdo it with the drink.' 'Why don't you stay here tonight with mum, we know you booked it out of respect for us. Let's all be together here for Christmas day.' Stanley said. Pete looked at Tilly, waiting for the signal of a smile, as to his answer, he would never want to overstep the boundaries of her family. He did not have to say anything, Edith was at the other end of the lounge, when she called out 'Please stay Pete, you are part of the family,' Tilly went over to him and put her arms around him. 'Why don't we go to the b&b, get your belongings. Let's see if we can cancel the rest of the time you have there, I'm sure he can rebook the room especially at this time of the year.' Pete was smiling from ear to ear, he had never thought he would have been accepted so quickly by Tilly's family. He was so happy. 'Ok, let's go and do that.' They got to the pub and went upstairs and put Petes clothes and belongings into the suitcase, went to the landlord, telling him of the situation, Pete offered to pay for the all the days, but the landlord, only charged him for last night and tonight, he had a list ready of people wanting a room should there be a cancellation.

    Tilly went upstairs to make room for Pete's clothes, he was following behind her with his case. She peeped into the childrens bedrooms, they were fast asleep, their little Christmas stockings filled to the brim, with some presents on the end of their beds. Pete followed Tilly, as she opened her wardrobe, pushing the coat hangers so tightly together to find some room in there. Pete sat aghast, at all the clothes, shoes and handbags that were surrounding him on the bed. 'Blimey, I can see you like a good selection in your wardrobe,' Pete said quietly laughing. As Tilly was trying with all her might to squeeze the hangers together, 'the thing is, I do love buying clothes, shoes and handbags, I just can't seem to resist,' she said with her puppy dog eyes. 'I will find some room, I promise,' still trying to shuffle the hangers as tightly as she could, so Pete had somewhere to put his clothes. 'So the first thing when we have our own home, said Pete, is to make sure you have your own dressing room, where you can put all the clothes, shoes and handbags in one place.' A warmth came over Tilly, this was the first time Pete had ever mentioned a home together, although they had discussed how to plan their future, there were not many details at the moment. There, all your clothes are away, they sat on the bed together, Pete got hold of Tillys hand and was gently stroking her hand. 'You know Tilly, I love you so much,' 'I love you to Pete very much.' they gazed into each other's eyes, and kissed each other. When they went back down stairs, Edith had gone to bed, Stanley and Martin were still playing cards, Frances and Sarah were busy clearing up the lounge, so it was all clean and tidy for the mayhem of excited children, opening up their presents Tilly and Pete, decided to sort out the Turkey, cooking it slowly through the night, finishing it off in the morning to make room for the rest of the food that needed to be cooked. Tilly was quite a light sleeper, as she started stirring, she could hear little voices, squealing with delight that Father Christmas had arrived, their biggest fear and most asked question was… " Is Father Christmas going to find us, as we wont be at the home he has been before." She got up and peeked through the door, they were opening their stockings and pulling out the goodies, eating chocolate reindeer, and playing with their new toys, she left them to play and went back to bed, snuggling back up to Pete. She heard Sarah sorting the children out, asking them to go back to bed as it was too early to be up, as they had a long and exciting day ahead of them. That seemed to do the trick.

As Tilly pulled back the curtains in the morning, she was greeted with a beautiful blue sky and the sun shining. It was a cold crisp Christmas morning, she left Pete in bed, attempting to try and sort out the turkey. By 9am everyone was up, the children so excited with the anticipation of opening up their presents, they had all had breakfast. It was time to open the presents, Pete had gone outside to get Tillys present, Pete's present from Tilly was already under the tree. Pete had given Tilly a beautiful heart shaped necklace, which he had engraved "Forever" on the back, a lovely art deco card, which he had written lovely words on the card. Tilly loved the art deco era, she would have made a good flapper girl. Tilly was not sure what to buy Pete, knowing he had a bucket list of things he wanted to do so she bought him an experience of flying in a hot air balloon. He was so pleased with the present that Tilly had bought him. The children were happily playing with their toys. Tilly, Frances and Sarah were getting the table ready for the Christmas dinner, and had a smaller table for the children to sit at. They had their own crackers, and new Christmas plastic tumblers laid out already for them. They all sat around the table where the beast of a turkey was placed in the centre of the table, with all the vegetables, and side dishes so everyone could help themselves. The children were sitting at their own little table, waiting for their dinners to arrive. They all thoroughly enjoyed their dinner, pulling crackers, laughing, 'cheers everyone' Stanley said, as they all raised their glasses, including the children. It was one of the best Christmases Tilly had ever had, made all the better with Pete being there beside her. Sarah had come into the kitchen, thanking her mum for everything, and the scrummy dinner. 'Oh my darling you are so welcome, I have loved being able to be with you all this year, seeing all my grandchildren open their presents, just being excited. Your nan has enjoyed this so much, she will probably sleep for a week when you have gone home,' Tilly said laughing. Sarah came over and gave her mum a big hug, Frances and I have decided that we are taking over tomorrow, you look a bit tired mum. 'Yes I suppose I do feel a bit tired, but it's a happy tired feeling, if you know what I mean.' 'That's why we are going to prepare the food, cook and clean everything up. You and Pete can have some time together. We are going to the beach in the morning. The kids want to see the sea, so how about we all go together, then leave the rest to us.' Sarah replied 'Yes that is a good idea, your nan can have a bit of peace for an hour or so. Sarah, don't take that the wrong way, but your nan does spend a lot of time napping.' 'Mum I never thought anything of it, I know she likes her naps, ' she replied smiling. 'Mum, I have to say, Sarah continued, that we love Pete already, he is such a lovely caring man. We can see that he adores you, you deserve that mum. How funny that you have known him for years and your paths have crossed again, certainly meant to be.' 'Thank you,' that means a lot to me Sarah. They all went for a walk to the beach. The little cafe was open, so they all had hot chocolate as they were walking while taking in the fresh air. 'I know I said it before, 'said Frances, 'but I could easily live up here,' looking at Stanley. 'Well maybe one day, I do love it here,' he replied. The tide was gradually coming in, and the children were running around, Martin and Stanley were showing them how to skim the water with stones, they were all enthralled with the way the stones made ripples. They were all picking up stones trying to copy their dads. They made their way back home, the dads were in charge of the children while the mums prepared the food for that day. They were putting out a cold buffet, so again everyone could help themselves.

Tilly and Pete, had a quick bite to eat, then went out for a few hours. There were some woods not far away, they were part of a public footpath, surrounded by fields, it was only a few minutes away by car. As they entered the woods, it looked beautiful. As they walked on the dry leaves that lay fallen, covered in frost they could hear the crunch of the frost as they made their steps into the woods. Pete had his camera, seeing spiderwebs patterns where the frost had formed around the web. He got lots of pictures of webs and the formation of the tree trunks. They felt so peaceful there, as they looked up and saw a canopy of trees gently nestling in with each other, like neighbours meeting up for a chat and putting the worlds to right. All the different eras of time that these trees had seen, the wisdom that they hold. Although most of them had been there a few hundred years or more. They had thoroughly enjoyed walking in the woods, when they stood still there was complete silence. They had been out a few hours and it was getting chilly, so they made their way back home again. When they got back, Sarah and Frances had cooked the meal, and were just dishing up the dinner for the children. The table was laid, and they were told to go and sit down. Tilly was quite enjoying not rushing about today. The last four weeks had been a bit of a whirlwind, but she would not have had that any other way. Boxing day had gone by very quickly, in fact the whole of Christmas had flown by so quick.

Later in the day Sarah and Frances were getting all their belongings together, to make room for all the extra toys and bits, as they were going home tomorrow. The house was buzzing, everybody was up. Breakfast was done in sittings, so the children were ready for their journey home. Tilly was rushing around making sure nothing had been left behind, Pete was helping the men load up the cars. It was time for them to set off, Tilly had tears in her eyes, Sarah had found her in the lounge, standing by the window. She knew her mum always got emotional when they left, she went over and gave her a big cuddle, thanking her for everything. 'Sarah, I will come down and visit you soon.' 'Mum, you know you and Pete are welcome to stay. Mum, I think Pete is such a good person, you seem good together. I just want you to be happy' Said Sarah. 'So dry your tears, I miss you too,' she continued, but this is where we are at the moment.' 'Thank you' said Tilly, 'I'm happy, we just need to work out how we are going to move forward as Pete is in Cornwall and I am here, but we can move anywhere really, but I am aware that your Nan is not feeling to well, and don't want to leave her on her own.' 'It always works out, you know that' said Sarah. 'There is no rush, you have found your man.' Everyone said their goodbyes, the grandchildren all cuddling themselves around Tilly as they did not want to leave her. Tilly stood with Pete, as she waved to them until the cars turned the corner out of site. Pete could see that Tilly was emotional, as he put his arms around her. 'Don't worry we will go and see your family as regularly as we can. Spending weekends enjoying our time together. They decided to have an early night, as they were both needing some time together. Edith was already tucked up in bed. They laid in bed, and kissed and cuddled each other, caressing each other's bodies, they finally made love, they were both so in tune with each other, it was pure ecstasy for them both. They lay there talking until the early hours, as Tilly asked Pete, about the comment he made regarding a dressing room in their home. 'Pete, you know that comment you made about the dressing room in our home, this has been bothering me, as we live opposite ends of the UK.' 'Yes of course I remember that, I do mean it. I have been thinking the same thing, moving forward. I am happy to move up here with you, you have your mum to look after, I can get my cottage and studio valued and put it on the market.' 'REALLY' Tilly sat bolt upright in bed 'really' she exclaimed. 'Yes really,' as Pete stroked Tilly's face. I don't have any ties down there, 'What about your work?' Tilly said. 'Well I can always work up here, I can rent a small studio, I get most of my work from my website or recommendations, not everybody comes and collects, plus I can advertise up here,' replied Pete. 'Tilly I do want to be with you, but this is all about timing, but I can at least get the ball rolling. So how about we take a step at a time, that way we are not trying to rush, it has to be right, I have a lot of things to sort out in my studio and get the logistics of things organised. Then I can find a studio and flat to rent. Tilly spoke over Pete,' you can live here, I know mum would love that, until we work out where we want to be. I don't think I can leave mum at the moment she is getting more frail.' 'What about your business idea Tilly?' Enquired Pete 'Well yes I still want to do that, so our businesses are incorporated together, but I agree with you, let's see how things unfold. if it's meant to be, it will happen. 'Yes, get your place valued and then we can start working through the rest.' 'I want you in my life forever Tilly, I want you to be my wife. I know this is not probably the right time and I'm not on bended knee in the Maldives, but would you marry me Tilly Fellowes.' Tilly, looked at Pete, 'they were both crying with happiness, 'I love you, and yes I would love to be your wife.' They both snuggled together totally in bliss looking forward to not only planning a small wedding ceremony, with a whole new future together. Their souls had met again, and this time it was for keeps.

Tilly had truly become, "The Butterfly that learnt to fly."

Simple Self Care Plan - using natural products

Essential oils…..Using essential oils can help greatly to alleviate any depression, anxiety and panic attacks that you may be experiencing to create a calm and uplifting feeling. The oils I used in the book are: Lavender, Geranium, Frankincense, Bergamot, Neroli and Grapefruit.
I recommend you use an Almond base oil to blend with the oils.
Uplifting oils: Lemon, Grapefruit, Bergamot
Calming: Neroli, Geranium, Frankincense, Lavender.
Anxiety, Depression and Panic: Lavender, Bergamot, Geranium, Neroli.

You do not need to have all the oils, so see what you are drawn to. The oils I have mentioned do not hold any contra-indications. Blend the base oil with the essential oil or oils that you have chosen. Add 2-3 drops to 10 ml of the base oil, mix together and you are ready to use.

Self Massage…… You can massage your feet, legs, arms, legs and tummy. Massaging all of these areas will allow the oils to absorb into your skin.
If you feel nauseous, massaging your tummy area in a clockwise motion should alleviate that feeling.
You can massage your face, neck with a Neroli blend. This oil is for self love, it calms the nervous system, and self love is what is needed.
Massaging your feet is very calming and soothing to the whole body, as it holds all the energy points of the body.
Please note that you don't have to massage every area at the same time, but do what is best for you at that time. I would recommend 10 minutes. Once you have massaged the said area, relax for another 10 minutes to allow the oils to absorb into your skin, and to let them do their work for you. The Aroma of the oils alone will affect the nerves directly to the brain, which is the emotional centre, this will calm the body as well, gaining a peaceful state of being.

A couple of quick techniques if you are feeling anxious or panicky at home or out.

1.   Place your right hand over your heart area and gently rub, saying to yourself that you are safe and all is well, continue to gently rub your heart area until you feel calmer.
2.   Take a deep breath in, then take another quick short breath in, exhale out, click the left hand fingers then the right hand fingers, then clap. This regulates the left and right side of the brain. This takes seconds to do, and gets you back into sync.

2. Hegu acupressure point

Place your finger and forefinger of your dominant hand between the webbed part of your thumb of your other hand. Press them together in the webbed area, so they are just above the thumb and base of the forefinger, and hold for a minute or so until you can feel the anxiety easing.

Homoeopathy: Bach flower Rescue remedy, is great to put in your bag, it calms the nervous system. There are various ways this remedy can be bought. Also Lavender essential oil has a similar effect, if you put some on a tissue, then inhale the essential oil it also has a wonderful calming effect on the body.

I hope this information has been helpful to you.

Should you need more help or information: Please contact me through my email address:

trish23butterfly@gmail.com

Milton Keynes UK
Ingram Content Group UK Ltd.
UKHW020818251023
431306UK00015B/378